CORINNA **BECHKO**   DANNY **LUCKERT**

THE SPACE BETWEEN ™

Published by

BOOM! ™
STUDIOS

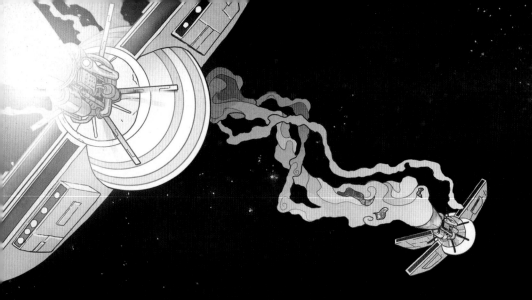

To Nathaniel, for creating the space I need to write while making our journey feel like home no matter where it takes us. -CB

To Waylon, who was always a shining star, even on the darkest of nights. -DL

ROSS RICHIE Chairman & Founder
JEN HARNED CFO
MATT GAGNON Editor-in-Chief
FILIP SABLIK President, Publishing & Marketing
STEPHEN CHRISTY President, Development
ADAM YOELIN Senior Vice President, Film
LANCE KREITER Vice President, Licensing & Merchandising
BRYCE CARLSON Vice President, Editorial & Creative Strategy
JOSH HAYES Vice President, Sales

METTE NORKJAER Vice President, Development
RYAN MATSUNAGA Director, Marketing
STEPHANIE LAZARSKI Director, Operations
ELYSE STRANDBERG Manager, Finance
MICHELLE ANKLEY Manager, Production Design
CHERYL PARKER Manager, Human Resources
ROSALIND MOREHEAD Manager, Retail Sales
JASON LEE Manager, Accounting

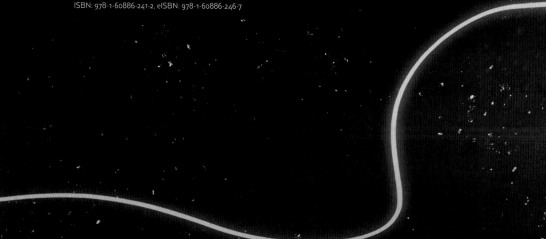

BOOM! Studios, 6920 Melrose Avenue, Los Angeles, CA 90038-3306. Printed in China. First Printing.

ISBN: 978-1-60886-241-2, eISBN: 978-1-60886-246-7

THE SPACE BETWEEN

CREATED BY
CORINNA BECHKO & **DANNY LUCKERT**

WRITTEN BY
CORINNA BECHKO

ILLUSTRATED BY
DANNY LUCKERT

LETTERED BY
JIM CAMPBELL

COVER BY
DANNY LUCKERT

LOGO DESIGNER
MARIE KRUPINA

SERIES DESIGNER
NANCY MOJICA

COLLECTION DESIGNER
VERONICA GUTIERREZ

EDITOR
SOPHIE PHILIPS-ROBERTS

SUPERVISING EDITOR
DAFNA PLEBAN

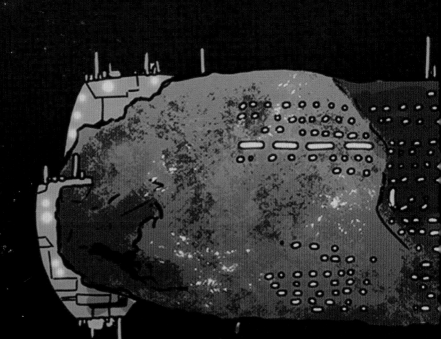

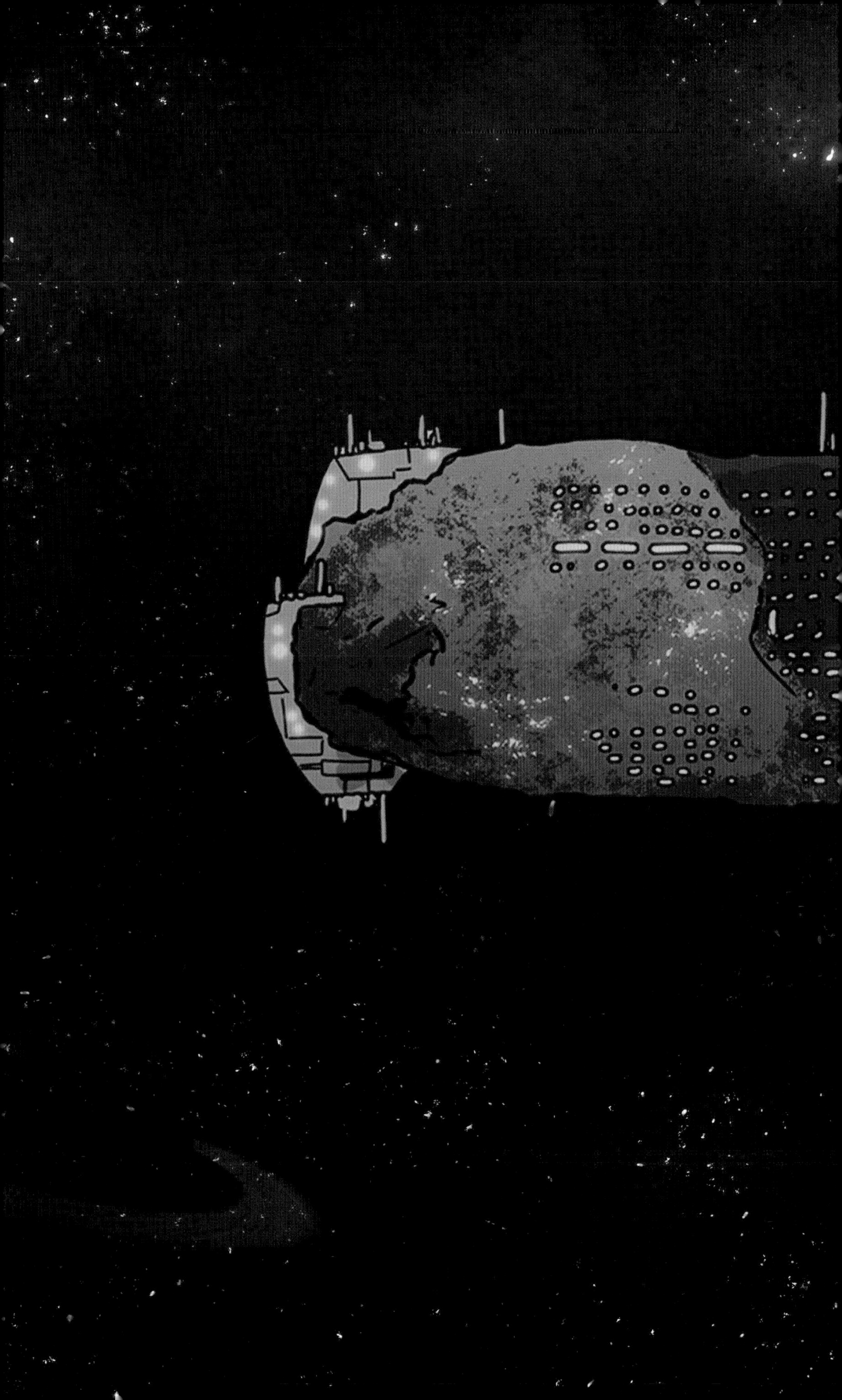

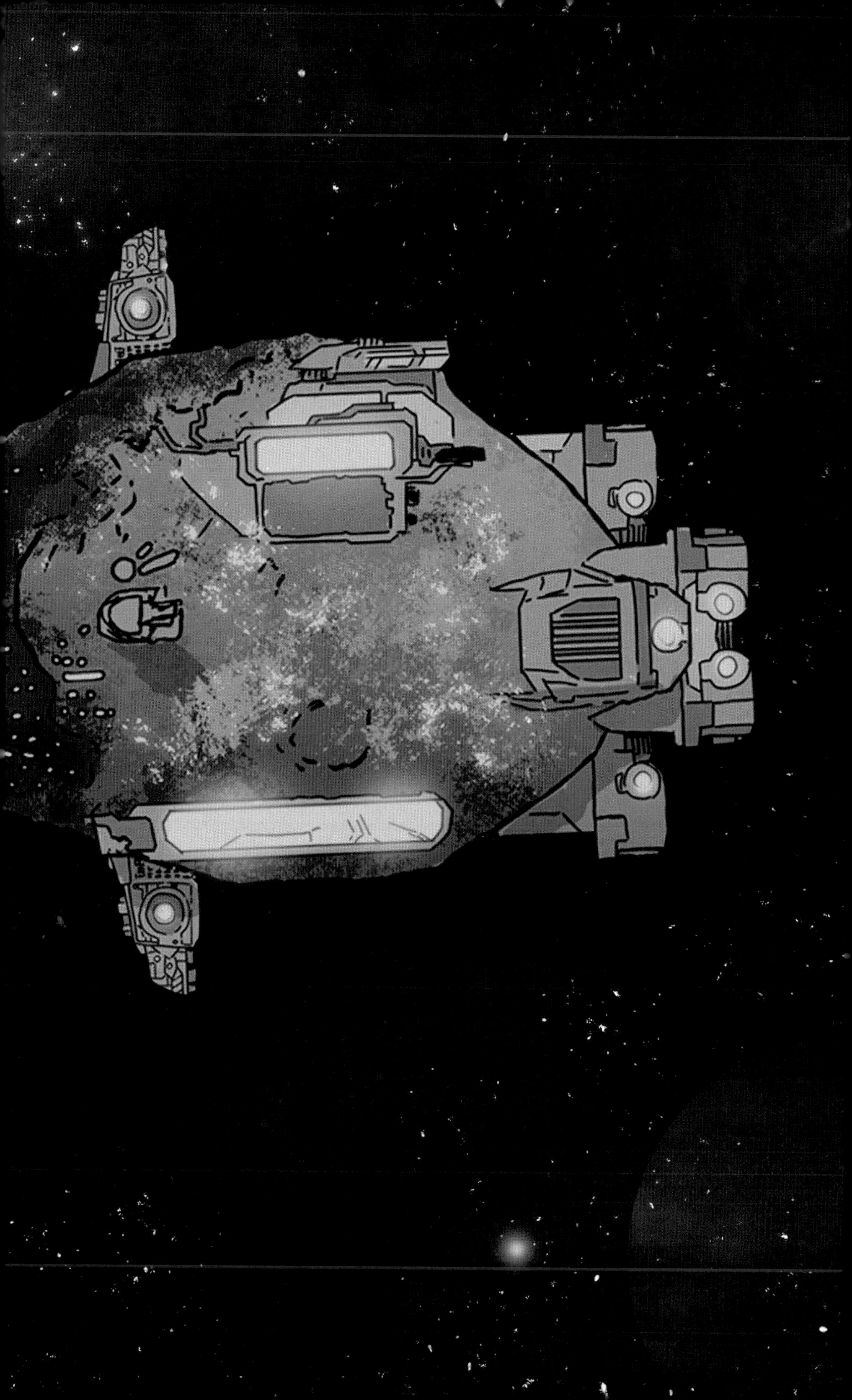

CHAPTER
ONE

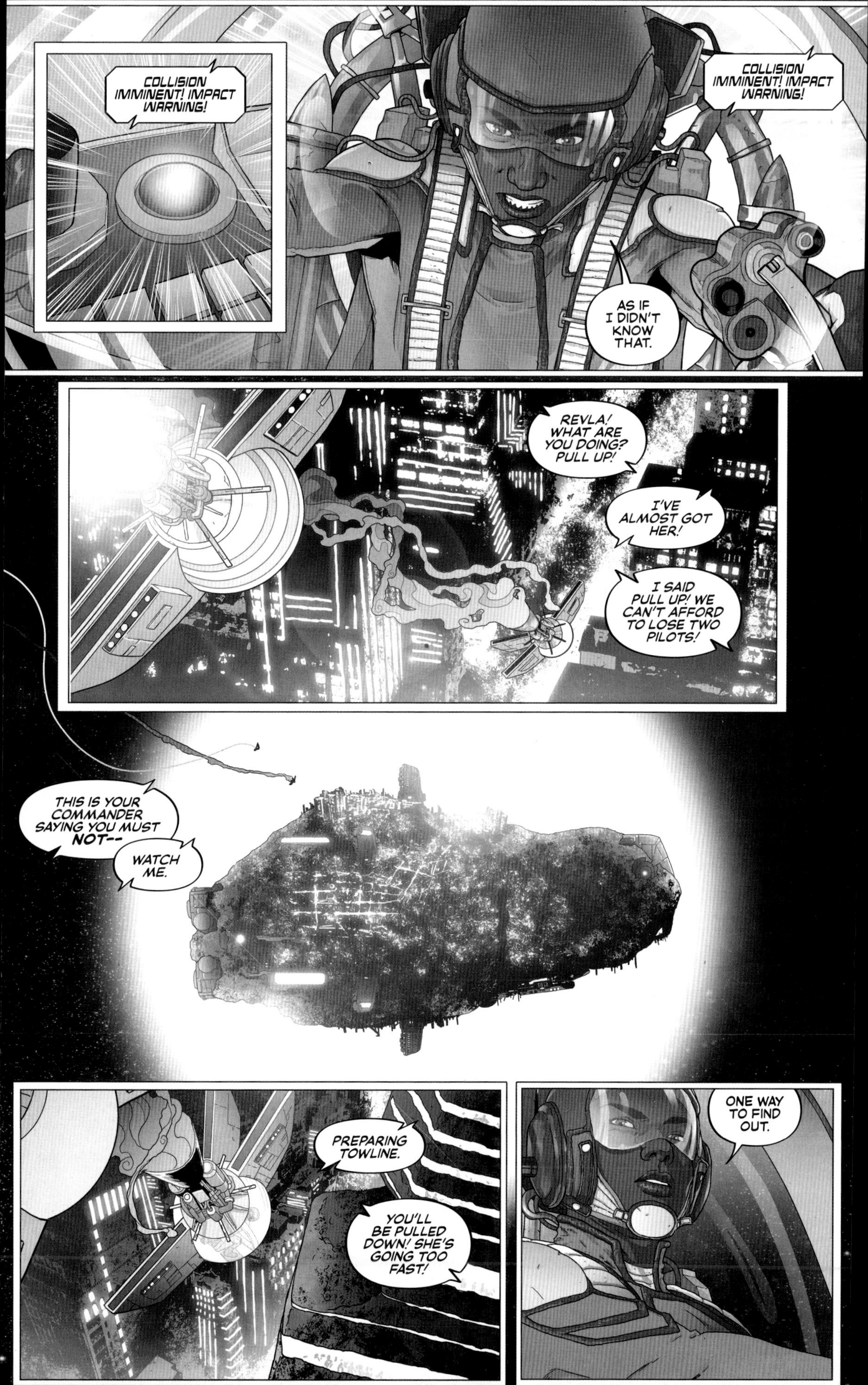
COLLISION IMMINENT! IMPACT WARNING!
COLLISION IMMINENT! IMPACT WARNING!
AS IF I DIDN'T KNOW THAT.
REVLA! WHAT ARE YOU DOING? PULL UP!
I'VE ALMOST GOT HER!
I SAID PULL UP! WE CAN'T AFFORD TO LOSE TWO PILOTS!
THIS IS YOUR COMMANDER SAYING YOU MUST NOT--
WATCH ME.
PREPARING TOWLINE.
YOU'LL BE PULLED DOWN! SHE'S GOING TOO FAST!
ONE WAY TO FIND OUT.

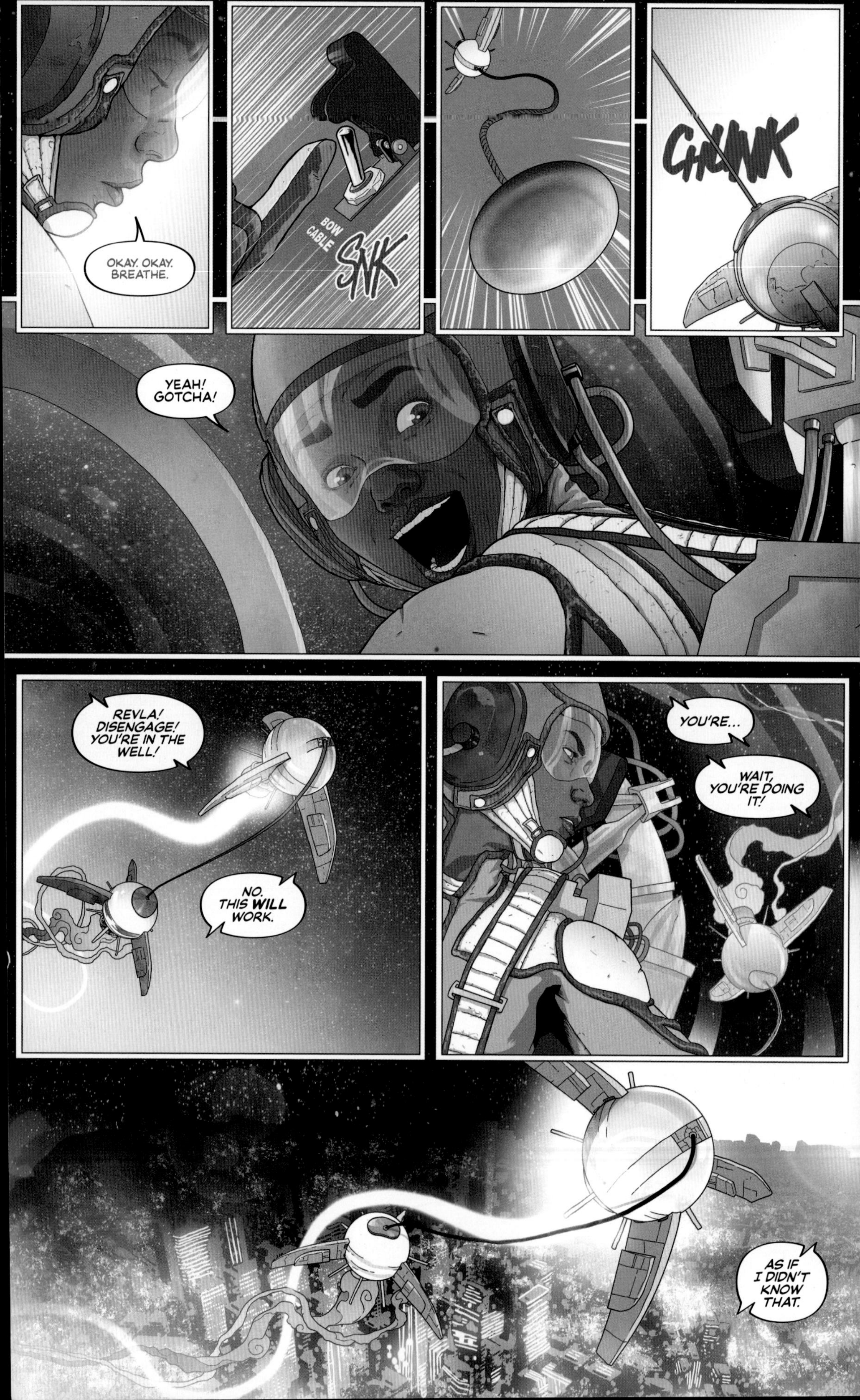

OKAY. OKAY. BREATHE.
BOW CABLE
SNK
CHUNK
YEAH! GOTCHA!
REVLA! DISENGAGE! YOU'RE IN THE WELL!
NO. THIS **WILL** WORK.
YOU'RE...
WAIT, YOU'RE DOING IT!
AS IF I DIDN'T KNOW THAT.

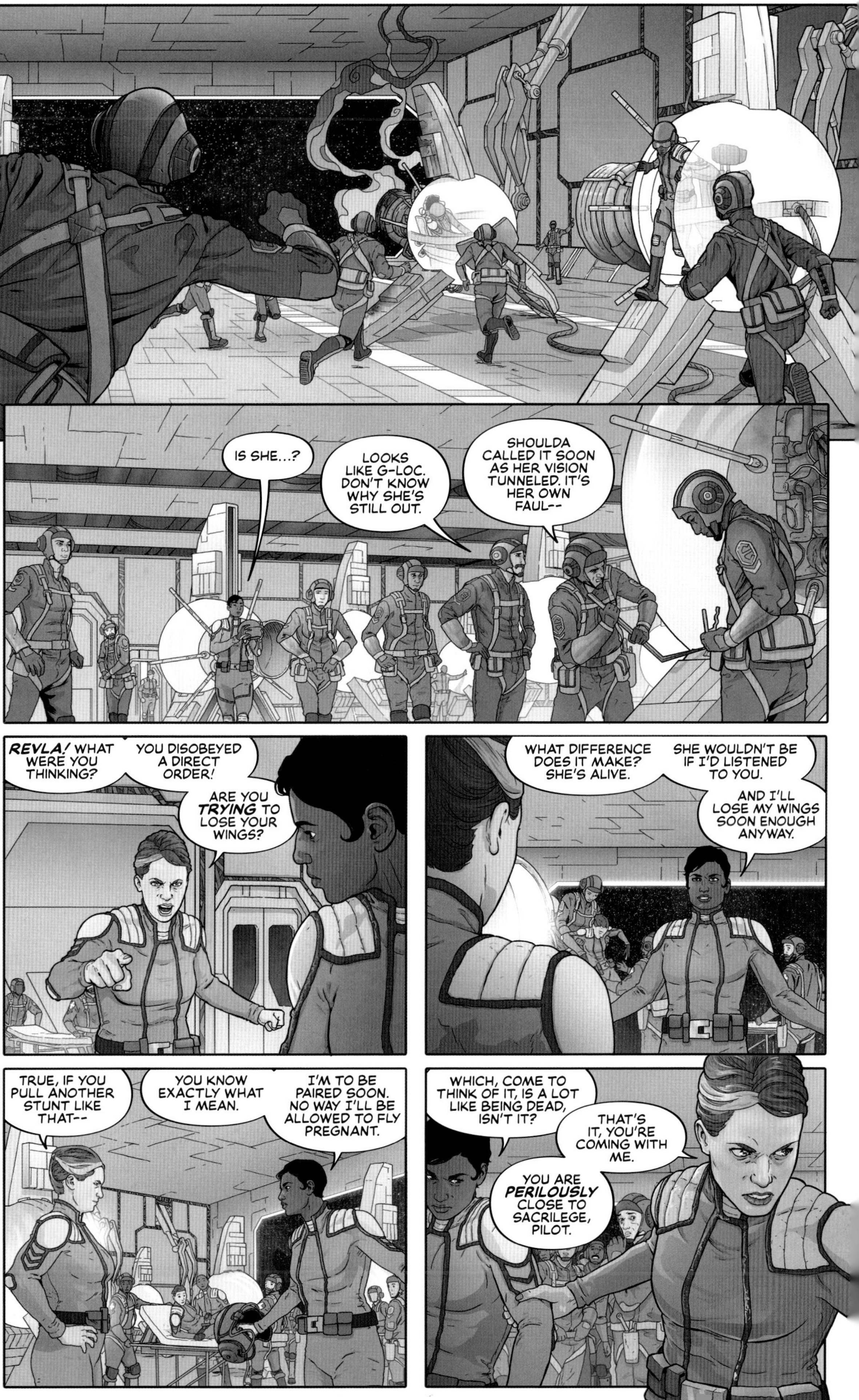
IS SHE...?
LOOKS LIKE G-LOC. DON'T KNOW WHY SHE'S STILL OUT.
SHOULDA CALLED IT SOON AS HER VISION TUNNELED. IT'S HER OWN FAUL--
REVLA! WHAT WERE YOU THINKING?
YOU DISOBEYED A DIRECT ORDER!
ARE YOU TRYING TO LOSE YOUR WINGS?
WHAT DIFFERENCE DOES IT MAKE? SHE'S ALIVE.
SHE WOULDN'T BE IF I'D LISTENED TO YOU.
AND I'LL LOSE MY WINGS SOON ENOUGH ANYWAY.
TRUE, IF YOU PULL ANOTHER STUNT LIKE THAT--
YOU KNOW EXACTLY WHAT I MEAN.
I'M TO BE PAIRED SOON. NO WAY I'LL BE ALLOWED TO FLY PREGNANT.
WHICH, COME TO THINK OF IT, IS A LOT LIKE BEING DEAD, ISN'T IT?
THAT'S IT, YOU'RE COMING WITH ME.
YOU ARE PERILOUSLY CLOSE TO SACRILEGE, PILOT.

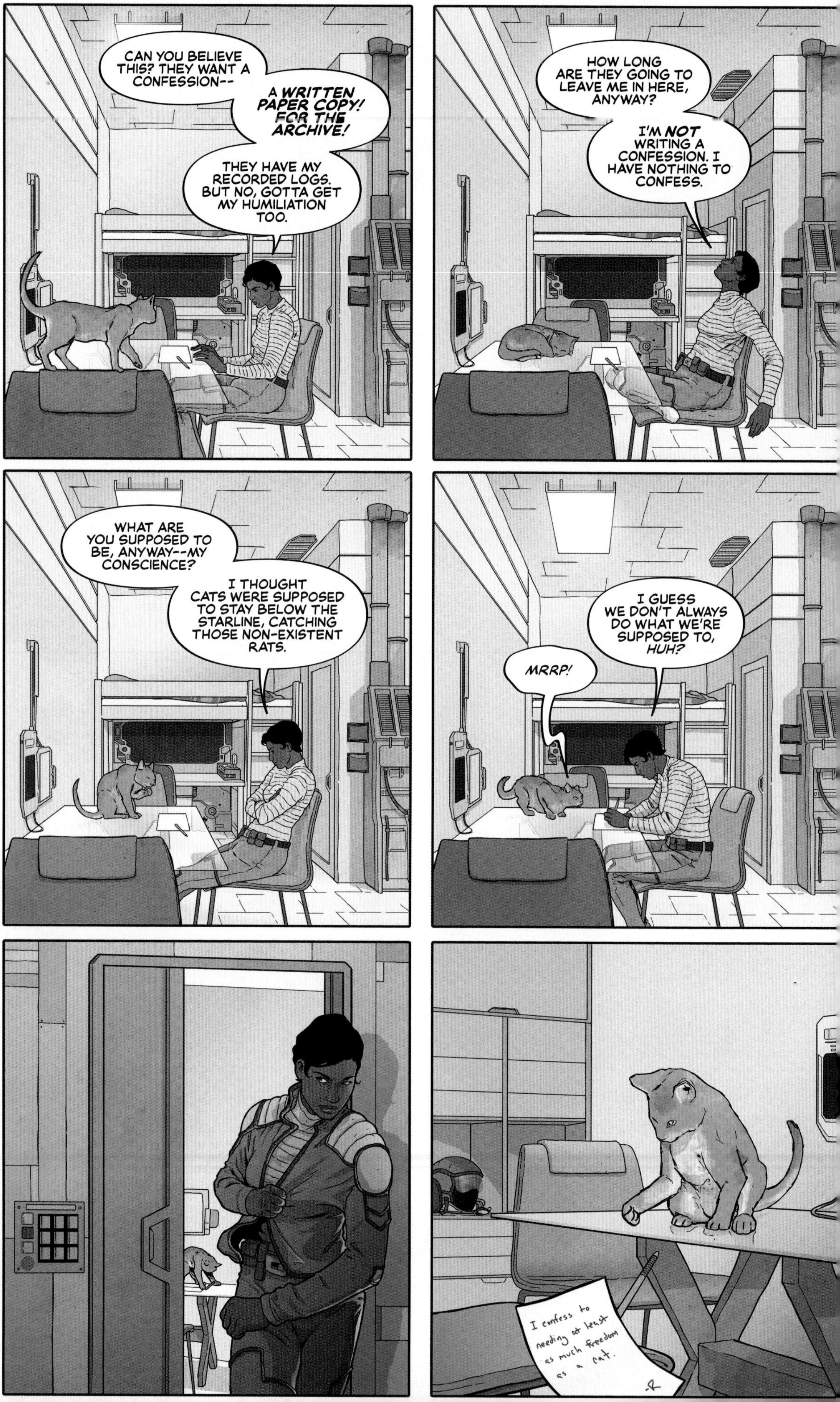
CAN YOU BELIEVE THIS? THEY WANT A CONFESSION--
A WRITTEN PAPER COPY! FOR THE ARCHIVE!
THEY HAVE MY RECORDED LOGS. BUT NO, GOTTA GET MY HUMILIATION TOO.
HOW LONG ARE THEY GOING TO LEAVE ME IN HERE, ANYWAY?
I'M NOT WRITING A CONFESSION. I HAVE NOTHING TO CONFESS.
WHAT ARE YOU SUPPOSED TO BE, ANYWAY--MY CONSCIENCE?
I THOUGHT CATS WERE SUPPOSED TO STAY BELOW THE STARLINE, CATCHING THOSE NON-EXISTENT RATS.
MRRP!
I GUESS WE DON'T ALWAYS DO WHAT WE'RE SUPPOSED TO, HUH?
I confess to needing at least as much freedom as a cat.
-R

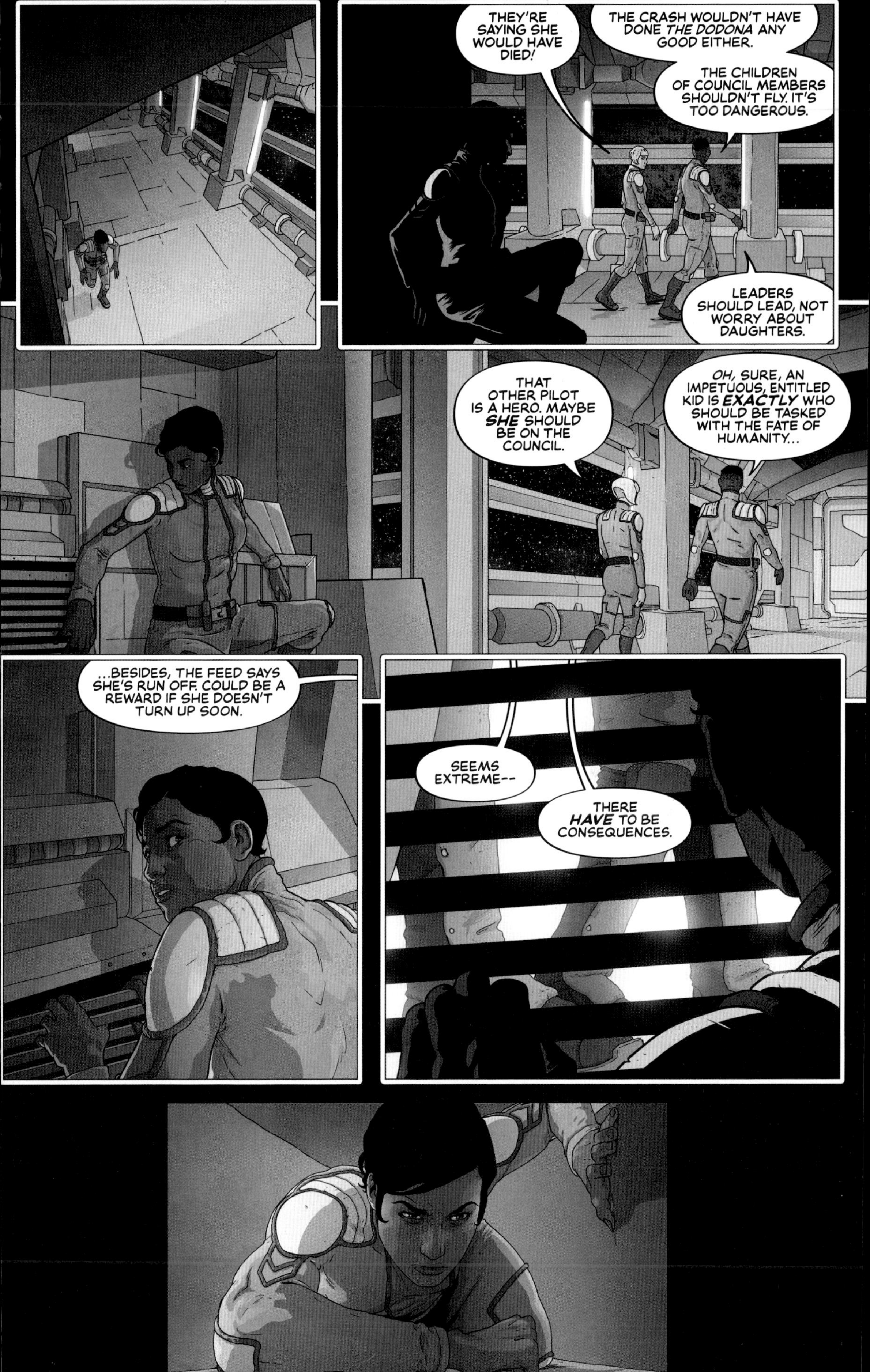
THEY'RE SAYING SHE WOULD HAVE DIED!
THE CRASH WOULDN'T HAVE DONE *THE DODONA* ANY GOOD EITHER.
THE CHILDREN OF COUNCIL MEMBERS SHOULDN'T FLY. IT'S TOO DANGEROUS.
LEADERS SHOULD LEAD, NOT WORRY ABOUT DAUGHTERS.
THAT OTHER PILOT IS A HERO. MAYBE ***SHE*** SHOULD BE ON THE COUNCIL.
OH, SURE, AN IMPETUOUS, ENTITLED KID IS ***EXACTLY*** WHO SHOULD BE TASKED WITH THE FATE OF HUMANITY...
...BESIDES, THE FEED SAYS SHE'S RUN OFF. COULD BE A REWARD IF SHE DOESN'T TURN UP SOON.
SEEMS EXTREME--
THERE ***HAVE*** TO BE CONSEQUENCES.

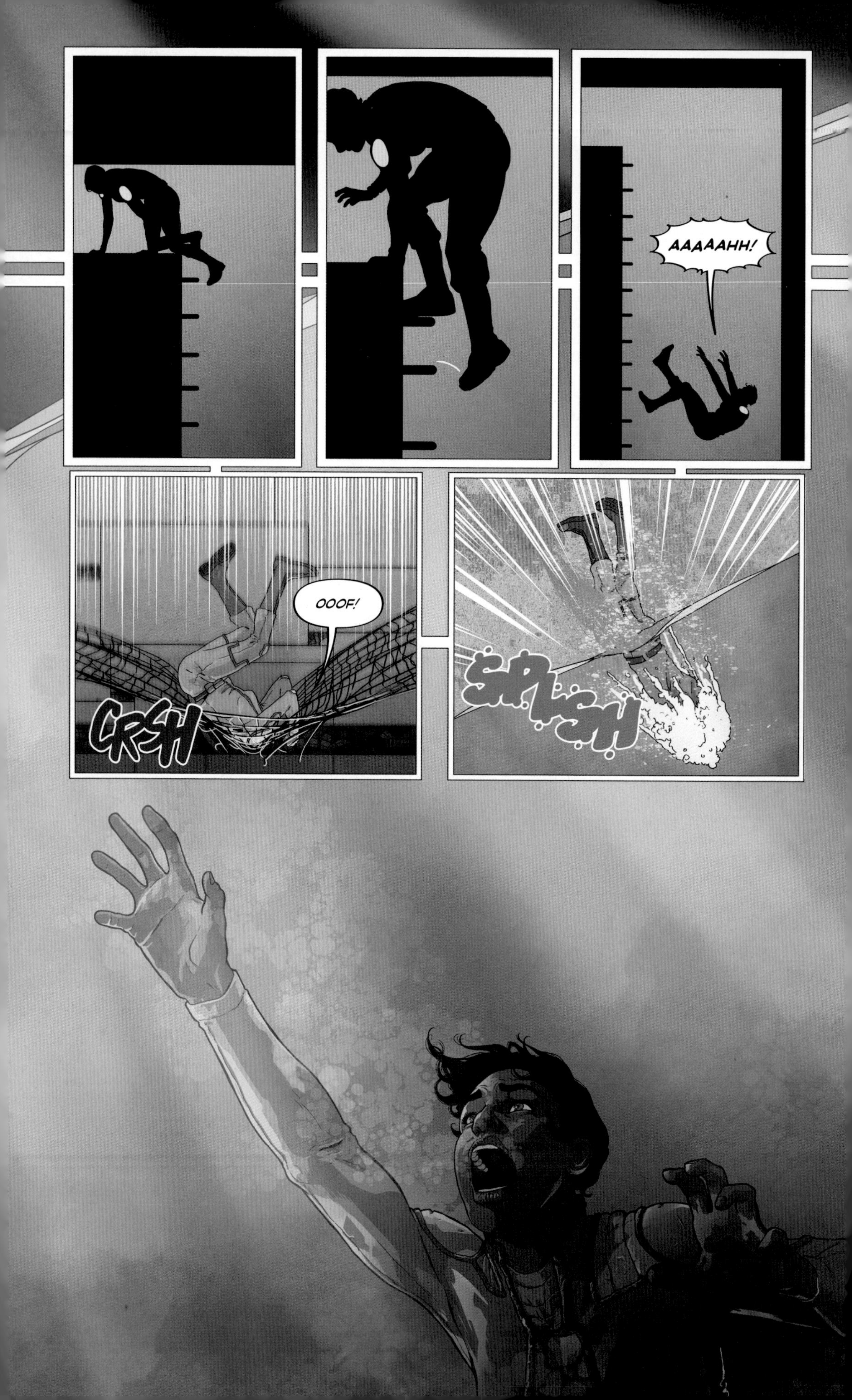
AAAAAHH!
OOOF!
CRSH
SPLSH

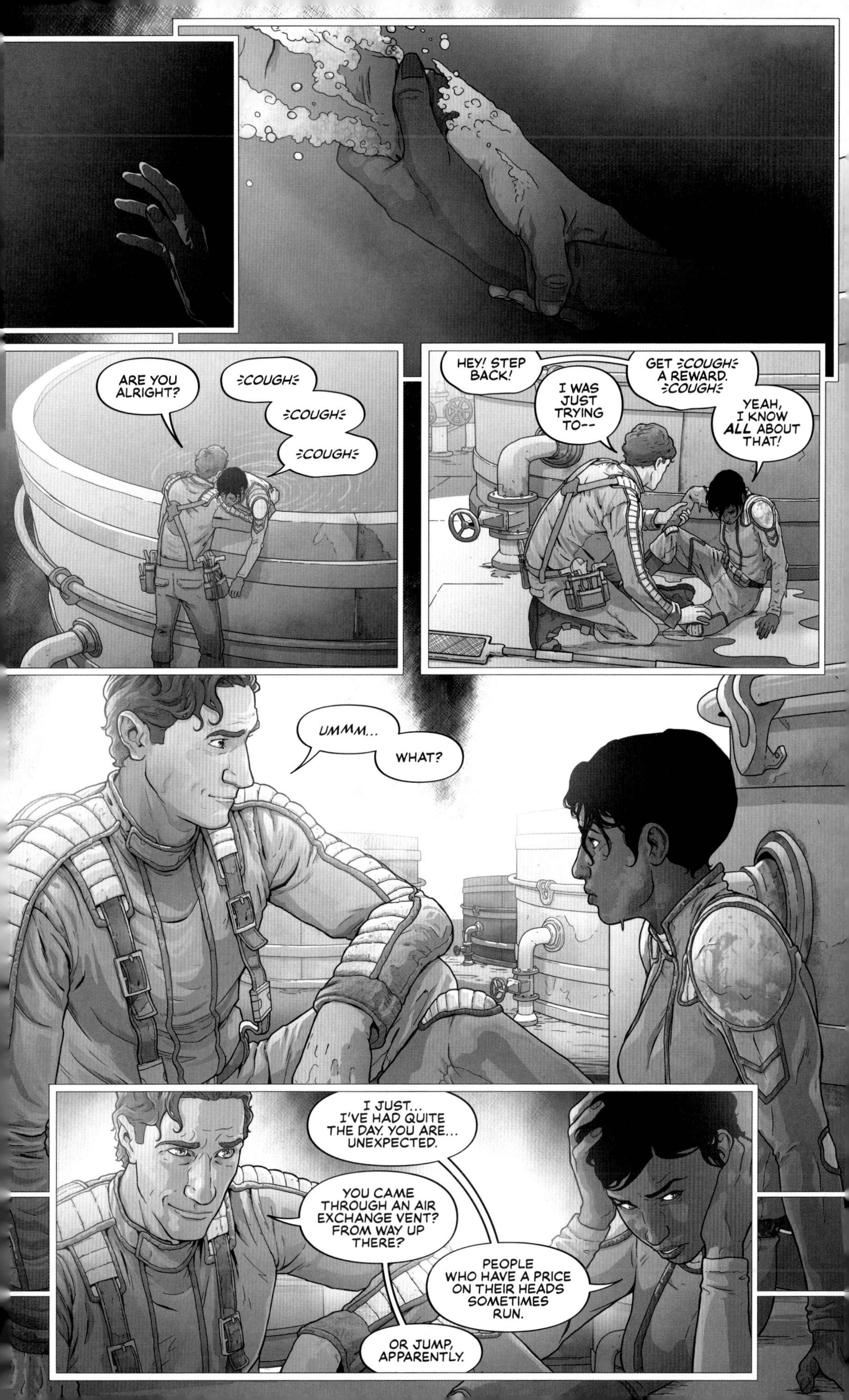
ARE YOU ALRIGHT?
≈COUGH≈
≈COUGH≈
≈COUGH≈
HEY! STEP BACK!
I WAS JUST TRYING TO--
GET ≈COUGH≈ A REWARD. ≈COUGH≈
YEAH, I KNOW ALL ABOUT THAT!
UMMM...
WHAT?
I JUST... I'VE HAD QUITE THE DAY. YOU ARE... UNEXPECTED.
YOU CAME THROUGH AN AIR EXCHANGE VENT? FROM WAY UP THERE?
PEOPLE WHO HAVE A PRICE ON THEIR HEADS SOMETIMES RUN.
OR JUMP, APPARENTLY.

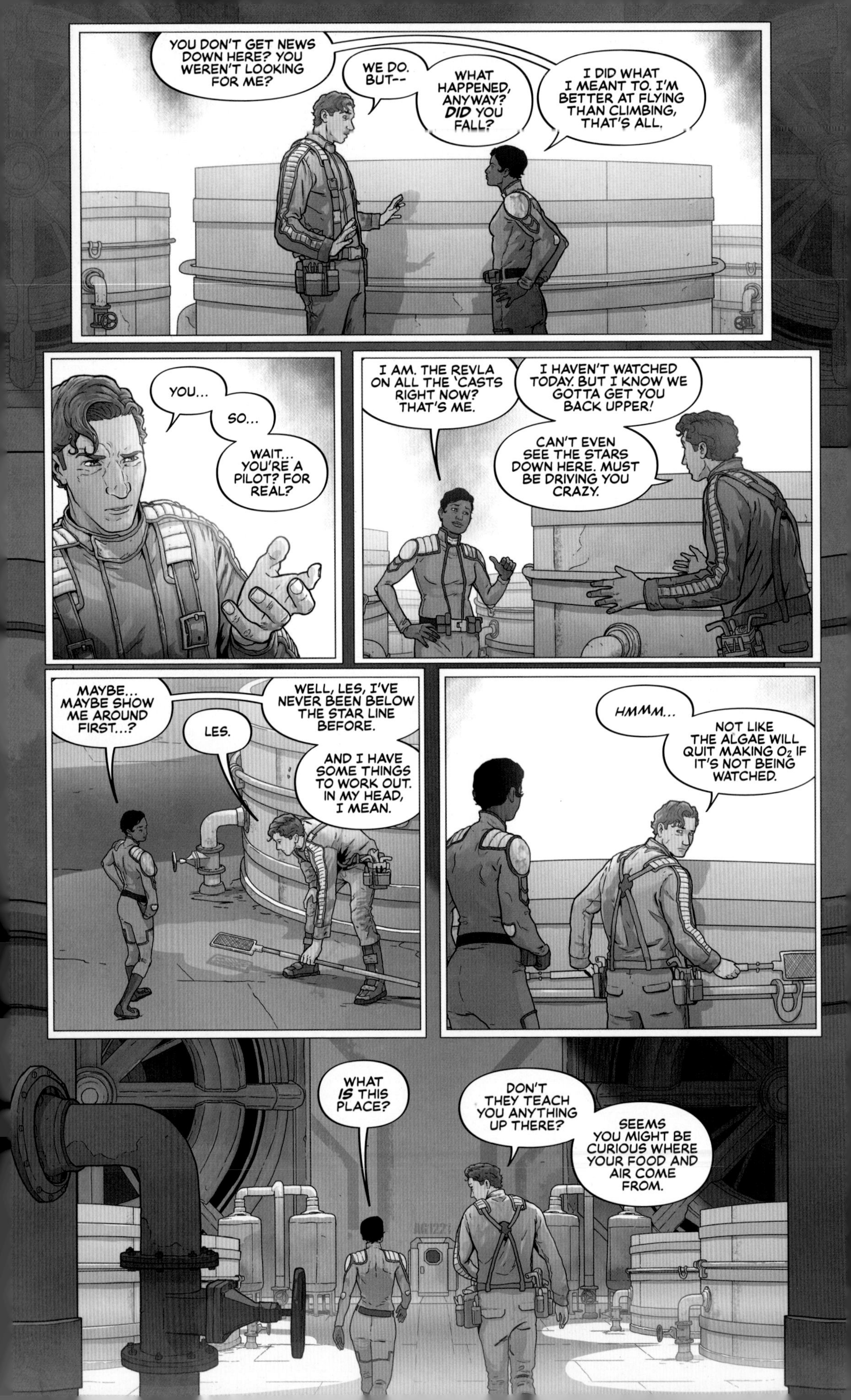
YOU DON'T GET NEWS DOWN HERE? YOU WEREN'T LOOKING FOR ME?
WE DO. BUT--
WHAT HAPPENED, ANYWAY? DID YOU FALL?
I DID WHAT I MEANT TO. I'M BETTER AT FLYING THAN CLIMBING, THAT'S ALL.
YOU...
SO...
WAIT... YOU'RE A PILOT? FOR REAL?
I AM. THE REVLA ON ALL THE 'CASTS RIGHT NOW? THAT'S ME.
I HAVEN'T WATCHED TODAY. BUT I KNOW WE GOTTA GET YOU BACK UPPER!
CAN'T EVEN SEE THE STARS DOWN HERE. MUST BE DRIVING YOU CRAZY.
MAYBE... MAYBE SHOW ME AROUND FIRST...?
LES.
WELL, LES, I'VE NEVER BEEN BELOW THE STAR LINE BEFORE.
AND I HAVE SOME THINGS TO WORK OUT. IN MY HEAD, I MEAN.
HMMM...
NOT LIKE THE ALGAE WILL QUIT MAKING O_2 IF IT'S NOT BEING WATCHED.
WHAT IS THIS PLACE?
DON'T THEY TEACH YOU ANYTHING UP THERE?
SEEMS YOU MIGHT BE CURIOUS WHERE YOUR FOOD AND AIR COME FROM.
JG122

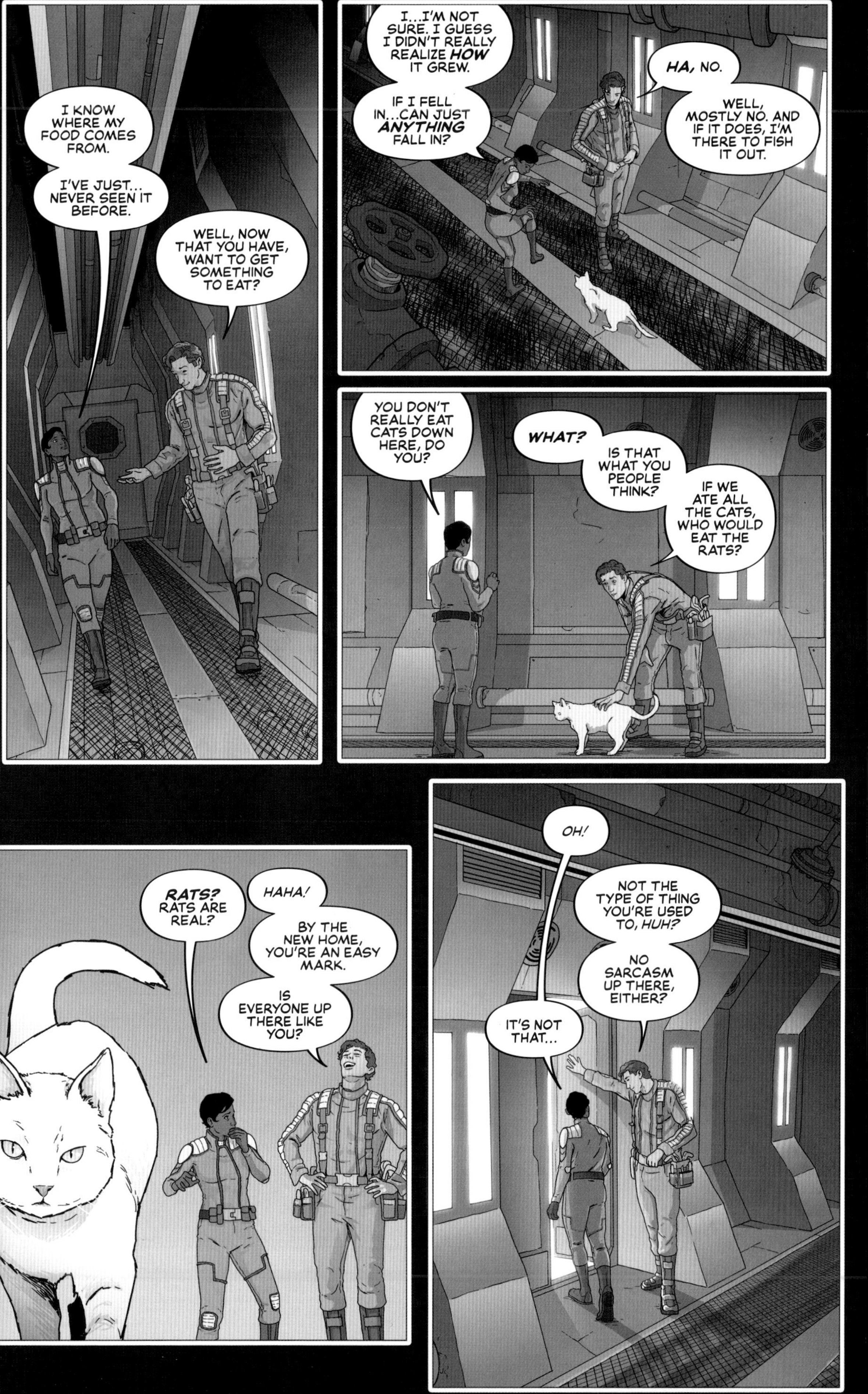
I KNOW WHERE MY FOOD COMES FROM.
I'VE JUST... NEVER SEEN IT BEFORE.
WELL, NOW THAT YOU HAVE, WANT TO GET SOMETHING TO EAT?
I...I'M NOT SURE. I GUESS I DIDN'T REALLY REALIZE HOW IT GREW.
IF I FELL IN...CAN JUST ANYTHING FALL IN?
HA, NO.
WELL, MOSTLY NO. AND IF IT DOES, I'M THERE TO FISH IT OUT.
YOU DON'T REALLY EAT CATS DOWN HERE, DO YOU?
WHAT?
IS THAT WHAT YOU PEOPLE THINK?
IF WE ATE ALL THE CATS, WHO WOULD EAT THE RATS?
RATS? RATS ARE REAL?
HAHA!
BY THE NEW HOME, YOU'RE AN EASY MARK.
IS EVERYONE UP THERE LIKE YOU?
OH!
NOT THE TYPE OF THING YOU'RE USED TO, HUH?
NO SARCASM UP THERE, EITHER?
IT'S NOT THAT...

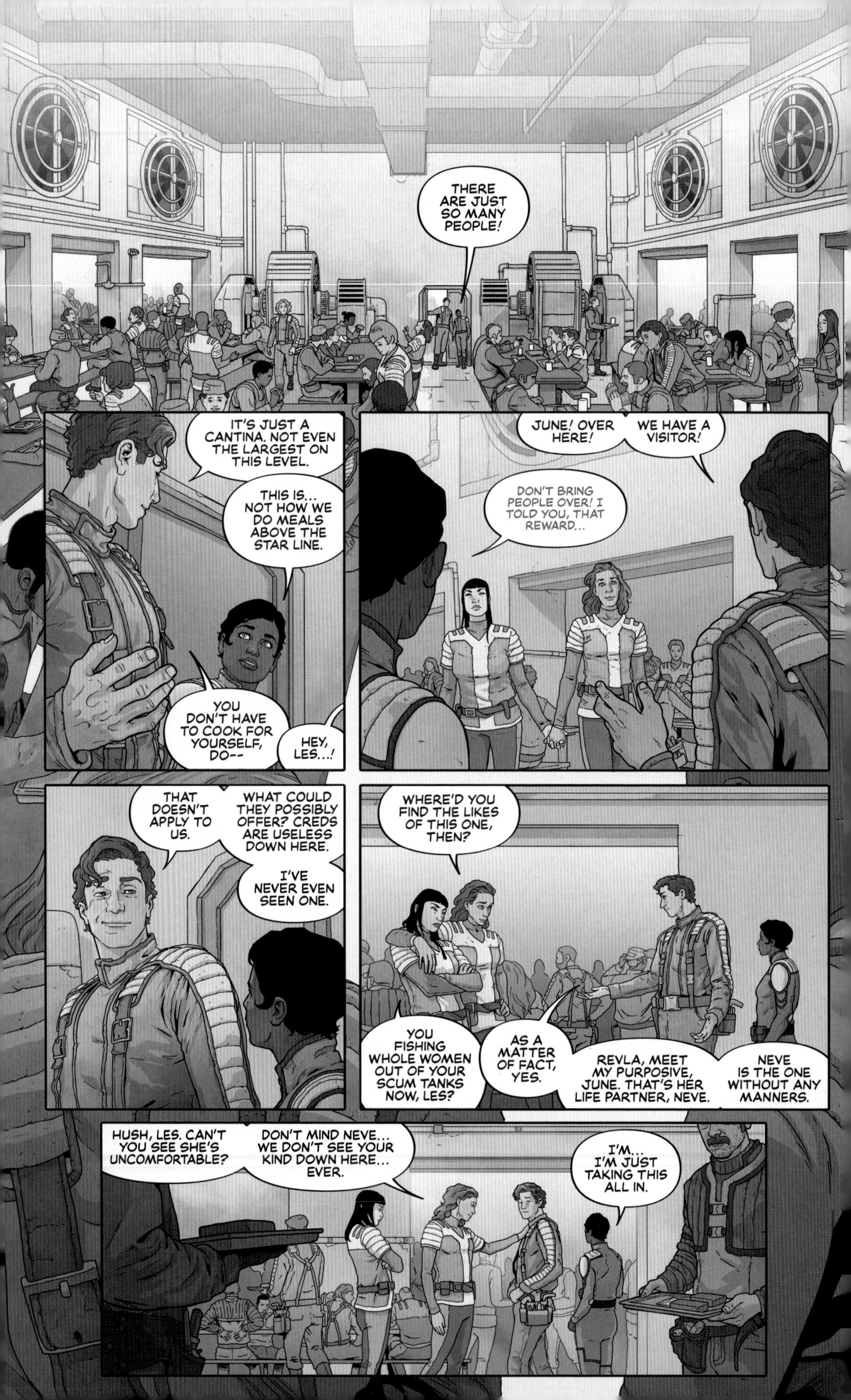
THERE ARE JUST SO MANY PEOPLE!
IT'S JUST A CANTINA. NOT EVEN THE LARGEST ON THIS LEVEL.
THIS IS... NOT HOW WE DO MEALS ABOVE THE STAR LINE.
YOU DON'T HAVE TO COOK FOR YOURSELF, DO--
HEY, LES...!
JUNE! OVER HERE!
WE HAVE A VISITOR!
DON'T BRING PEOPLE OVER! I TOLD YOU, THAT REWARD...
THAT DOESN'T APPLY TO US.
WHAT COULD THEY POSSIBLY OFFER? CREDS ARE USELESS DOWN HERE.
I'VE NEVER EVEN SEEN ONE.
WHERE'D YOU FIND THE LIKES OF THIS ONE, THEN?
YOU FISHING WHOLE WOMEN OUT OF YOUR SCUM TANKS NOW, LES?
AS A MATTER OF FACT, YES.
REVLA, MEET MY PURPOSIVE, JUNE. THAT'S HER LIFE PARTNER, NEVE.
NEVE IS THE ONE WITHOUT ANY MANNERS.
HUSH, LES. CAN'T YOU SEE SHE'S UNCOMFORTABLE?
DON'T MIND NEVE... WE DON'T SEE YOUR KIND DOWN HERE... EVER.
I'M... I'M JUST TAKING THIS ALL IN.

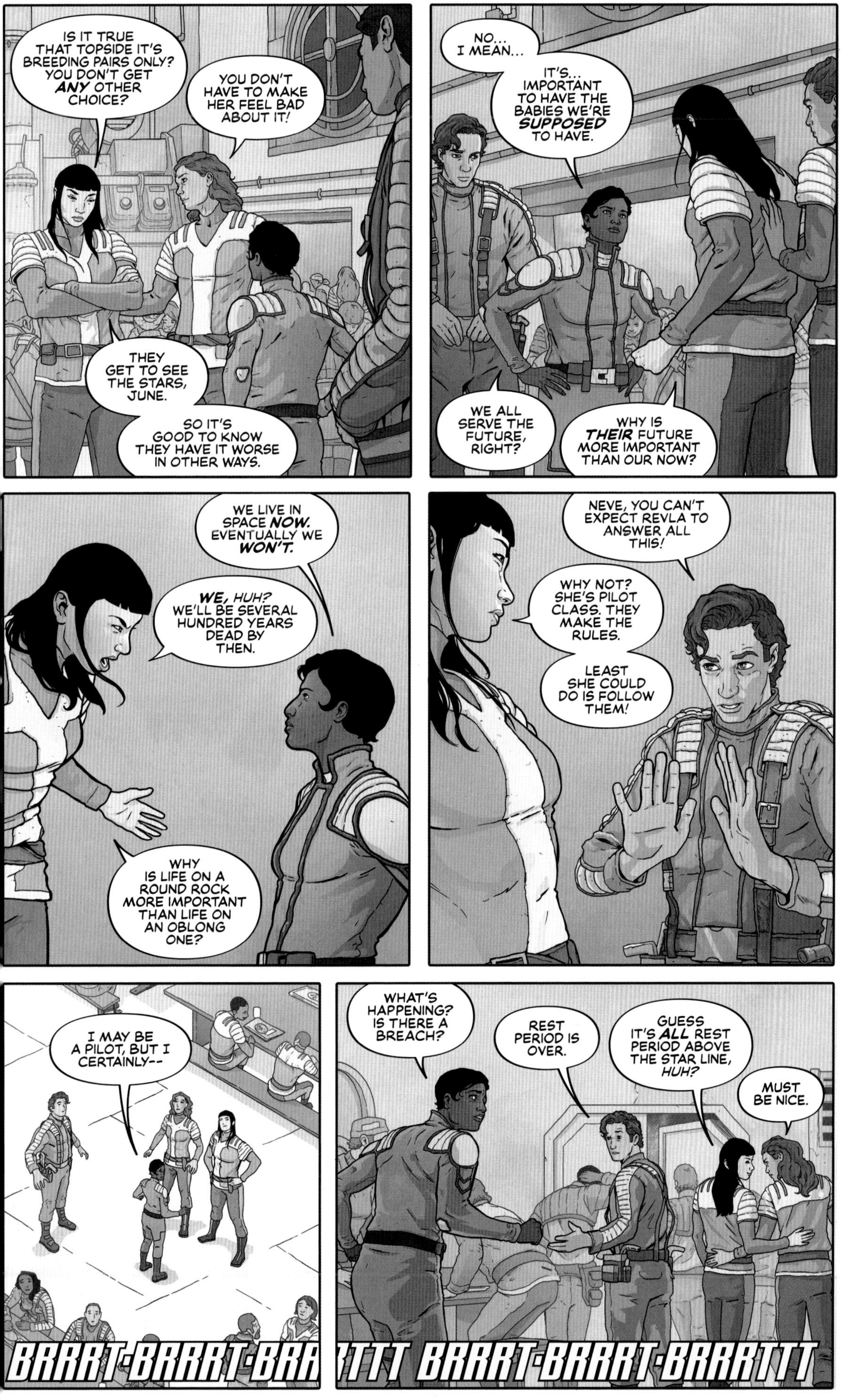
IS IT TRUE THAT TOPSIDE IT'S BREEDING PAIRS ONLY? YOU DON'T GET ANY OTHER CHOICE?
YOU DON'T HAVE TO MAKE HER FEEL BAD ABOUT IT!
THEY GET TO SEE THE STARS, JUNE.
SO IT'S GOOD TO KNOW THEY HAVE IT WORSE IN OTHER WAYS.
NO... I MEAN...
IT'S... IMPORTANT TO HAVE THE BABIES WE'RE SUPPOSED TO HAVE.
WE ALL SERVE THE FUTURE, RIGHT?
WHY IS THEIR FUTURE MORE IMPORTANT THAN OUR NOW?
WE LIVE IN SPACE NOW. EVENTUALLY WE WON'T.
WE, HUH? WE'LL BE SEVERAL HUNDRED YEARS DEAD BY THEN.
WHY IS LIFE ON A ROUND ROCK MORE IMPORTANT THAN LIFE ON AN OBLONG ONE?
NEVE, YOU CAN'T EXPECT REVLA TO ANSWER ALL THIS!
WHY NOT? SHE'S PILOT CLASS. THEY MAKE THE RULES.
LEAST SHE COULD DO IS FOLLOW THEM!
I MAY BE A PILOT, BUT I CERTAINLY--
BRRRT-BRRRT-BRRRTTT
WHAT'S HAPPENING? IS THERE A BREACH?
REST PERIOD IS OVER.
GUESS IT'S ALL REST PERIOD ABOVE THE STAR LINE, HUH?
MUST BE NICE.
BRRRT-BRRRT-BRRRTTT

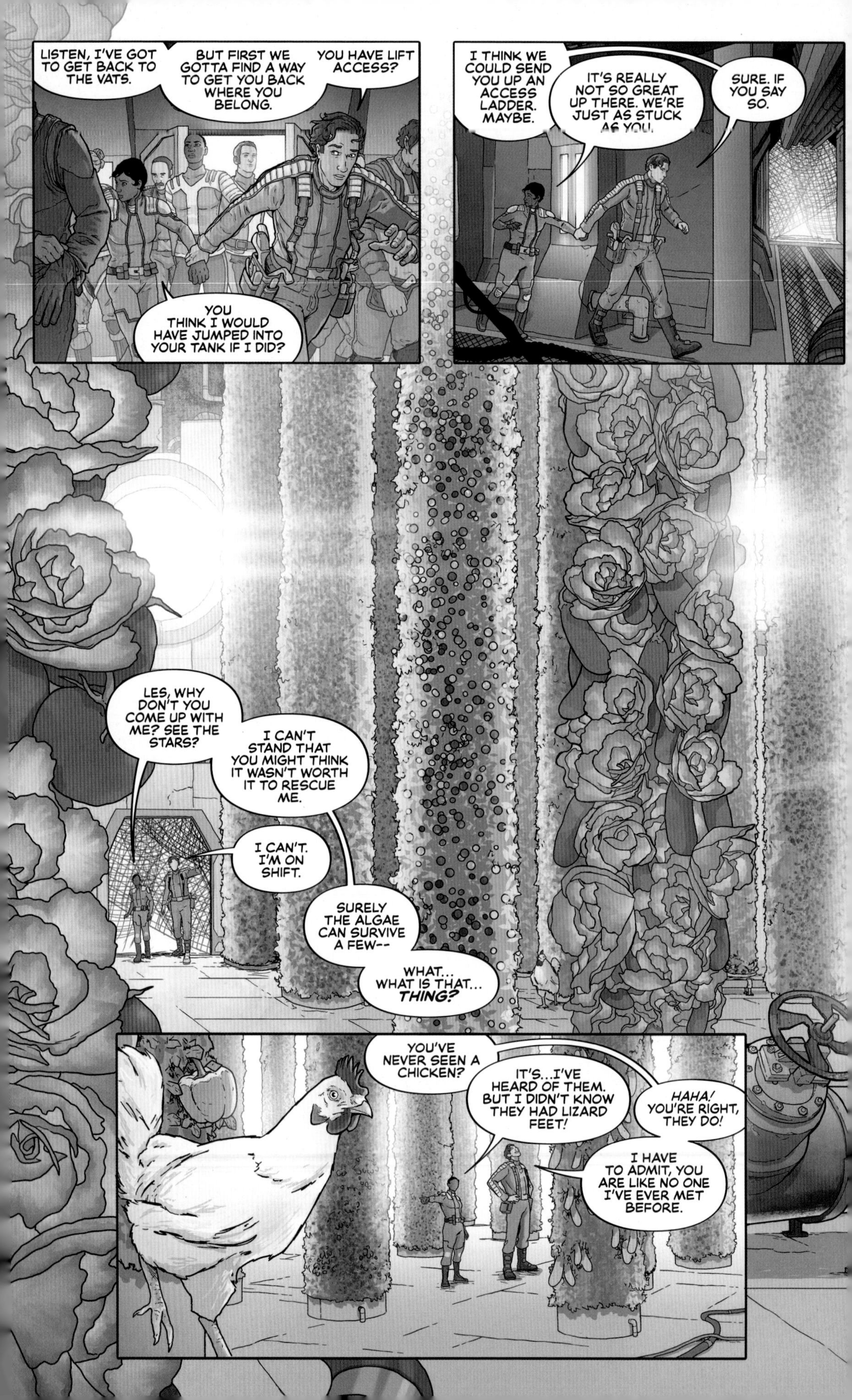
LISTEN, I'VE GOT TO GET BACK TO THE VATS.
BUT FIRST WE GOTTA FIND A WAY TO GET YOU BACK WHERE YOU BELONG.
YOU HAVE LIFT ACCESS?
YOU THINK I WOULD HAVE JUMPED INTO YOUR TANK IF I DID?
I THINK WE COULD SEND YOU UP AN ACCESS LADDER. MAYBE.
IT'S REALLY NOT SO GREAT UP THERE. WE'RE JUST AS STUCK AS YOU.
SURE. IF YOU SAY SO.
LES, WHY DON'T YOU COME UP WITH ME? SEE THE STARS?
I CAN'T STAND THAT YOU MIGHT THINK IT WASN'T WORTH IT TO RESCUE ME.
I CAN'T. I'M ON SHIFT.
SURELY THE ALGAE CAN SURVIVE A FEW--
WHAT... WHAT IS THAT... *THING?*
YOU'VE NEVER SEEN A CHICKEN?
IT'S...I'VE HEARD OF THEM. BUT I DIDN'T KNOW THEY HAD LIZARD FEET!
HAHA! YOU'RE RIGHT, THEY *DO!*
I HAVE TO ADMIT, YOU ARE LIKE NO ONE I'VE EVER MET BEFORE.

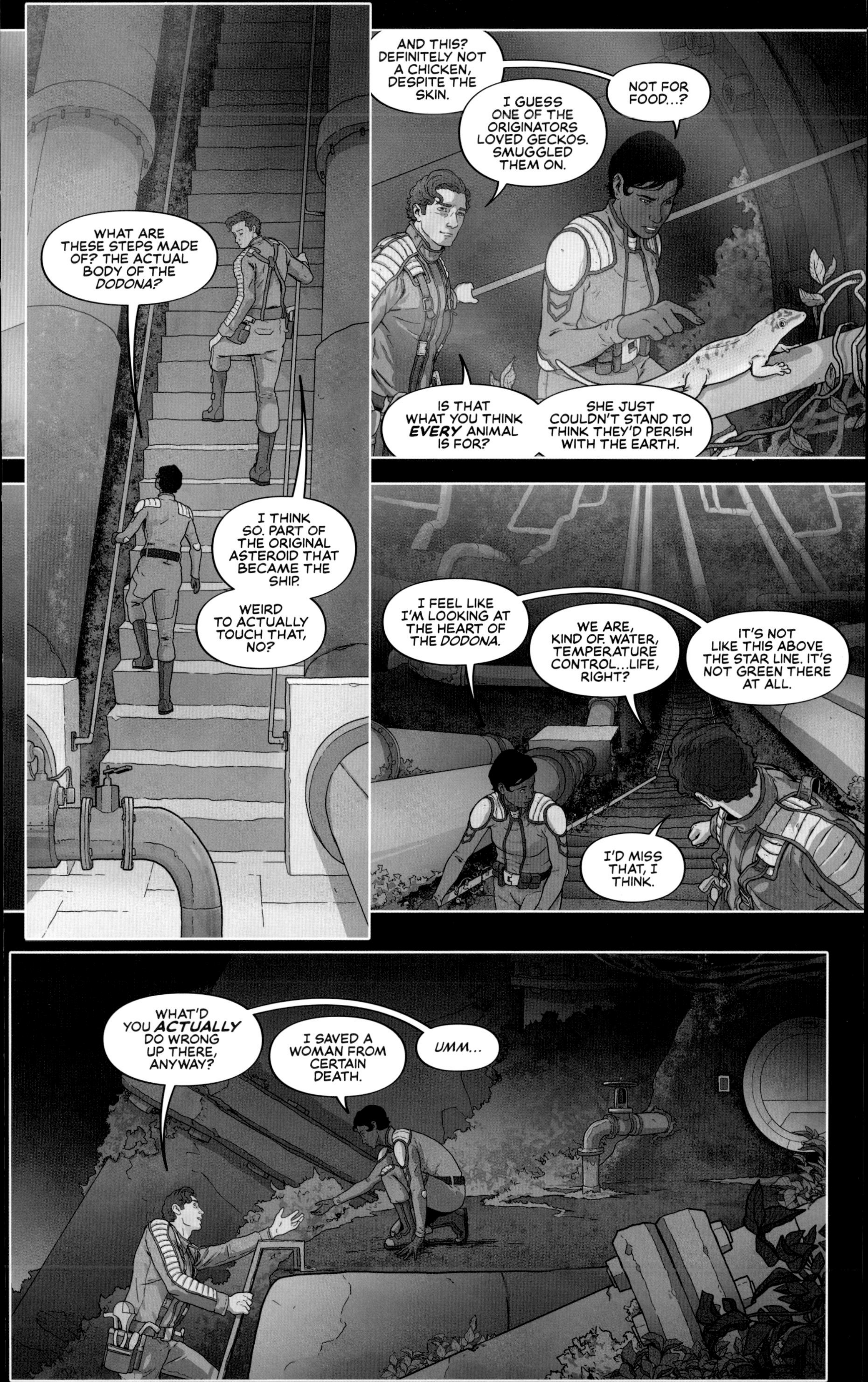
WHAT ARE THESE STEPS MADE OF? THE ACTUAL BODY OF THE *DODONA?*
I THINK SO. PART OF THE ORIGINAL ASTEROID THAT BECAME THE SHIP.
WEIRD TO ACTUALLY TOUCH THAT, NO?
AND THIS? DEFINITELY NOT A CHICKEN, DESPITE THE SKIN.
NOT FOR FOOD...?
I GUESS ONE OF THE ORIGINATORS LOVED GECKOS. SMUGGLED THEM ON.
IS THAT WHAT YOU THINK ***EVERY*** ANIMAL IS FOR?
SHE JUST COULDN'T STAND TO THINK THEY'D PERISH WITH THE EARTH.
I FEEL LIKE I'M LOOKING AT THE HEART OF THE *DODONA.*
WE ARE, KIND OF. WATER, TEMPERATURE CONTROL...LIFE, RIGHT?
IT'S NOT LIKE THIS ABOVE THE STAR LINE. IT'S NOT GREEN THERE AT ALL.
I'D MISS THAT, I THINK.
WHAT'D YOU ***ACTUALLY*** DO WRONG UP THERE, ANYWAY?
I SAVED A WOMAN FROM CERTAIN DEATH.
UMM...

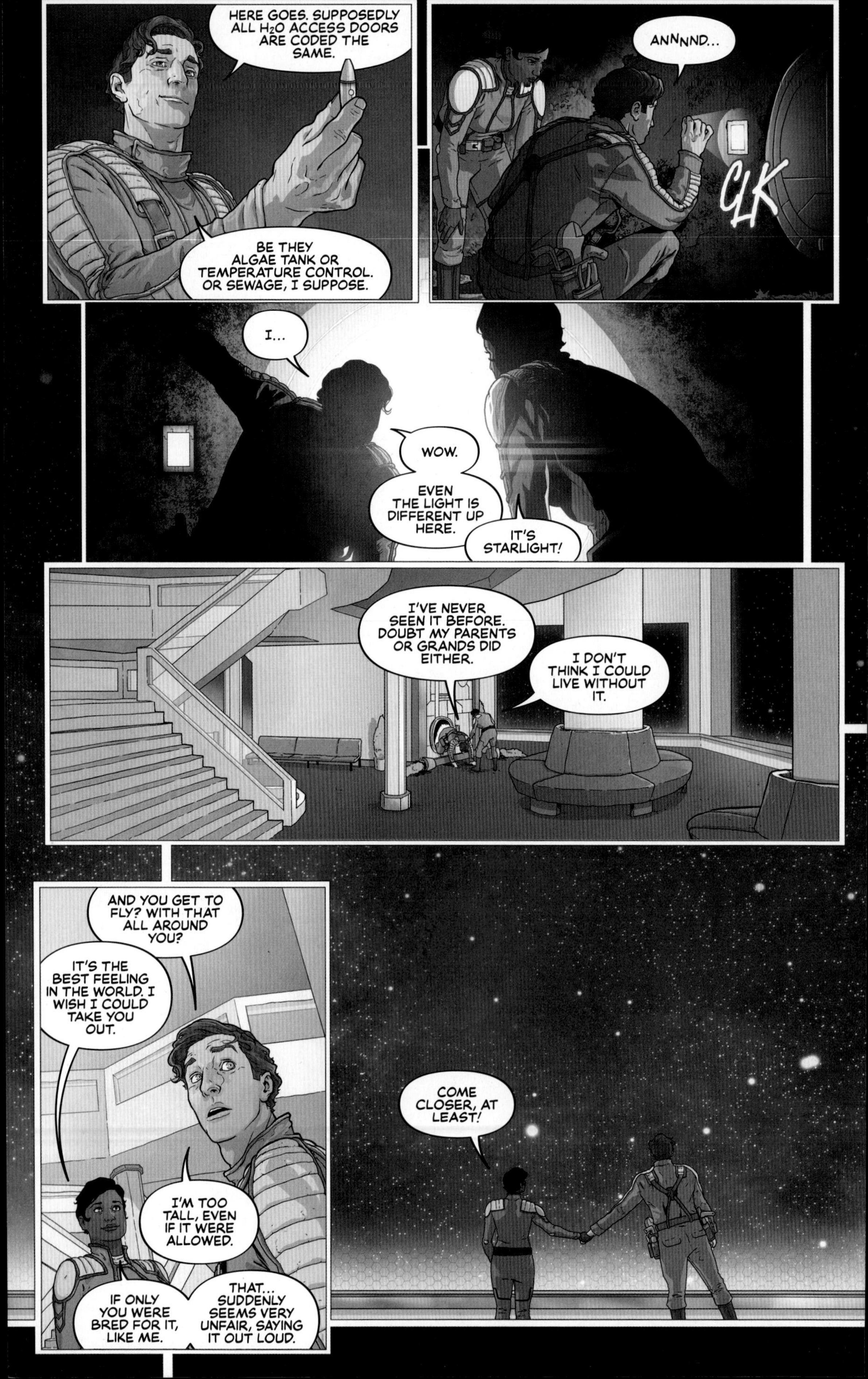
HERE GOES. SUPPOSEDLY ALL H_2O ACCESS DOORS ARE CODED THE SAME.
BE THEY ALGAE TANK OR TEMPERATURE CONTROL. OR SEWAGE, I SUPPOSE.
ANNNND...
CLK
I...
WOW.
EVEN THE LIGHT IS DIFFERENT UP HERE.
IT'S STARLIGHT!
I'VE NEVER SEEN IT BEFORE. DOUBT MY PARENTS OR GRANDS DID EITHER.
I DON'T THINK I COULD LIVE WITHOUT IT.
AND YOU GET TO FLY? WITH THAT ALL AROUND YOU?
IT'S THE BEST FEELING IN THE WORLD. I WISH I COULD TAKE YOU OUT.
I'M TOO TALL, EVEN IF IT WERE ALLOWED.
IF ONLY YOU WERE BRED FOR IT, LIKE ME.
THAT... SUDDENLY SEEMS VERY UNFAIR, SAYING IT OUT LOUD.
COME CLOSER, AT LEAST!

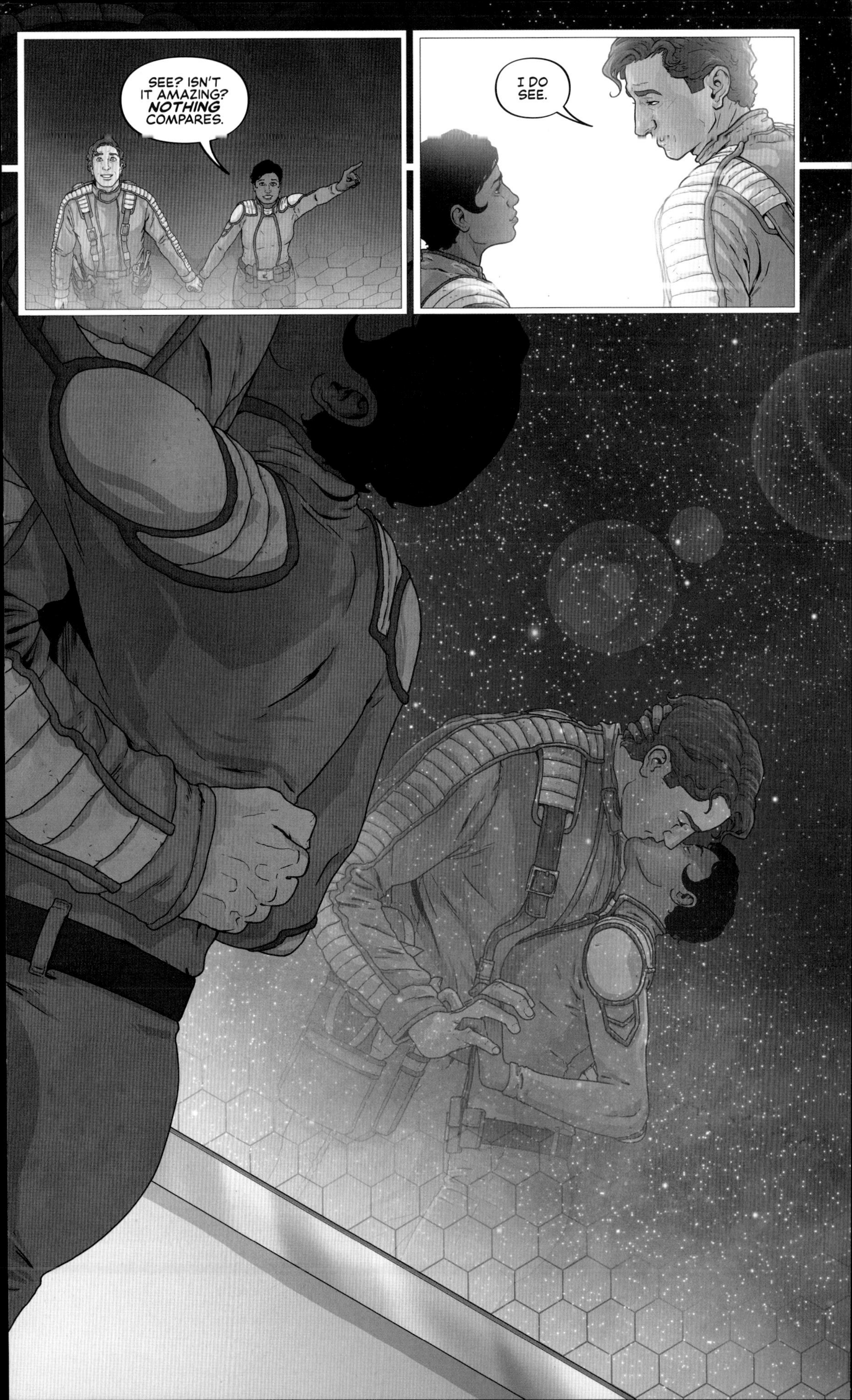
SEE? ISN'T IT AMAZING? NOTHING COMPARES.
I DO SEE.

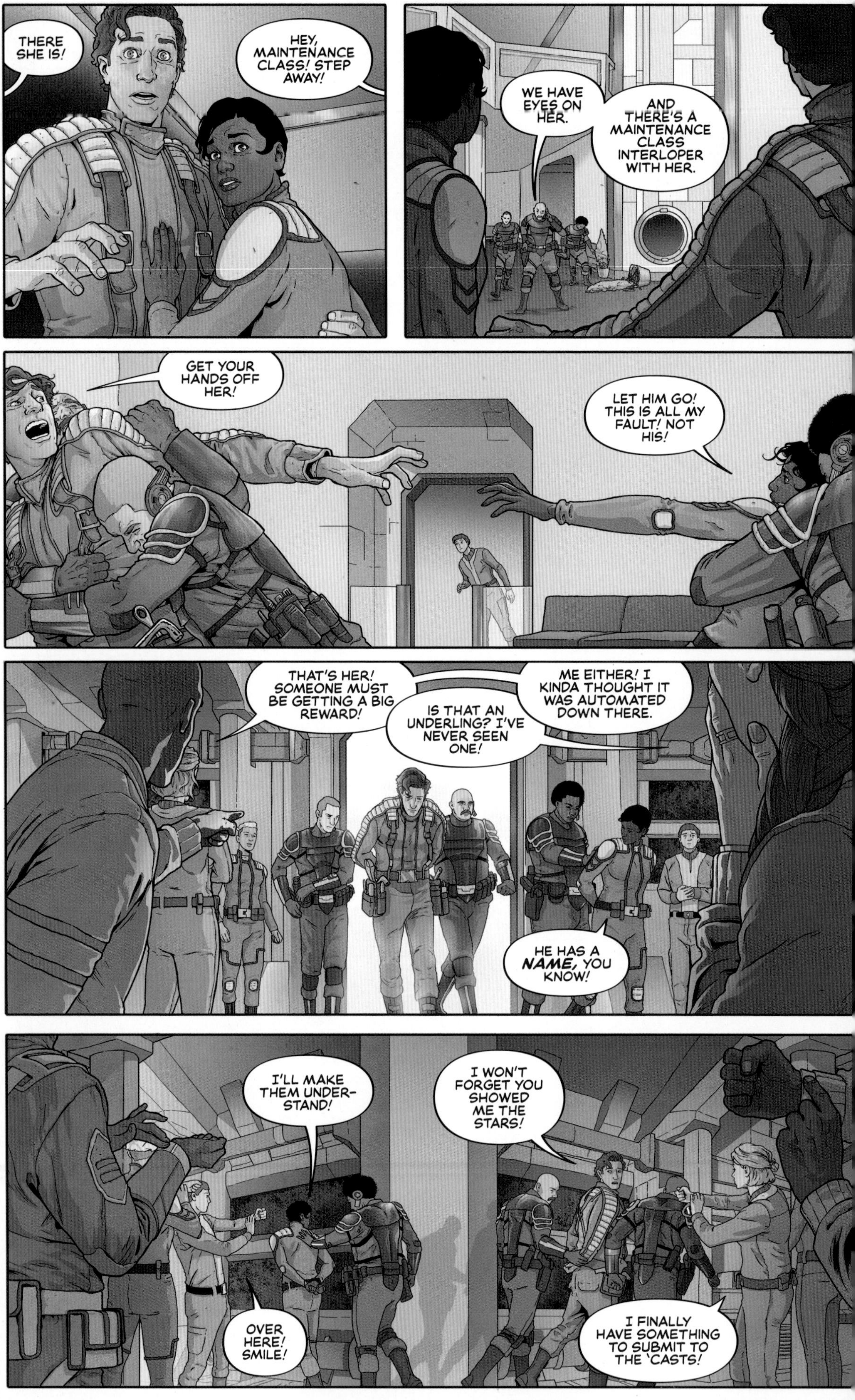
THERE SHE IS!
HEY, MAINTENANCE CLASS! STEP AWAY!
WE HAVE EYES ON HER.
AND THERE'S A MAINTENANCE CLASS INTERLOPER WITH HER.
GET YOUR HANDS OFF HER!
LET HIM GO! THIS IS ALL MY FAULT! NOT HIS!
THAT'S HER! SOMEONE MUST BE GETTING A BIG REWARD!
IS THAT AN UNDERLING? I'VE NEVER SEEN ONE!
ME EITHER! I KINDA THOUGHT IT WAS AUTOMATED DOWN THERE.
HE HAS A ***NAME,*** YOU KNOW!
I'LL MAKE THEM UNDER-STAND!
I WON'T FORGET YOU SHOWED ME THE STARS!
OVER HERE! SMILE!
I FINALLY HAVE SOMETHING TO SUBMIT TO THE 'CASTS!

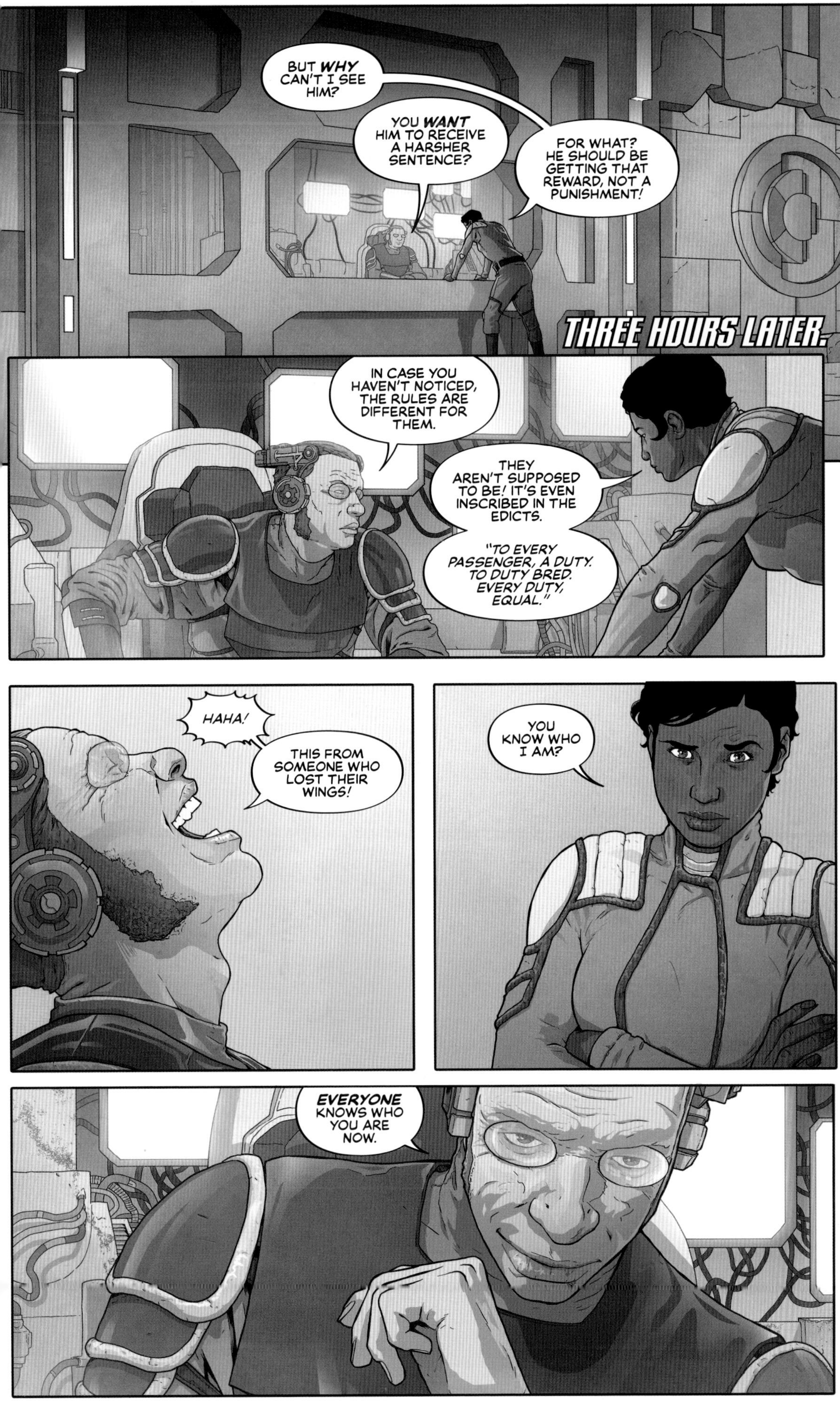
BUT WHY CAN'T I SEE HIM?
YOU WANT HIM TO RECEIVE A HARSHER SENTENCE?
FOR WHAT? HE SHOULD BE GETTING THAT REWARD, NOT A PUNISHMENT!
THREE HOURS LATER.
IN CASE YOU HAVEN'T NOTICED, THE RULES ARE DIFFERENT FOR THEM.
THEY AREN'T SUPPOSED TO BE! IT'S EVEN INSCRIBED IN THE EDICTS.
"TO EVERY PASSENGER, A DUTY. TO DUTY BRED. EVERY DUTY, EQUAL."
HAHA!
THIS FROM SOMEONE WHO LOST THEIR WINGS!
YOU KNOW WHO I AM?
EVERYONE KNOWS WHO YOU ARE NOW.

WHAT ARE YOU DOING HERE, CAT? I'M NOT ALLOWED TO HAVE VISITORS.

DON'T YOU KNOW WHO I AM? APPARENTLY, I'M INFAMOUS.

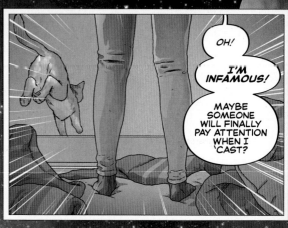

OH!

I'M INFAMOUS!

MAYBE SOMEONE WILL FINALLY PAY ATTENTION WHEN I 'CAST?

I SPEAK NOW NOT TO EXPLAIN OR EXCUSE MYSELF...

BUT BECAUSE ANOTHER IS UNFAIRLY TREATED BECAUSE OF MY ACTIONS.

WHILE I MERELY CHAFE UNDER CONFINEMENT...

WE DEMAND TO SPEAK TO THE PRISONER!

IS IT TRUE HE'S BEING MADE AN EXAMPLE?

NOW WAIT, I'M NOT AUTHORIZED TO--

IT'S BEEN FIFTY-FOUR YEARS SINCE THE LAST EXECUTION! YOUR COMMENT?

...A MAINTENANCE CLASS WORKER NAMED LES IS AWAITING TRIAL FOR MY INSUBORDINATION.

HIS CRIME? DOING WHAT THE DODONA'S LEADERS ASKED OF HIM.

BY THE NEW HOME, I NEVER EXPECTED THE LIKES OF HER TO STEP UP.

NOW HE'S ACCUSED OF SEDITION. JUST FOR LOOKING AT THE STARS!

SO THAT PILOT IS A LEGAL SCHOLAR NOW?

A CASUAL RULE THAT HAS SOLIDIFIED INTO LAW...

DESPITE HAVING NO PRECEDENT IN THE EDICTS.

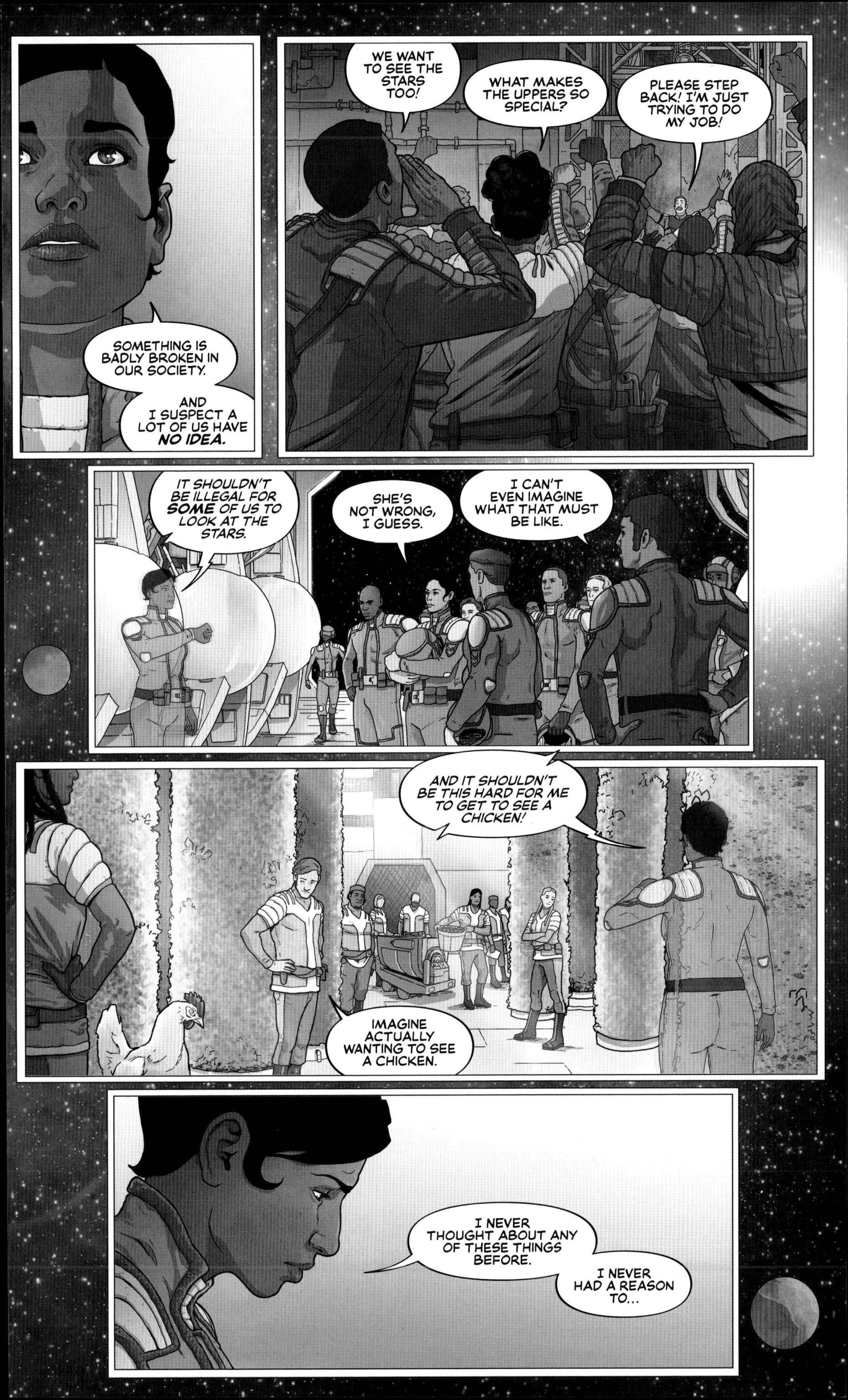
SOMETHING IS BADLY BROKEN IN OUR SOCIETY.
AND I SUSPECT A LOT OF US HAVE **NO IDEA.**
WE WANT TO SEE THE STARS TOO!
WHAT MAKES THE UPPERS SO SPECIAL?
PLEASE STEP BACK! I'M JUST TRYING TO DO MY JOB!
*IT SHOULDN'T BE ILLEGAL FOR **SOME** OF US TO LOOK AT THE STARS.*
SHE'S NOT WRONG, I GUESS.
I CAN'T EVEN IMAGINE WHAT THAT MUST BE LIKE.
AND IT SHOULDN'T BE THIS HARD FOR ME TO GET TO SEE A CHICKEN!
IMAGINE ACTUALLY WANTING TO SEE A CHICKEN.
I NEVER THOUGHT ABOUT ANY OF THESE THINGS BEFORE.
I NEVER HAD A REASON TO...

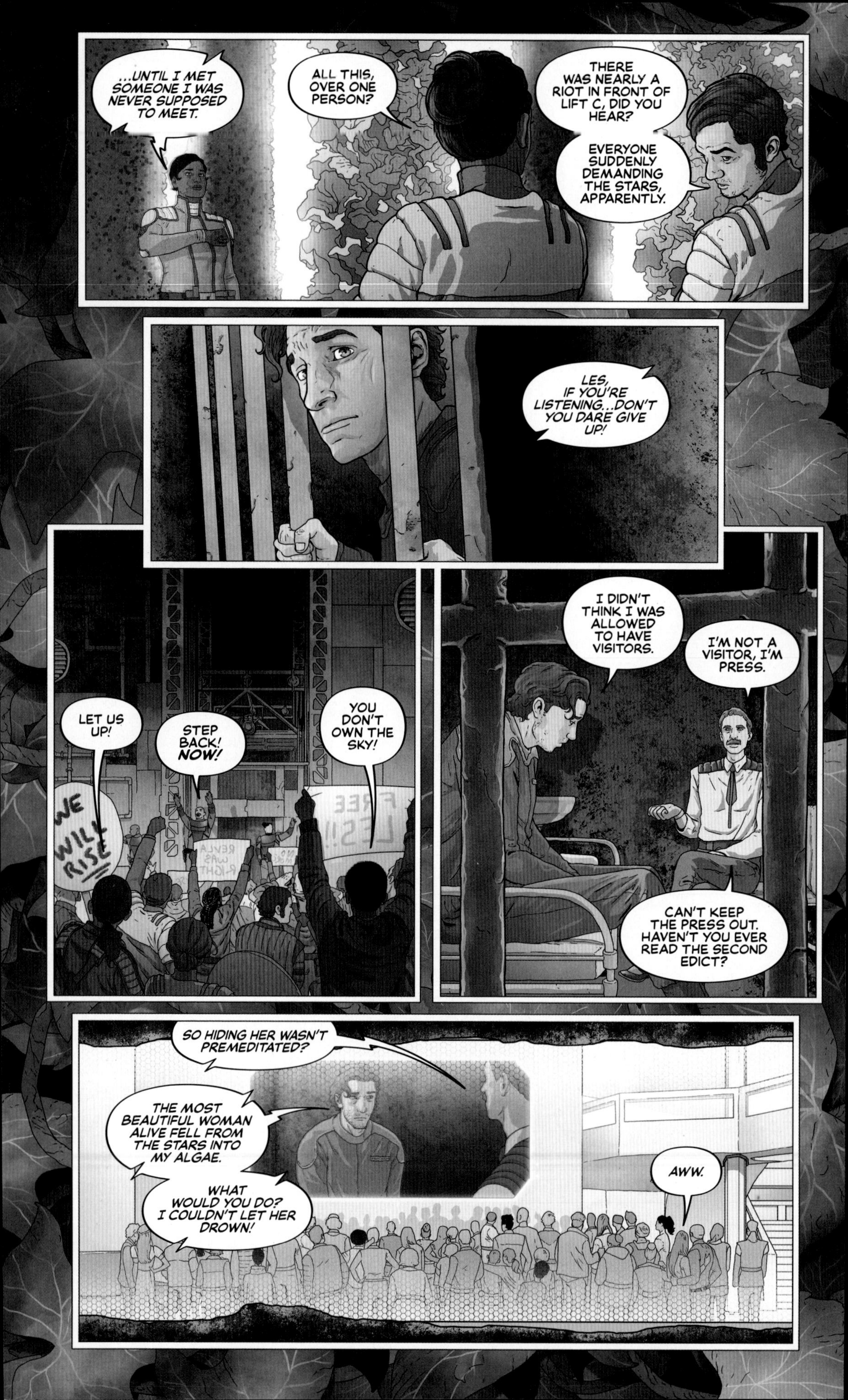
...UNTIL I MET SOMEONE I WAS NEVER SUPPOSED TO MEET.
ALL THIS, OVER ONE PERSON?
THERE WAS NEARLY A RIOT IN FRONT OF LIFT C, DID YOU HEAR?
EVERYONE SUDDENLY DEMANDING THE STARS, APPARENTLY.
LES, IF YOU'RE LISTENING...DON'T YOU DARE GIVE UP!
LET US UP!
STEP BACK! **NOW!**
YOU DON'T OWN THE SKY!
WE WILL RISE
REVLA WAS RIGHT
FREE LES!!
I DIDN'T THINK I WAS ALLOWED TO HAVE VISITORS.
I'M NOT A VISITOR, I'M PRESS.
CAN'T KEEP THE PRESS OUT. HAVEN'T YOU EVER READ THE SECOND EDICT?
SO HIDING HER WASN'T PREMEDITATED?
THE MOST BEAUTIFUL WOMAN ALIVE FELL FROM THE STARS INTO MY ALGAE.
WHAT WOULD YOU DO? I COULDN'T LET HER DROWN!
AWW.

EVERY DUTY. EQUAL.
OF COURSE I CALLED THIS MEETING TO ADDRESS THE UNREST! IT'S--
SO THEY GET RESTLESS NOW AND THEN. BEST THING IS TO IGNORE IT.
WE'RE THE COUNCIL! WE HAVE TO AT LEAST LISTEN.
WHY? WE TELL THEM HOW IT IS, NOT THE OTHER WAY AROUND.
ONE MONTH LATER.
YOU'D THINK I'D HAVE FIGURED OUT HOW YOU GET IN HERE BY NOW.
MRRRP
WELL, SURE. BUT I HAVE THUMBS.
MRRRR
I KNOW, IT'S TIME FOR MY 'CAST. HAVEN'T MISSED ONE YET.
SIX MONTHS LATER.
NOT TO BELABOR THE POINT BUT IGNORING THEM DIDN'T WORK.
THAT'S NOT A REASON TO GIVE THEM MORE SPACE TO COMPLAIN.
AN INSURRECTION COULD DOOM THE ENTIRE SHIP!
I'D HARDLY CALL THIS AN INSURRECTION.
ONE YEAR LATER.
THIS IS GOOD NEWS! WE'VE GOT THE SENTENCE DOWN TO FOUR YEARS!
IT COULD BE WORSE. MUCH WORSE.
I KNOW. BUT I'M SO SICK OF STARING AT THESE WALLS!
TWO YEARS LATER.
THEN IT'S AGREED? WE AT LEAST HEAR THEIR DEMANDS?
IF THEY AGREE TO PICK A REPRESENTATIVE.
AND IT CAN'T BE THE ONE IN JAIL. HE'S ENTIRELY TOO POPULAR.
OF COURSE NOT. THE FOCUS SHOULD BE POLICY, NOT THEATRICS.
THREE YEARS LATER.
I CAN'T BELIEVE IT! YOU'LL BE OUT IN A FEW DAYS!
I QUIT FLYING.
ONLY BECAUSE YOU DON'T KNOW HOW TO QUIT.
NOT BY CHOICE. BUT WE'LL GET YOU BACK OUT THERE.
FOUR YEARS LATER.

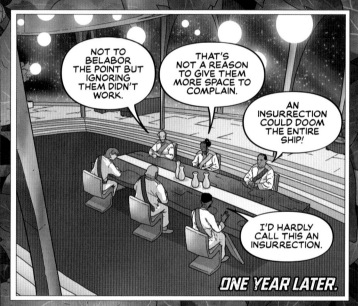

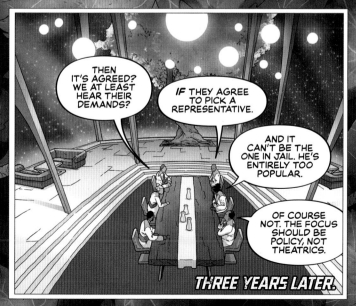

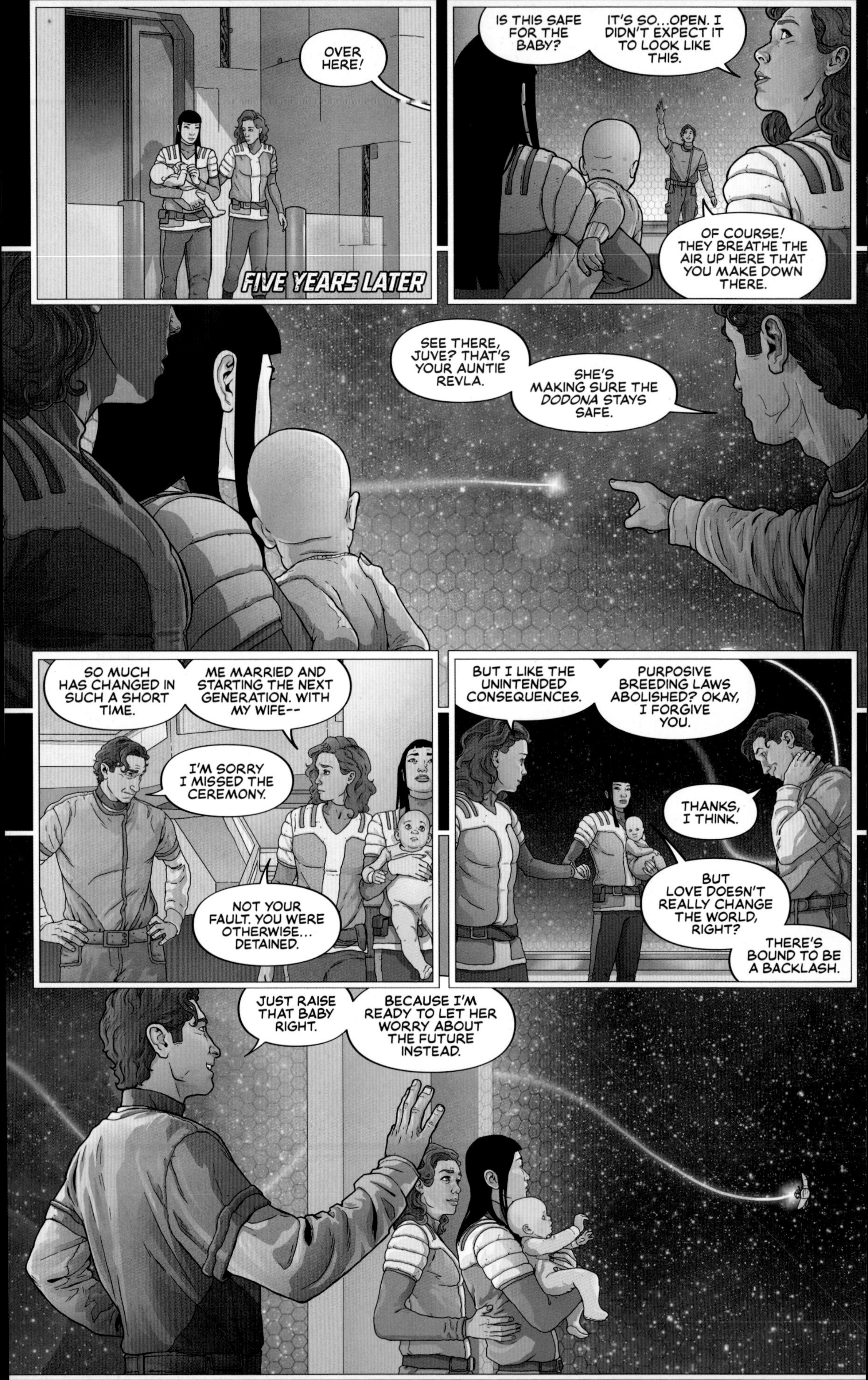
OVER HERE!
FIVE YEARS LATER
IS THIS SAFE FOR THE BABY?
IT'S SO...OPEN. I DIDN'T EXPECT IT TO LOOK LIKE THIS.
OF COURSE! THEY BREATHE THE AIR UP HERE THAT YOU MAKE DOWN THERE.
SEE THERE, JUVE? THAT'S YOUR AUNTIE REVLA.
SHE'S MAKING SURE THE *DODONA* STAYS SAFE.
SO MUCH HAS CHANGED IN SUCH A SHORT TIME.
ME MARRIED AND STARTING THE NEXT GENERATION. WITH MY WIFE--
I'M SORRY I MISSED THE CEREMONY.
NOT YOUR FAULT. YOU WERE OTHERWISE... DETAINED.
BUT I LIKE THE UNINTENDED CONSEQUENCES.
PURPOSIVE BREEDING LAWS ABOLISHED? OKAY, I FORGIVE YOU.
THANKS, I THINK.
BUT LOVE DOESN'T REALLY CHANGE THE WORLD, RIGHT?
THERE'S BOUND TO BE A BACKLASH.
JUST RAISE THAT BABY RIGHT.
BECAUSE I'M READY TO LET HER WORRY ABOUT THE FUTURE INSTEAD.

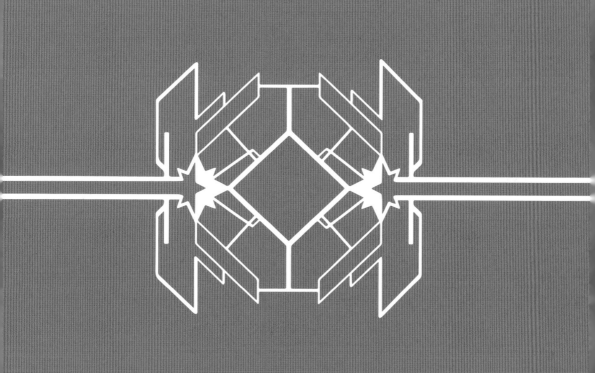

CHAPTER
TWO

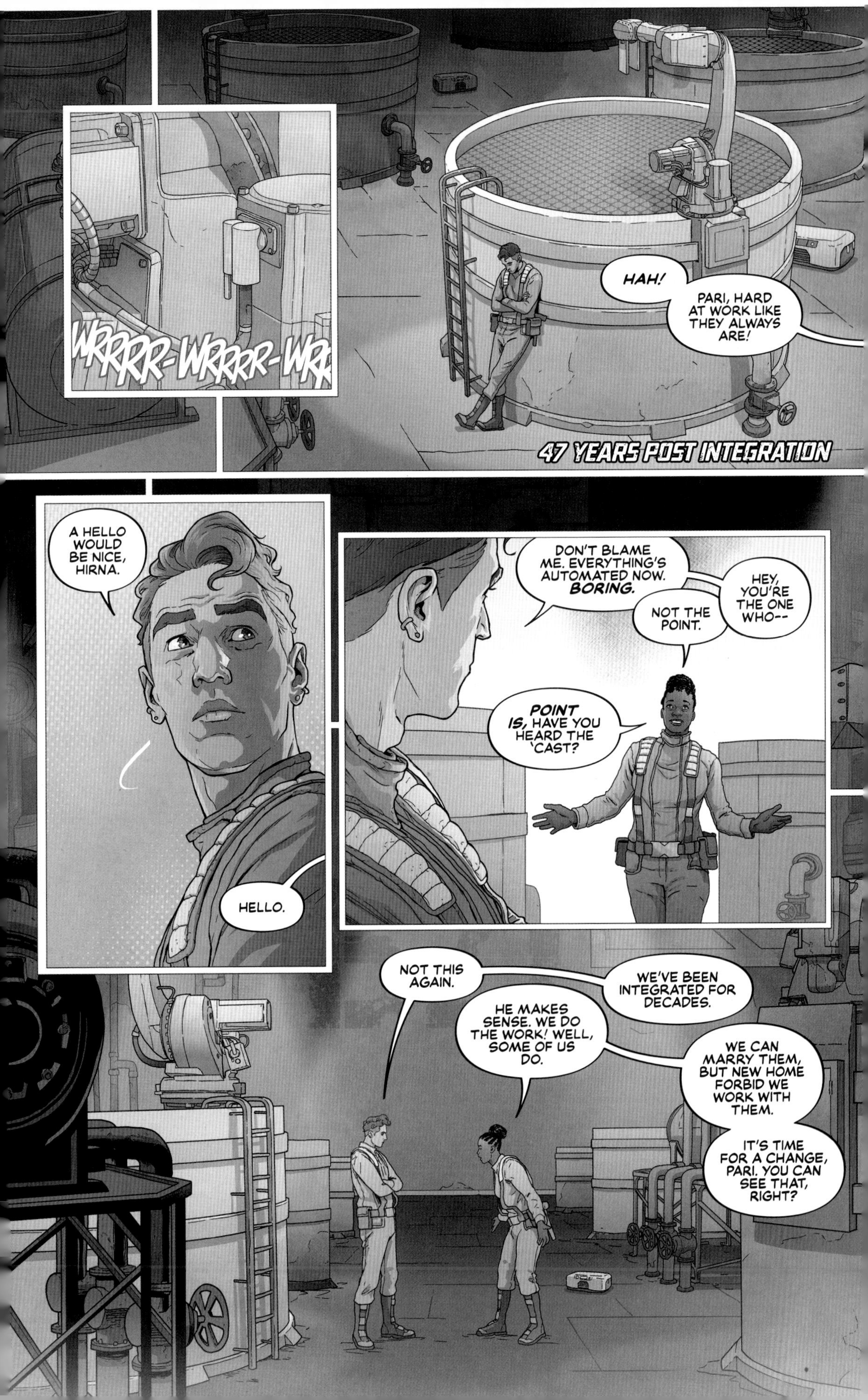
WRRRR-WRRRR-WRR
HAH!
PARI, HARD AT WORK LIKE THEY ALWAYS ARE!
47 YEARS POST INTEGRATION
A HELLO WOULD BE NICE, HIRNA.
HELLO.
DON'T BLAME ME. EVERYTHING'S AUTOMATED NOW. BORING.
HEY, YOU'RE THE ONE WHO--
NOT THE POINT.
POINT IS, HAVE YOU HEARD THE 'CAST?
NOT THIS AGAIN.
WE'VE BEEN INTEGRATED FOR DECADES.
HE MAKES SENSE. WE DO THE WORK! WELL, SOME OF US DO.
WE CAN MARRY THEM, BUT NEW HOME FORBID WE WORK WITH THEM.
IT'S TIME FOR A CHANGE, PARI. YOU CAN SEE THAT, RIGHT?

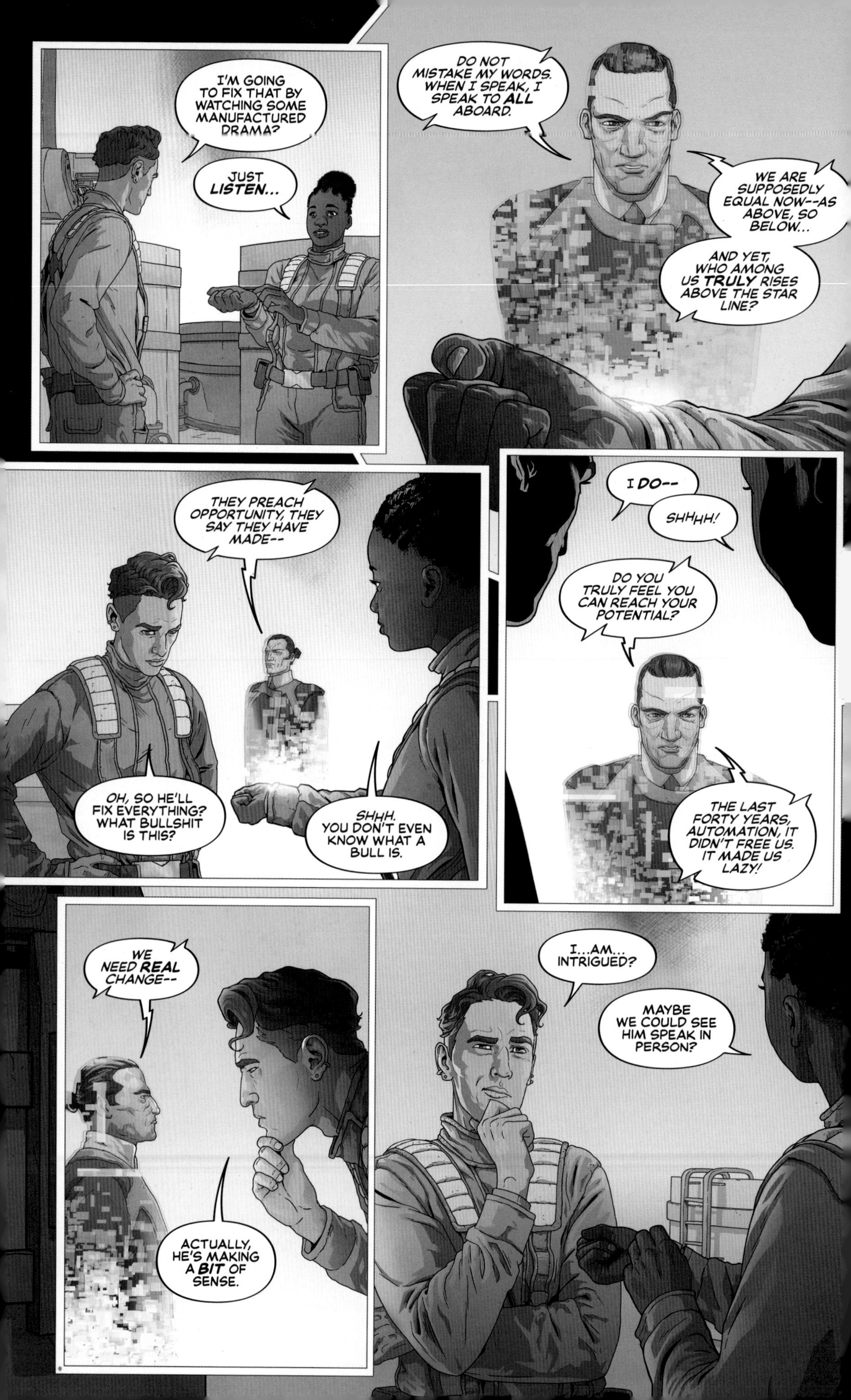
I'M GOING TO FIX THAT BY WATCHING SOME MANUFACTURED DRAMA?
JUST **LISTEN...**
DO NOT MISTAKE MY WORDS. WHEN I SPEAK, I SPEAK TO **ALL** ABOARD.
WE ARE SUPPOSEDLY EQUAL NOW--AS ABOVE, SO BELOW...
AND YET, WHO AMONG US **TRULY** RISES ABOVE THE STAR LINE?
THEY PREACH OPPORTUNITY, THEY SAY THEY HAVE MADE--
OH, SO HE'LL FIX EVERYTHING? WHAT BULLSHIT IS THIS?
SHHH. YOU DON'T EVEN KNOW WHAT A BULL IS.
I **DO--**
SHHHH!
DO YOU TRULY FEEL YOU CAN REACH YOUR POTENTIAL?
THE LAST FORTY YEARS, AUTOMATION, IT DIDN'T FREE US. IT MADE US LAZY!
WE NEED **REAL** CHANGE--
ACTUALLY, HE'S MAKING A **BIT** OF SENSE.
I...AM... INTRIGUED?
MAYBE WE COULD SEE HIM SPEAK IN PERSON?

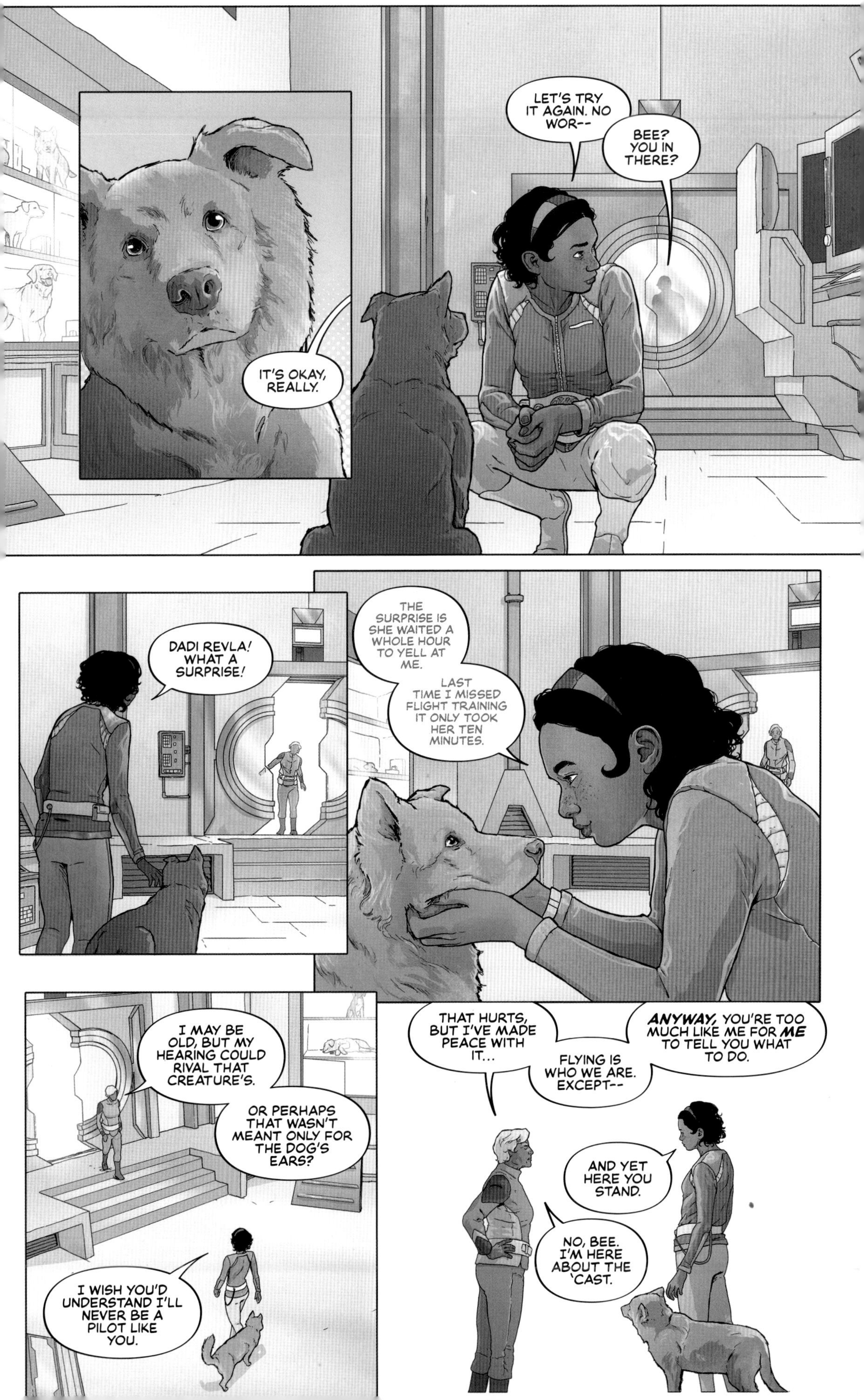
IT'S OKAY, REALLY.
LET'S TRY IT AGAIN. NO WOR--
BEE? YOU IN THERE?
DADI REVLA! WHAT A SURPRISE!
THE SURPRISE IS SHE WAITED A WHOLE HOUR TO YELL AT ME.
LAST TIME I MISSED FLIGHT TRAINING IT ONLY TOOK HER TEN MINUTES.
I MAY BE OLD, BUT MY HEARING COULD RIVAL THAT CREATURE'S.
OR PERHAPS THAT WASN'T MEANT ONLY FOR THE DOG'S EARS?
I WISH YOU'D UNDERSTAND I'LL NEVER BE A PILOT LIKE YOU.
THAT HURTS, BUT I'VE MADE PEACE WITH IT...
FLYING IS WHO WE ARE. EXCEPT--
ANYWAY, YOU'RE TOO MUCH LIKE ME FOR ME TO TELL YOU WHAT TO DO.
AND YET HERE YOU STAND.
NO, BEE. I'M HERE ABOUT THE 'CAST.

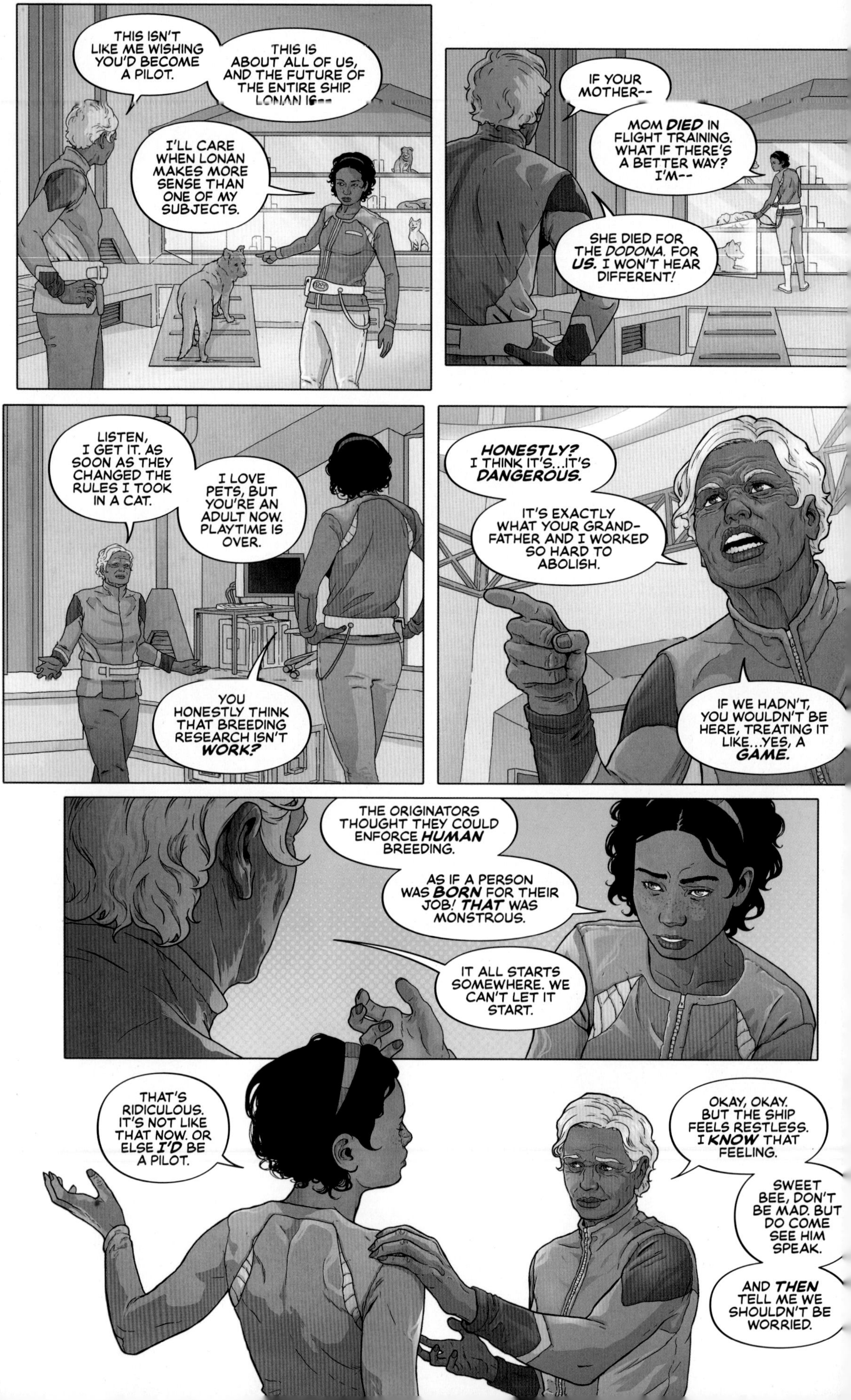
THIS ISN'T LIKE ME WISHING YOU'D BECOME A PILOT.
THIS IS ABOUT ALL OF US, AND THE FUTURE OF THE ENTIRE SHIP. LONAN IS--
I'LL CARE WHEN LONAN MAKES MORE SENSE THAN ONE OF MY SUBJECTS.
IF YOUR MOTHER--
MOM DIED IN FLIGHT TRAINING. WHAT IF THERE'S A BETTER WAY? I'M--
SHE DIED FOR THE DODONA. FOR US. I WON'T HEAR DIFFERENT!
LISTEN, I GET IT. AS SOON AS THEY CHANGED THE RULES I TOOK IN A CAT.
I LOVE PETS, BUT YOU'RE AN ADULT NOW. PLAYTIME IS OVER.
YOU HONESTLY THINK THAT BREEDING RESEARCH ISN'T WORK?
HONESTLY? I THINK IT'S...IT'S DANGEROUS.
IT'S EXACTLY WHAT YOUR GRAND-FATHER AND I WORKED SO HARD TO ABOLISH.
IF WE HADN'T, YOU WOULDN'T BE HERE, TREATING IT LIKE...YES, A GAME.
THE ORIGINATORS THOUGHT THEY COULD ENFORCE HUMAN BREEDING.
AS IF A PERSON WAS BORN FOR THEIR JOB! THAT WAS MONSTROUS.
IT ALL STARTS SOMEWHERE. WE CAN'T LET IT START.
THAT'S RIDICULOUS. IT'S NOT LIKE THAT NOW. OR ELSE I'D BE A PILOT.
OKAY, OKAY. BUT THE SHIP FEELS RESTLESS. I KNOW THAT FEELING.
SWEET BEE, DON'T BE MAD. BUT DO COME SEE HIM SPEAK.
AND THEN TELL ME WE SHOULDN'T BE WORRIED.

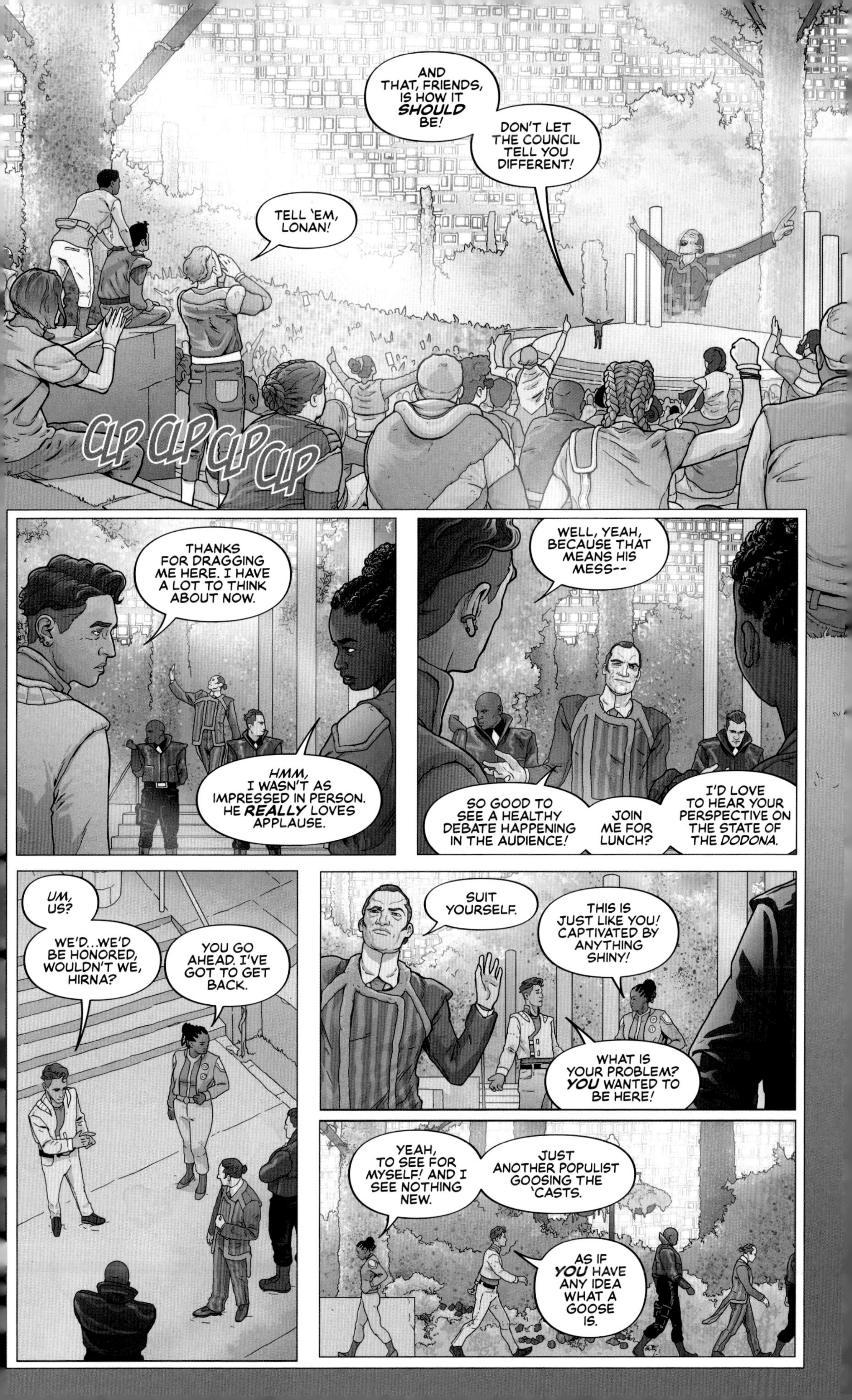
AND THAT, FRIENDS, IS HOW IT SHOULD BE!
DON'T LET THE COUNCIL TELL YOU DIFFERENT!
TELL 'EM, LONAN!
CLAP CLAP CLAP CLAP
THANKS FOR DRAGGING ME HERE. I HAVE A LOT TO THINK ABOUT NOW.
HMM, I WASN'T AS IMPRESSED IN PERSON. HE REALLY LOVES APPLAUSE.
WELL, YEAH, BECAUSE THAT MEANS HIS MESS--
SO GOOD TO SEE A HEALTHY DEBATE HAPPENING IN THE AUDIENCE!
JOIN ME FOR LUNCH?
I'D LOVE TO HEAR YOUR PERSPECTIVE ON THE STATE OF THE DODONA.
UM, US?
WE'D...WE'D BE HONORED, WOULDN'T WE, HIRNA?
YOU GO AHEAD. I'VE GOT TO GET BACK.
SUIT YOURSELF.
THIS IS JUST LIKE YOU! CAPTIVATED BY ANYTHING SHINY!
WHAT IS YOUR PROBLEM? YOU WANTED TO BE HERE!
YEAH, TO SEE FOR MYSELF! AND I SEE NOTHING NEW.
JUST ANOTHER POPULIST GOOSING THE 'CASTS.
AS IF YOU HAVE ANY IDEA WHAT A GOOSE IS.

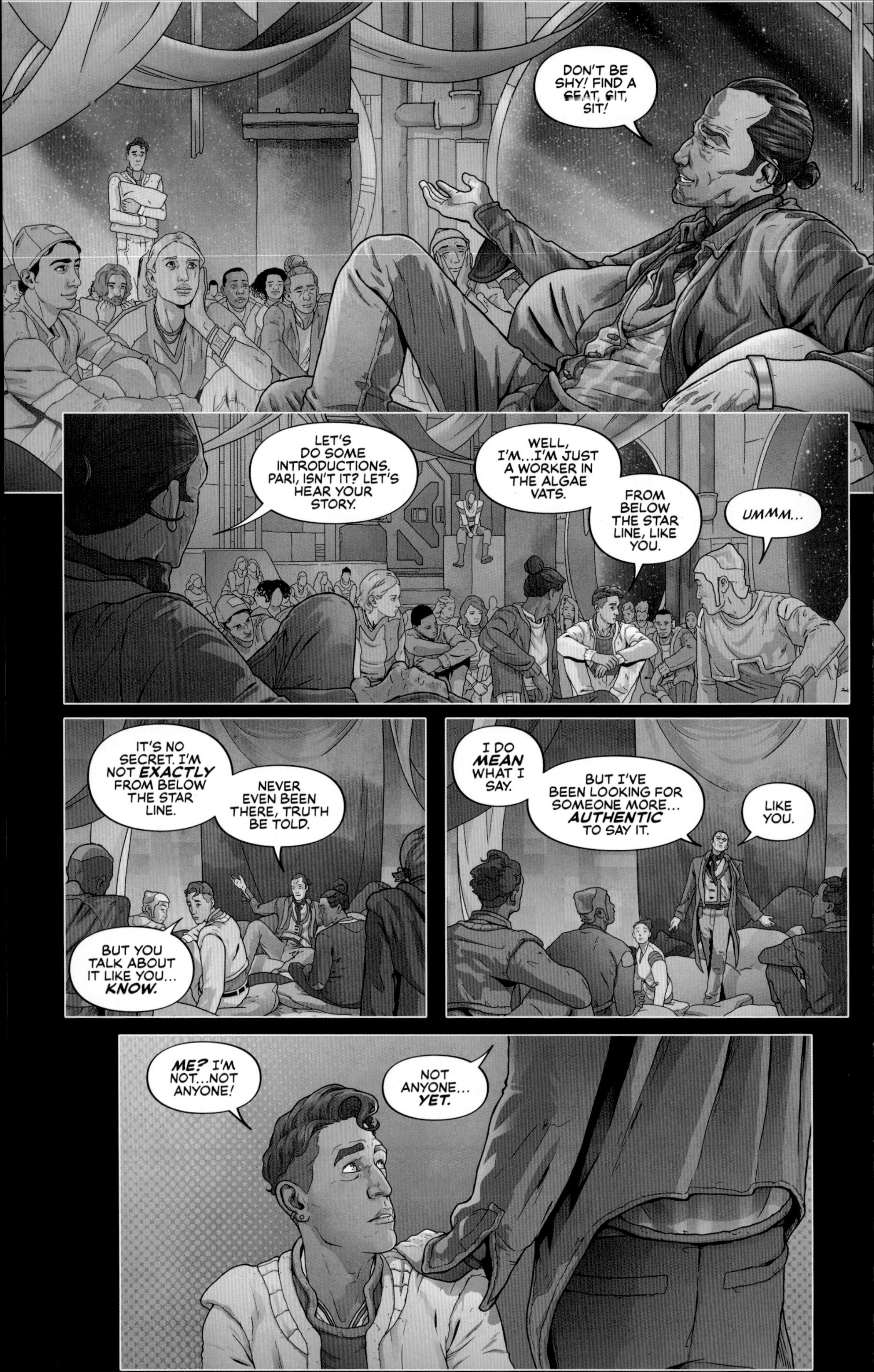

DON'T BE SHY! FIND A SEAT, SIT, SIT!
LET'S DO SOME INTRODUCTIONS. PARI, ISN'T IT? LET'S HEAR YOUR STORY.
WELL, I'M...I'M JUST A WORKER IN THE ALGAE VATS.
FROM BELOW THE STAR LINE, LIKE YOU.
UMMM...
IT'S NO SECRET. I'M NOT **EXACTLY** FROM BELOW THE STAR LINE.
NEVER EVEN BEEN THERE, TRUTH BE TOLD.
BUT YOU TALK ABOUT IT LIKE YOU... **KNOW.**
I DO **MEAN** WHAT I SAY.
BUT I'VE BEEN LOOKING FOR SOMEONE MORE... **AUTHENTIC** TO SAY IT.
LIKE YOU.
ME? I'M NOT...NOT ANYONE!
NOT ANYONE... **YET.**

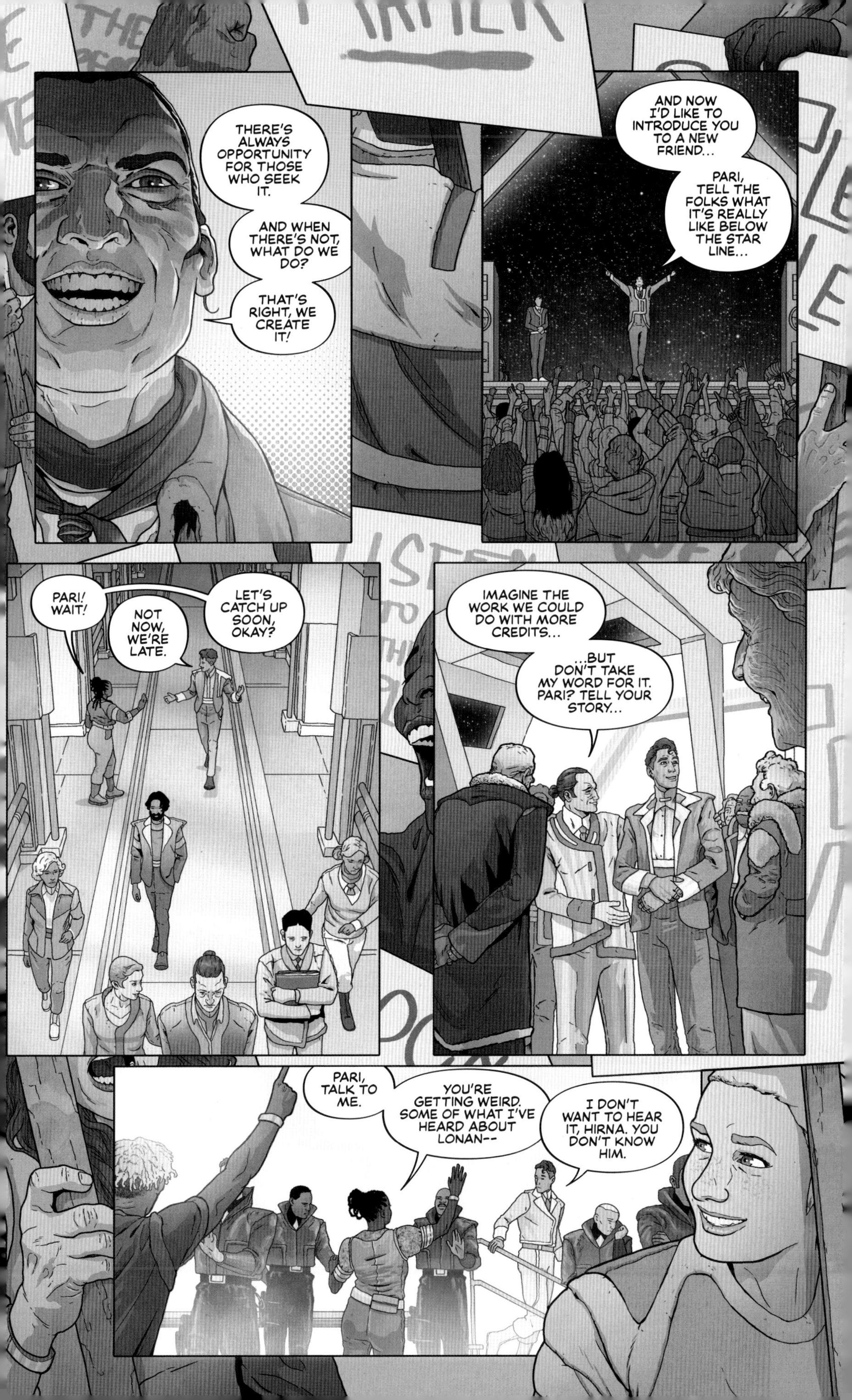
THERE'S ALWAYS OPPORTUNITY FOR THOSE WHO SEEK IT.
AND WHEN THERE'S NOT, WHAT DO WE DO?
THAT'S RIGHT, WE CREATE IT!
AND NOW I'D LIKE TO INTRODUCE YOU TO A NEW FRIEND...
PARI, TELL THE FOLKS WHAT IT'S REALLY LIKE BELOW THE STAR LINE...
PARI! WAIT!
NOT NOW, WE'RE LATE.
LET'S CATCH UP SOON, OKAY?
IMAGINE THE WORK WE COULD DO WITH MORE CREDITS...
...BUT DON'T TAKE MY WORD FOR IT. PARI? TELL YOUR STORY...
PARI, TALK TO ME.
YOU'RE GETTING WEIRD. SOME OF WHAT I'VE HEARD ABOUT LONAN--
I DON'T WANT TO HEAR IT, HIRNA. YOU DON'T KNOW HIM.

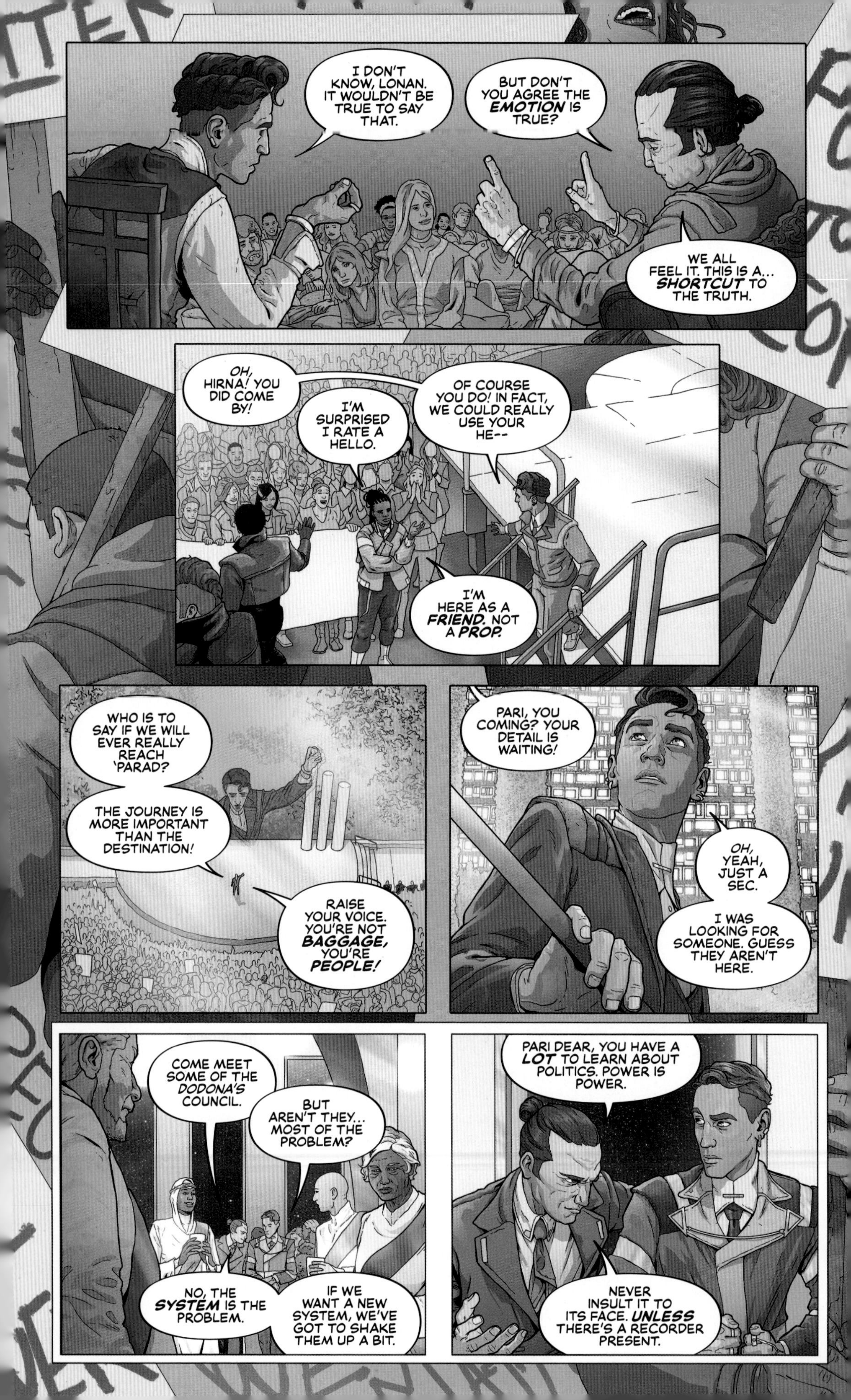
I DON'T KNOW, LONAN. IT WOULDN'T BE TRUE TO SAY THAT.
BUT DON'T YOU AGREE THE EMOTION IS TRUE?
WE ALL FEEL IT. THIS IS A... SHORTCUT TO THE TRUTH.
OH, HIRNA! YOU DID COME BY!
I'M SURPRISED I RATE A HELLO.
OF COURSE YOU DO! IN FACT, WE COULD REALLY USE YOUR HE--
I'M HERE AS A FRIEND. NOT A PROP.
WHO IS TO SAY IF WE WILL EVER REALLY REACH 'PARAD?
THE JOURNEY IS MORE IMPORTANT THAN THE DESTINATION!
RAISE YOUR VOICE. YOU'RE NOT BAGGAGE, YOU'RE PEOPLE!
PARI, YOU COMING? YOUR DETAIL IS WAITING!
OH, YEAH, JUST A SEC.
I WAS LOOKING FOR SOMEONE. GUESS THEY AREN'T HERE.
COME MEET SOME OF THE DODONA'S COUNCIL.
BUT AREN'T THEY... MOST OF THE PROBLEM?
NO, THE SYSTEM IS THE PROBLEM.
IF WE WANT A NEW SYSTEM, WE'VE GOT TO SHAKE THEM UP A BIT.
PARI DEAR, YOU HAVE A LOT TO LEARN ABOUT POLITICS. POWER IS POWER.
NEVER INSULT IT TO ITS FACE. UNLESS THERE'S A RECORDER PRESENT.

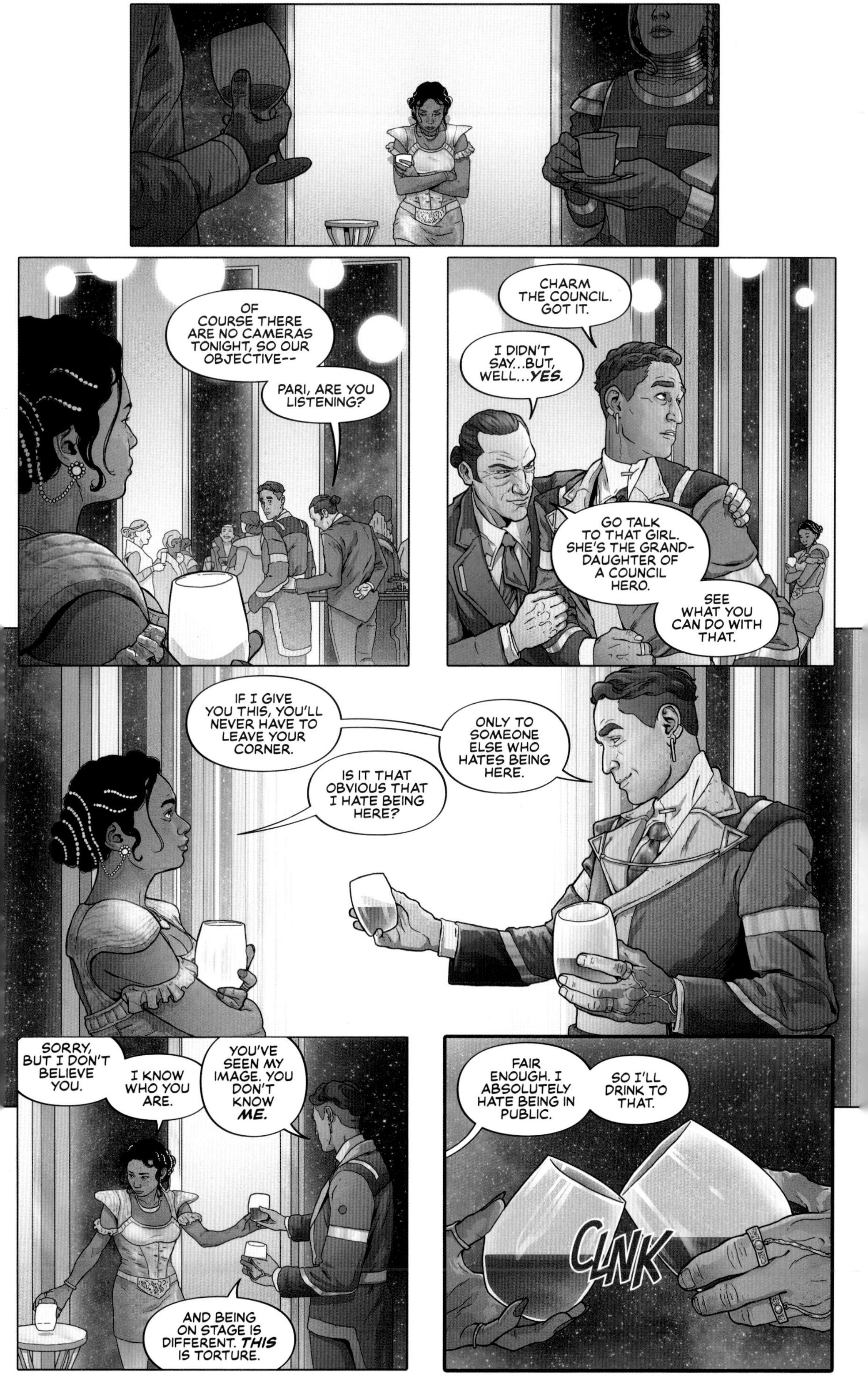
OF COURSE THERE ARE NO CAMERAS TONIGHT, SO OUR OBJECTIVE--
PARI, ARE YOU LISTENING?
CHARM THE COUNCIL. GOT IT.
I DIDN'T SAY...BUT, WELL...YES.
GO TALK TO THAT GIRL. SHE'S THE GRAND-DAUGHTER OF A COUNCIL HERO.
SEE WHAT YOU CAN DO WITH THAT.
IF I GIVE YOU THIS, YOU'LL NEVER HAVE TO LEAVE YOUR CORNER.
ONLY TO SOMEONE ELSE WHO HATES BEING HERE.
IS IT THAT OBVIOUS THAT I HATE BEING HERE?
SORRY, BUT I DON'T BELIEVE YOU.
I KNOW WHO YOU ARE.
YOU'VE SEEN MY IMAGE. YOU DON'T KNOW ME.
AND BEING ON STAGE IS DIFFERENT. THIS IS TORTURE.
FAIR ENOUGH. I ABSOLUTELY HATE BEING IN PUBLIC.
SO I'LL DRINK TO THAT.
CLNK

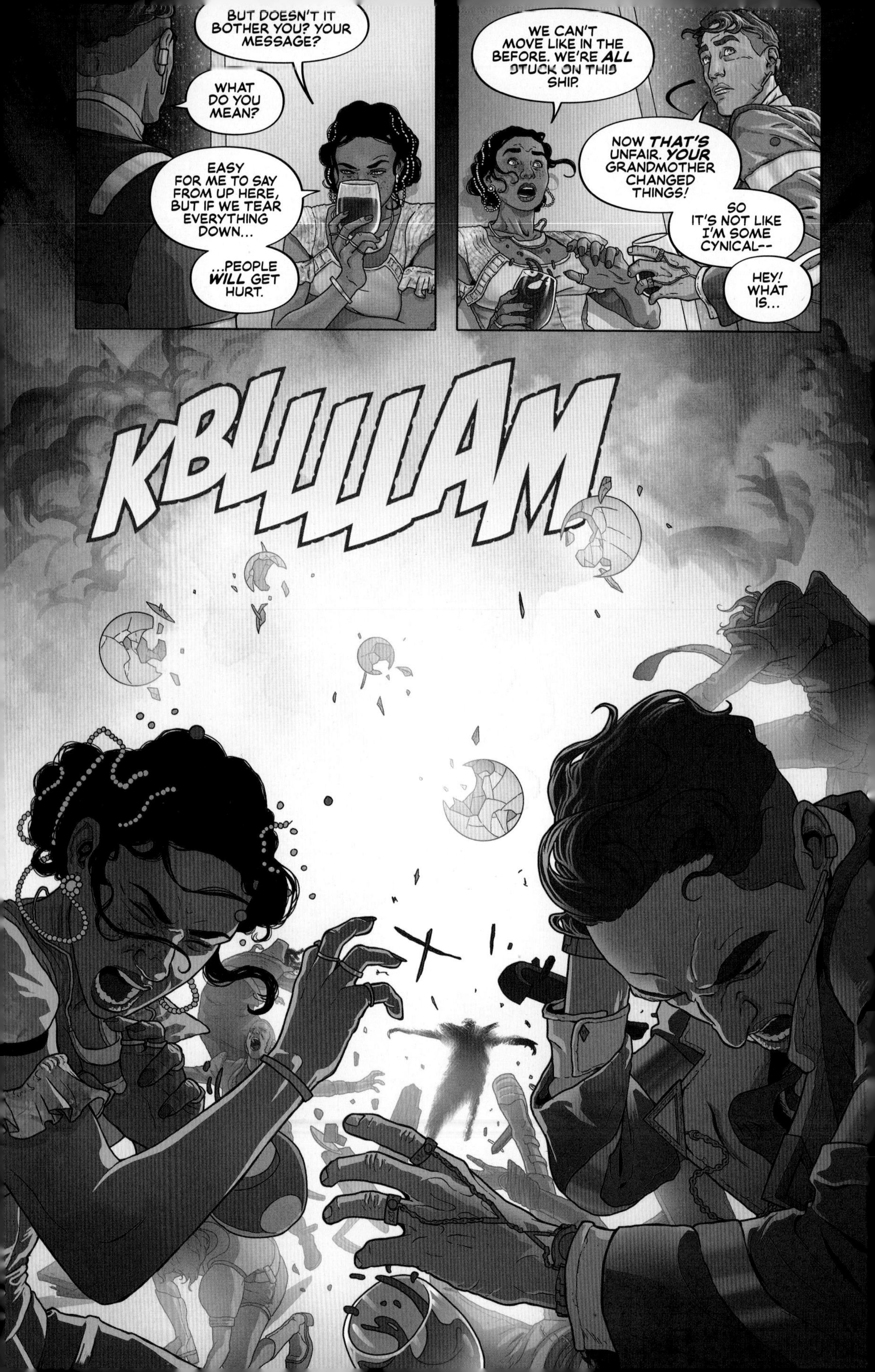
BUT DOESN'T IT BOTHER YOU? YOUR MESSAGE?
WHAT DO YOU MEAN?
EASY FOR ME TO SAY FROM UP HERE, BUT IF WE TEAR EVERYTHING DOWN...
...PEOPLE WILL GET HURT.
WE CAN'T MOVE LIKE IN THE BEFORE. WE'RE ALL STUCK ON THIS SHIP.
NOW THAT'S UNFAIR. YOUR GRANDMOTHER CHANGED THINGS!
SO IT'S NOT LIKE I'M SOME CYNICAL--
HEY! WHAT IS...
KBLLLLAM

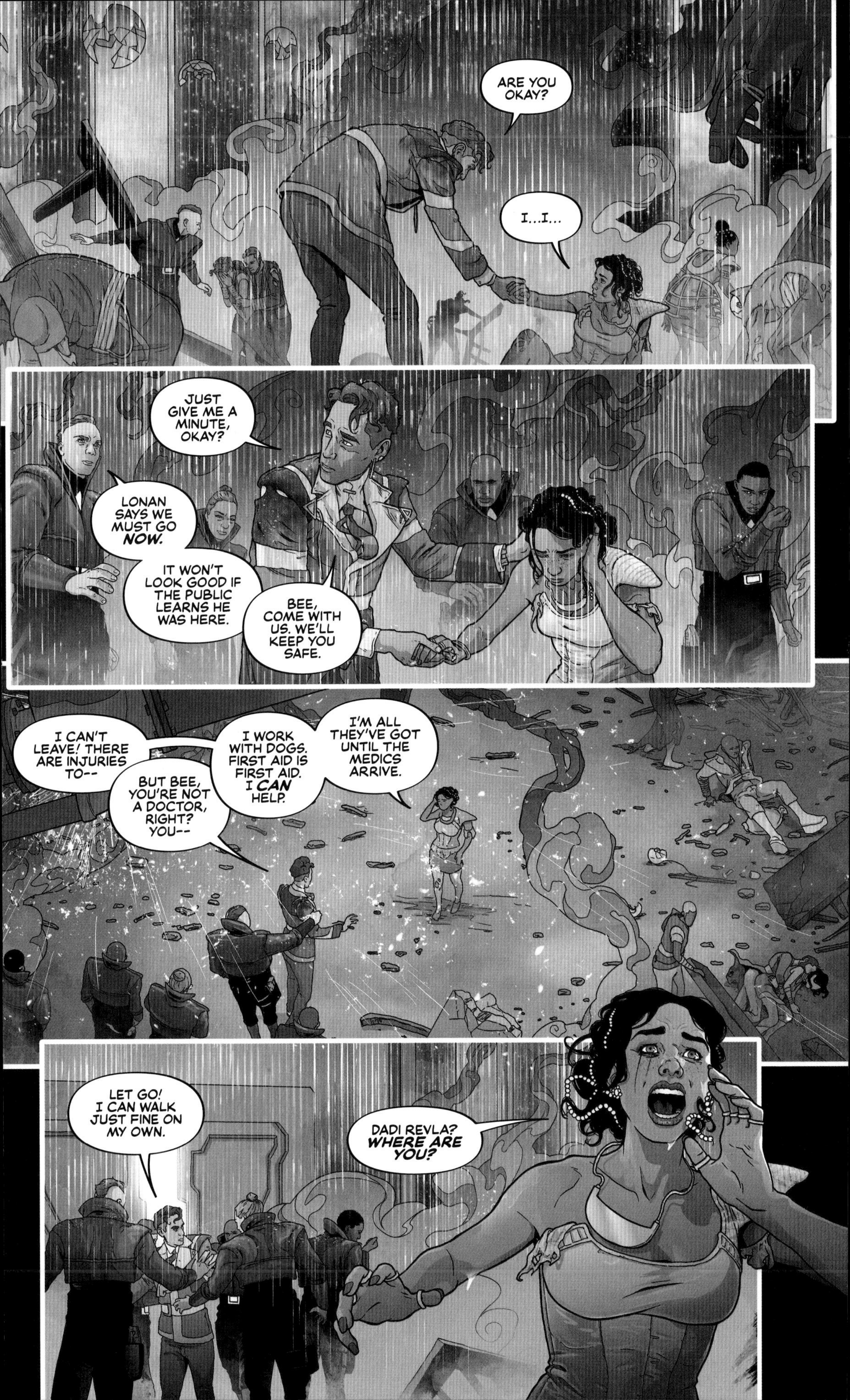
ARE YOU OKAY?
I...I...
JUST GIVE ME A MINUTE, OKAY?
LONAN SAYS WE MUST GO NOW.
IT WON'T LOOK GOOD IF THE PUBLIC LEARNS HE WAS HERE.
BEE, COME WITH US. WE'LL KEEP YOU SAFE.
I CAN'T LEAVE! THERE ARE INJURIES TO--
BUT BEE, YOU'RE NOT A DOCTOR, RIGHT? YOU--
I WORK WITH DOGS. FIRST AID IS FIRST AID. I CAN HELP.
I'M ALL THEY'VE GOT UNTIL THE MEDICS ARRIVE.
LET GO! I CAN WALK JUST FINE ON MY OWN.
DADI REVLA? WHERE ARE YOU?

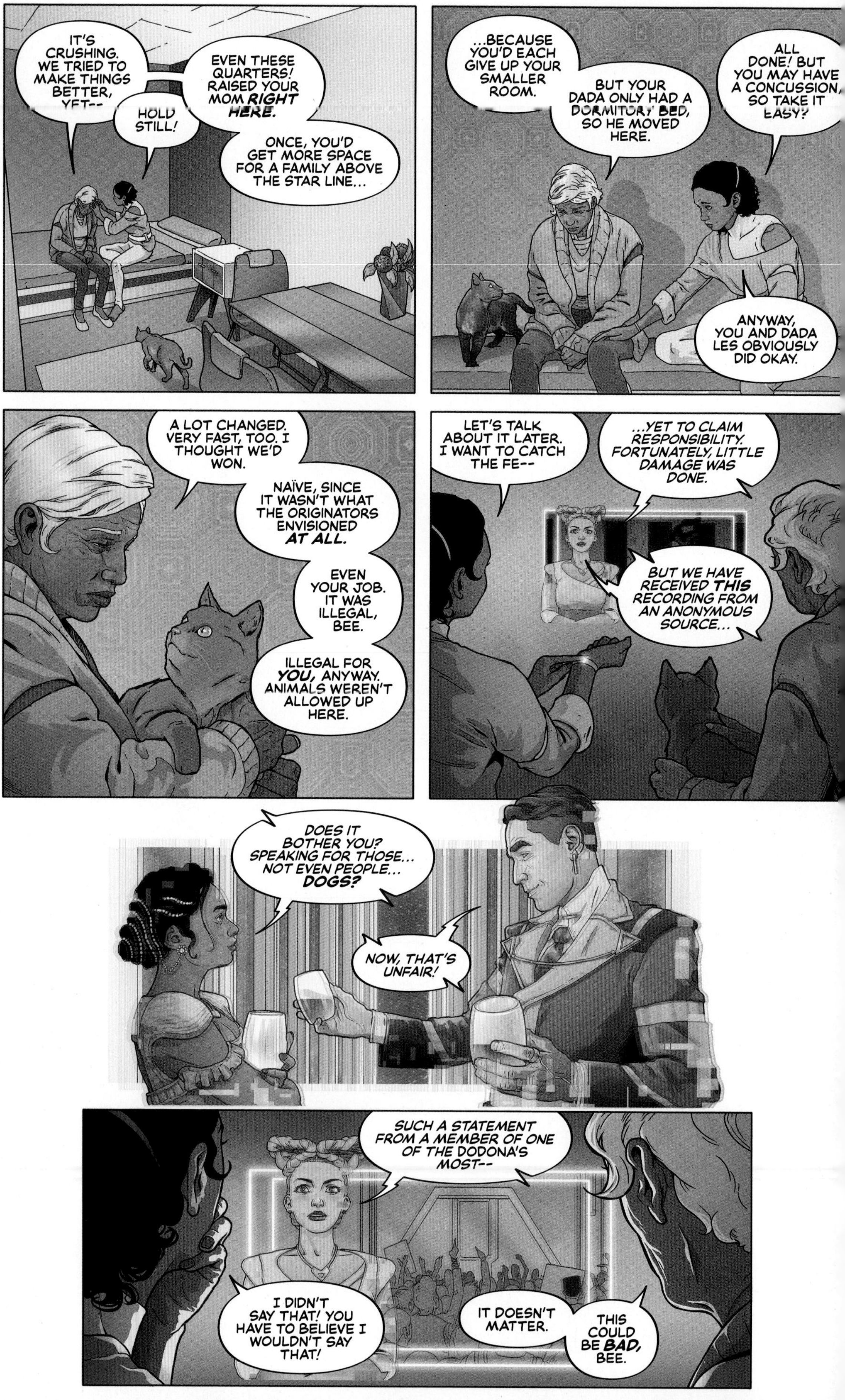
IT'S CRUSHING. WE TRIED TO MAKE THINGS BETTER, YET--
HOLD STILL!
EVEN THESE QUARTERS! RAISED YOUR MOM RIGHT HERE.
ONCE, YOU'D GET MORE SPACE FOR A FAMILY ABOVE THE STAR LINE...
...BECAUSE YOU'D EACH GIVE UP YOUR SMALLER ROOM.
BUT YOUR DADA ONLY HAD A DORMITORY BED, SO HE MOVED HERE.
ALL DONE! BUT YOU MAY HAVE A CONCUSSION, SO TAKE IT EASY?
ANYWAY, YOU AND DADA LES OBVIOUSLY DID OKAY.
A LOT CHANGED. VERY FAST, TOO. I THOUGHT WE'D WON.
NAÏVE, SINCE IT WASN'T WHAT THE ORIGINATORS ENVISIONED AT ALL.
EVEN YOUR JOB. IT WAS ILLEGAL, BEE.
ILLEGAL FOR YOU, ANYWAY. ANIMALS WEREN'T ALLOWED UP HERE.
LET'S TALK ABOUT IT LATER. I WANT TO CATCH THE FE--
...YET TO CLAIM RESPONSIBILITY. FORTUNATELY, LITTLE DAMAGE WAS DONE.
BUT WE HAVE RECEIVED THIS RECORDING FROM AN ANONYMOUS SOURCE...
DOES IT BOTHER YOU? SPEAKING FOR THOSE... NOT EVEN PEOPLE... DOGS?
NOW, THAT'S UNFAIR!
SUCH A STATEMENT FROM A MEMBER OF ONE OF THE DODONA'S MOST--
I DIDN'T SAY THAT! YOU HAVE TO BELIEVE I WOULDN'T SAY THAT!
IT DOESN'T MATTER.
THIS COULD BE BAD, BEE.

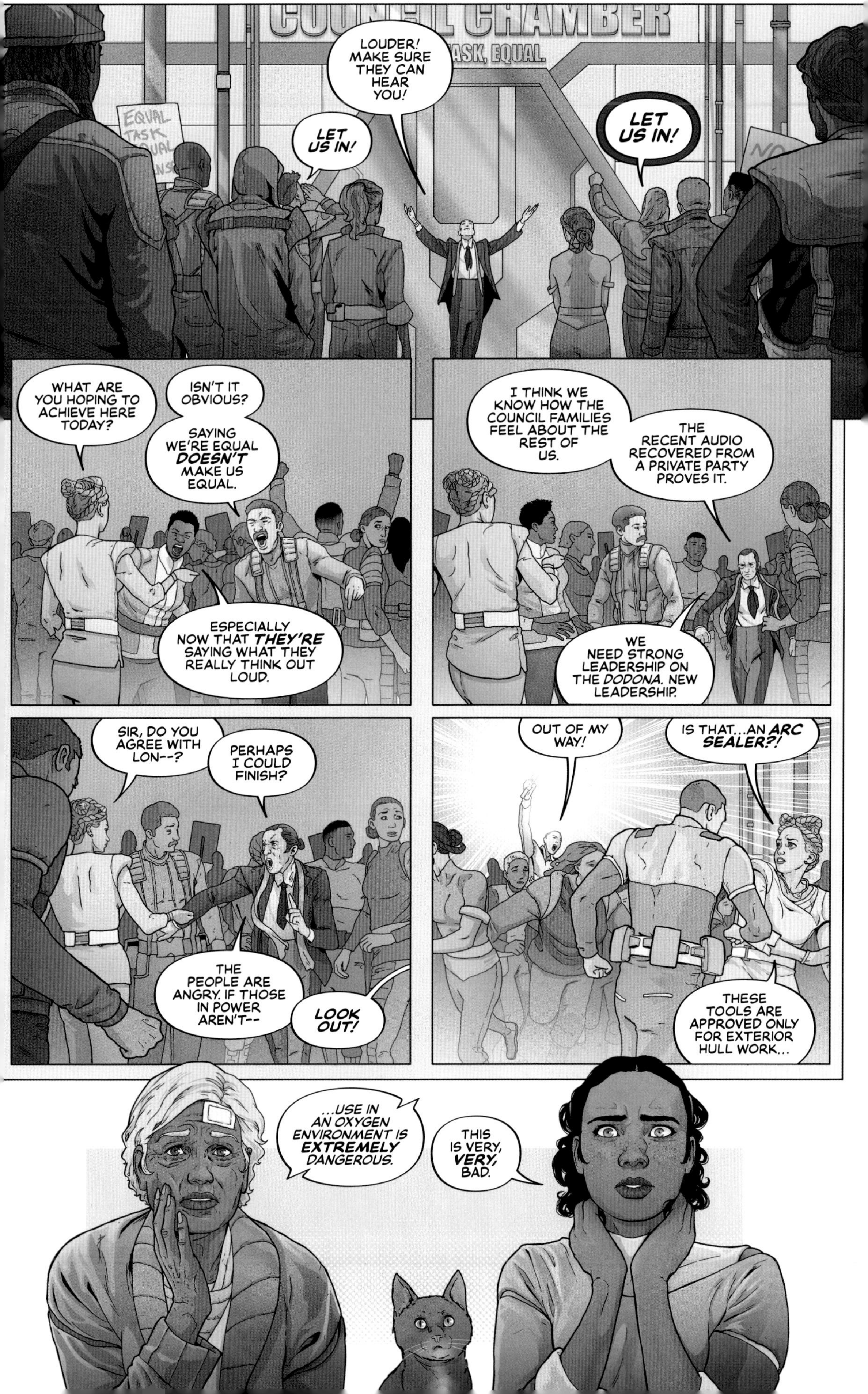

LOUDER! MAKE SURE THEY CAN HEAR YOU!
LET US IN!
LET US IN!
WHAT ARE YOU HOPING TO ACHIEVE HERE TODAY?
ISN'T IT OBVIOUS?
SAYING WE'RE EQUAL ***DOESN'T*** MAKE US EQUAL.
ESPECIALLY NOW THAT ***THEY'RE*** SAYING WHAT THEY REALLY THINK OUT LOUD.
I THINK WE KNOW HOW THE COUNCIL FAMILIES FEEL ABOUT THE REST OF US.
THE RECENT AUDIO RECOVERED FROM A PRIVATE PARTY PROVES IT.
WE NEED STRONG LEADERSHIP ON THE *DODONA*. NEW LEADERSHIP.
SIR, DO YOU AGREE WITH LON--?
PERHAPS I COULD FINISH?
THE PEOPLE ARE ANGRY. IF THOSE IN POWER AREN'T--
LOOK OUT!
OUT OF MY WAY!
IS THAT...AN ***ARC SEALER?!***
THESE TOOLS ARE APPROVED ONLY FOR EXTERIOR HULL WORK...
*...USE IN AN OXYGEN ENVIRONMENT IS **EXTREMELY** DANGEROUS.*
THIS IS VERY, ***VERY,*** BAD.

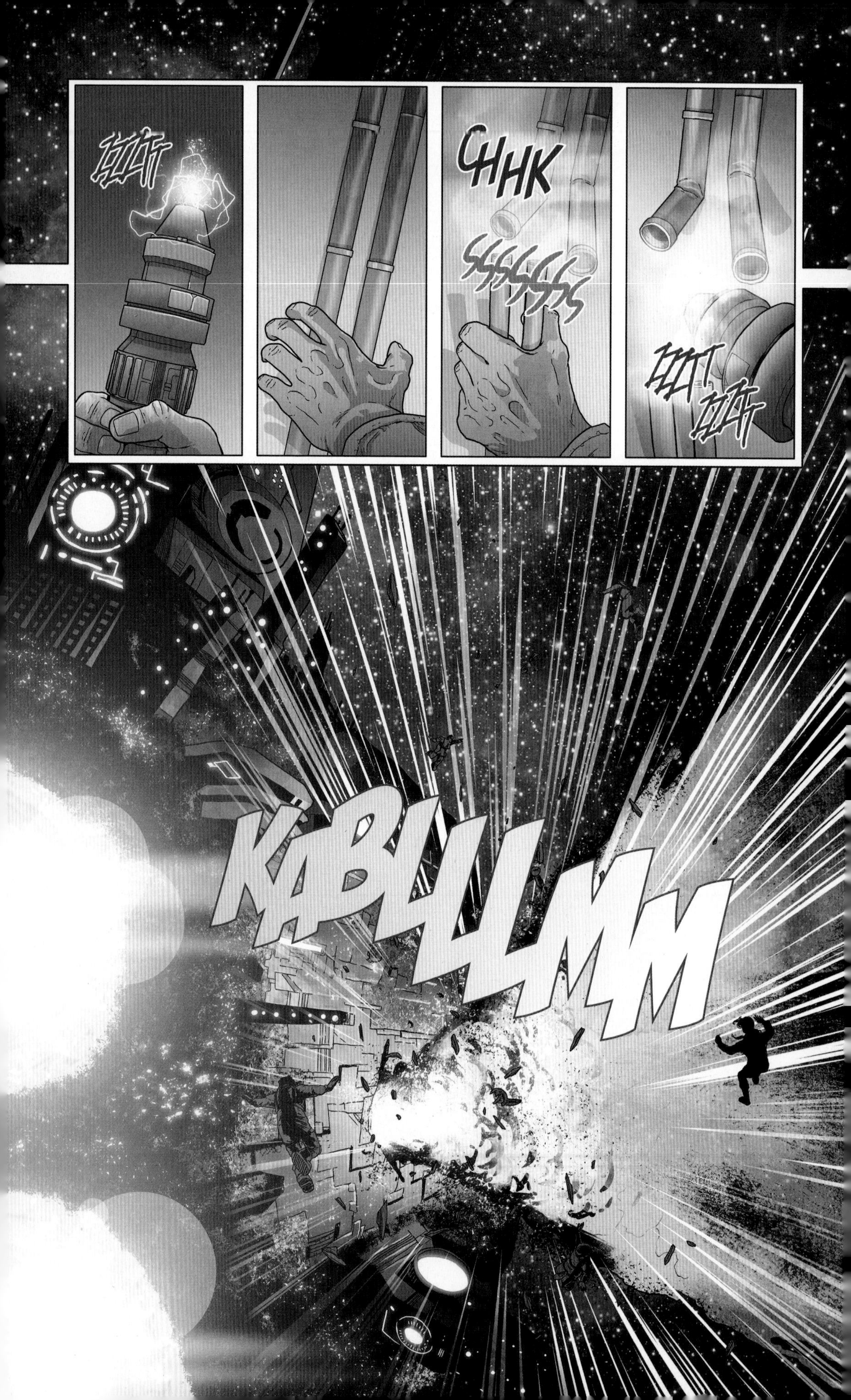
ZZZAT
CHHK
SSSSSSSS
ZZZT
ZZZAT
KABLLMM

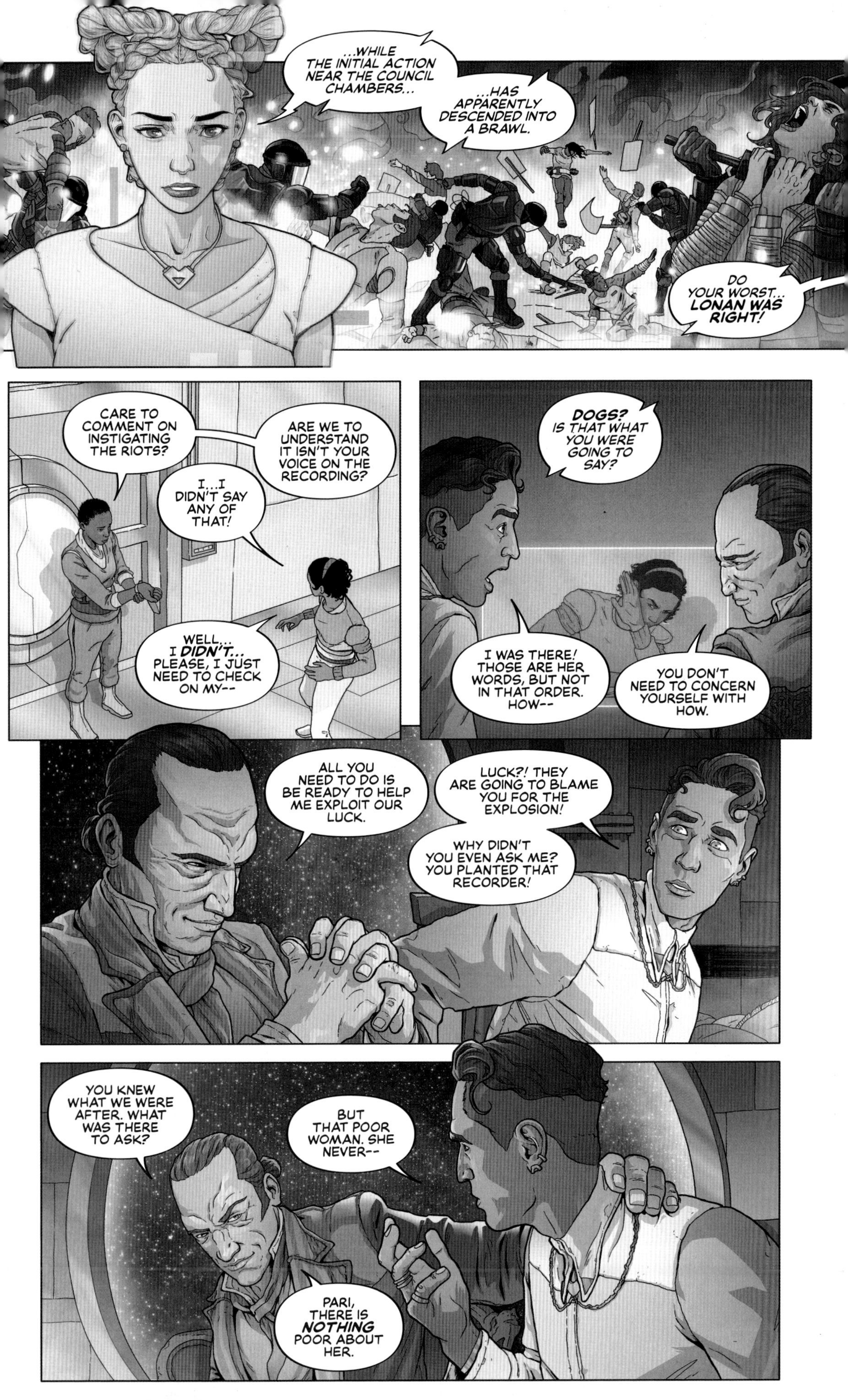
...WHILE THE INITIAL ACTION NEAR THE COUNCIL CHAMBERS...
...HAS APPARENTLY DESCENDED INTO A BRAWL.
DO YOUR WORST... **LONAN WAS RIGHT!**
CARE TO COMMENT ON INSTIGATING THE RIOTS?
ARE WE TO UNDERSTAND IT ISN'T YOUR VOICE ON THE RECORDING?
I...I DIDN'T SAY ANY OF THAT!
WELL... I ***DIDN'T...*** PLEASE, I JUST NEED TO CHECK ON MY--
DOGS? IS THAT WHAT YOU WERE GOING TO SAY?
I WAS THERE! THOSE ARE HER WORDS, BUT NOT IN THAT ORDER. HOW--
YOU DON'T NEED TO CONCERN YOURSELF WITH HOW.
ALL YOU NEED TO DO IS BE READY TO HELP ME EXPLOIT OUR LUCK.
LUCK?! THEY ARE GOING TO BLAME YOU FOR THE EXPLOSION!
WHY DIDN'T YOU EVEN ASK ME? YOU PLANTED THAT RECORDER!
YOU KNEW WHAT WE WERE AFTER. WHAT WAS THERE TO ASK?
BUT THAT POOR WOMAN. SHE NEVER--
PARI, THERE IS ***NOTHING*** POOR ABOUT HER.

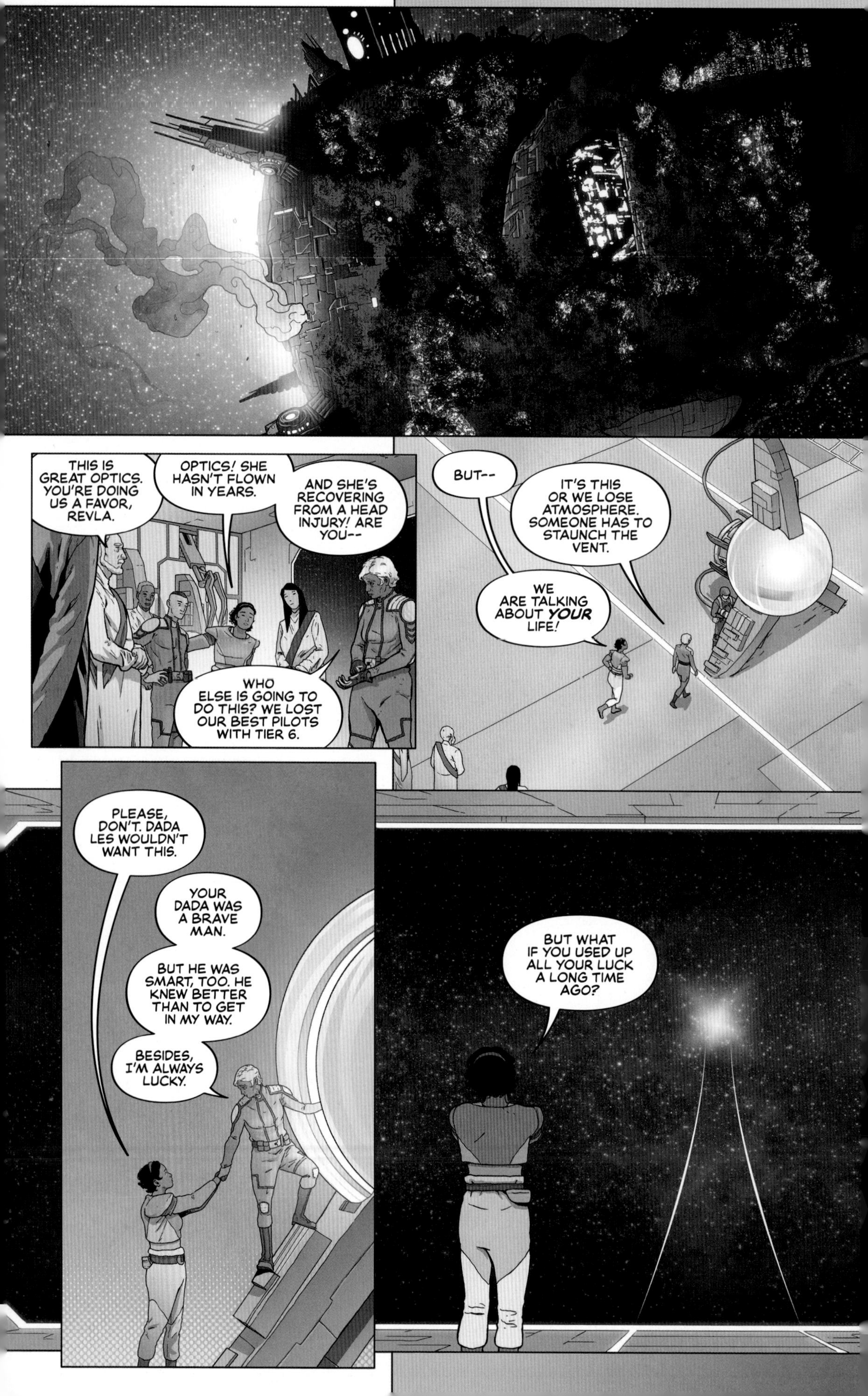
THIS IS GREAT OPTICS. YOU'RE DOING US A FAVOR, REVLA.
OPTICS! SHE HASN'T FLOWN IN YEARS.
AND SHE'S RECOVERING FROM A HEAD INJURY! ARE YOU--
WHO ELSE IS GOING TO DO THIS? WE LOST OUR BEST PILOTS WITH TIER 6.
BUT--
IT'S THIS OR WE LOSE ATMOSPHERE. SOMEONE HAS TO STAUNCH THE VENT.
WE ARE TALKING ABOUT ***YOUR*** LIFE!
PLEASE, DON'T. DADA LES WOULDN'T WANT THIS.
YOUR DADA WAS A BRAVE MAN.
BUT HE WAS SMART, TOO. HE KNEW BETTER THAN TO GET IN MY WAY.
BESIDES, I'M ALWAYS LUCKY.
BUT WHAT IF YOU USED UP ALL YOUR LUCK A LONG TIME AGO?

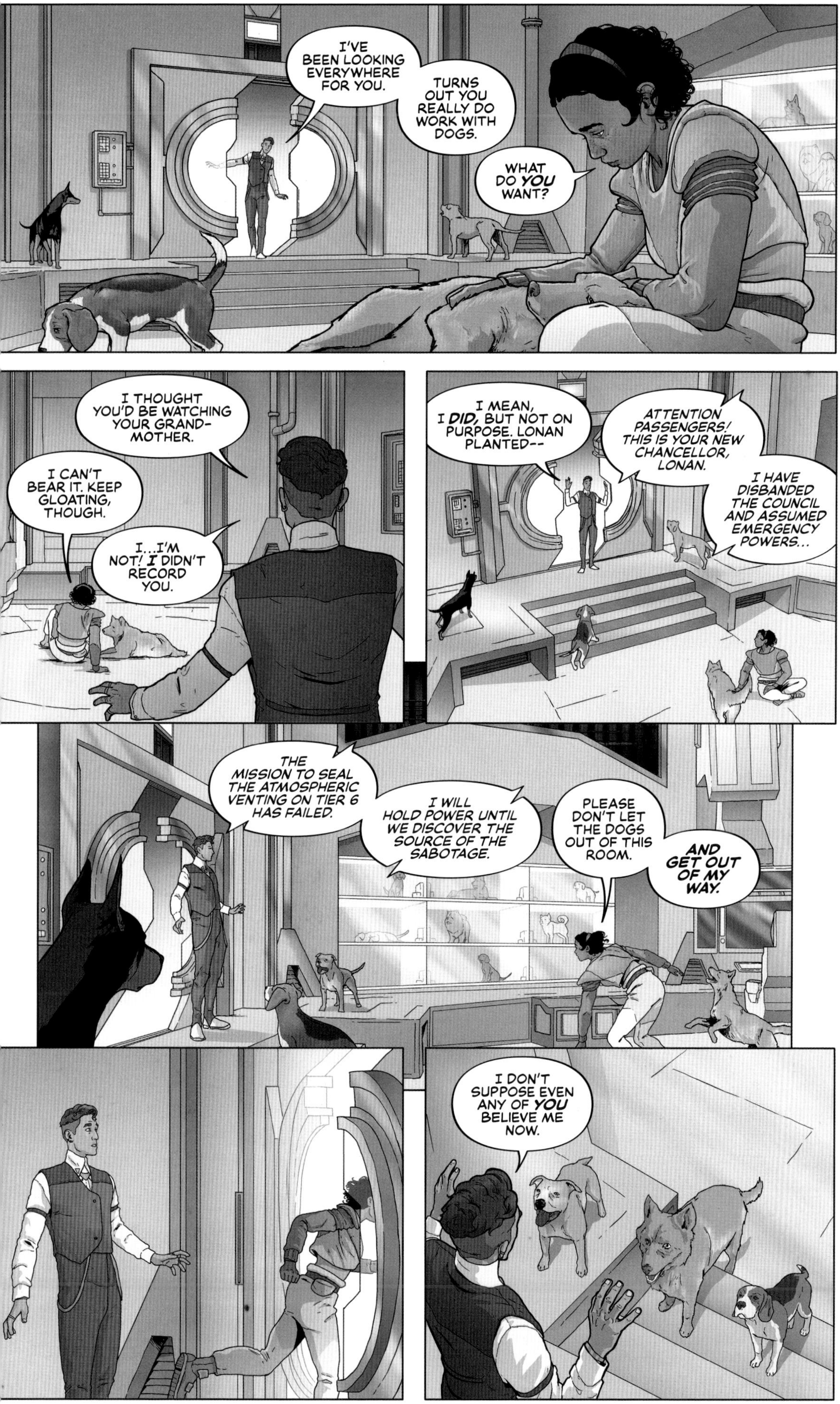
I'VE BEEN LOOKING EVERYWHERE FOR YOU.
TURNS OUT YOU REALLY DO WORK WITH DOGS.
WHAT DO YOU WANT?
I THOUGHT YOU'D BE WATCHING YOUR GRAND-MOTHER.
I CAN'T BEAR IT. KEEP GLOATING, THOUGH.
I...I'M NOT! I DIDN'T RECORD YOU.
I MEAN, I DID, BUT NOT ON PURPOSE. LONAN PLANTED--
ATTENTION PASSENGERS! THIS IS YOUR NEW CHANCELLOR, LONAN.
I HAVE DISBANDED THE COUNCIL AND ASSUMED EMERGENCY POWERS...
THE MISSION TO SEAL THE ATMOSPHERIC VENTING ON TIER 6 HAS FAILED.
I WILL HOLD POWER UNTIL WE DISCOVER THE SOURCE OF THE SABOTAGE.
PLEASE DON'T LET THE DOGS OUT OF THIS ROOM.
AND GET OUT OF MY WAY.
I DON'T SUPPOSE EVEN ANY OF YOU BELIEVE ME NOW.

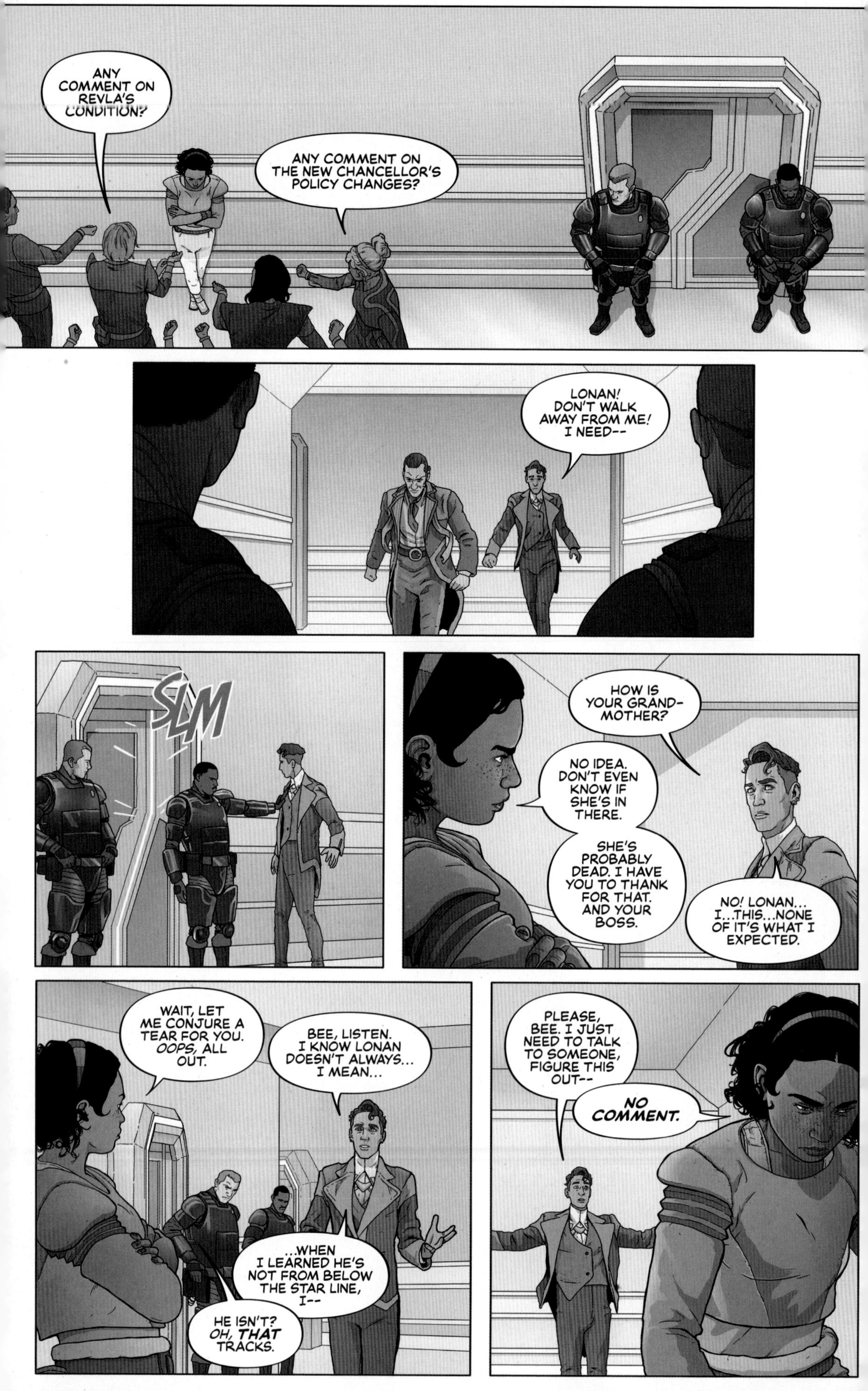
ANY COMMENT ON REVLA'S CONDITION?
ANY COMMENT ON THE NEW CHANCELLOR'S POLICY CHANGES?
LONAN! DON'T WALK AWAY FROM ME! I NEED--
SLM
HOW IS YOUR GRAND-MOTHER?
NO IDEA. DON'T EVEN KNOW IF SHE'S IN THERE.
SHE'S PROBABLY DEAD. I HAVE YOU TO THANK FOR THAT. AND YOUR BOSS.
NO! LONAN... I...THIS...NONE OF IT'S WHAT I EXPECTED.
WAIT, LET ME CONJURE A TEAR FOR YOU. OOPS, ALL OUT.
BEE, LISTEN. I KNOW LONAN DOESN'T ALWAYS... I MEAN...
...WHEN I LEARNED HE'S NOT FROM BELOW THE STAR LINE, I--
HE ISN'T? OH, THAT TRACKS.
PLEASE, BEE. I JUST NEED TO TALK TO SOMEONE, FIGURE THIS OUT--
NO COMMENT.

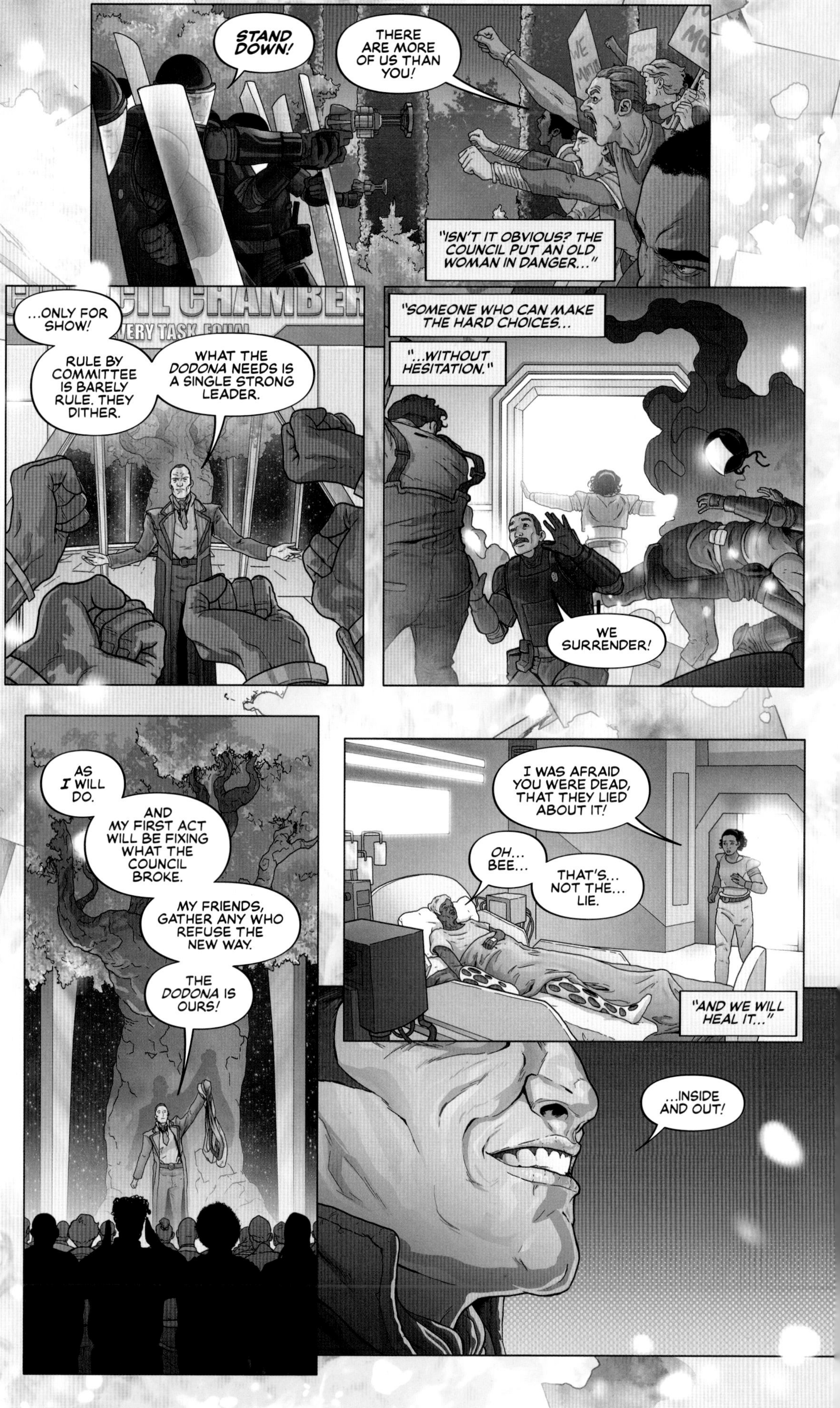
STAND DOWN!
THERE ARE MORE OF US THAN YOU!
"ISN'T IT OBVIOUS? THE COUNCIL PUT AN OLD WOMAN IN DANGER..."
...ONLY FOR SHOW!
RULE BY COMMITTEE IS BARELY RULE. THEY DITHER.
WHAT THE *DODONA* NEEDS IS A SINGLE STRONG LEADER.
"SOMEONE WHO CAN MAKE THE HARD CHOICES...
"...WITHOUT HESITATION."
WE SURRENDER!
AS *I* WILL DO.
AND MY FIRST ACT WILL BE FIXING WHAT THE COUNCIL BROKE.
MY FRIENDS, GATHER ANY WHO REFUSE THE NEW WAY.
THE *DODONA* IS OURS!
I WAS AFRAID YOU WERE DEAD, THAT THEY LIED ABOUT IT!
OH... BEE...
THAT'S... NOT THE... LIE.
"AND WE WILL HEAL IT..."
...INSIDE AND OUT!

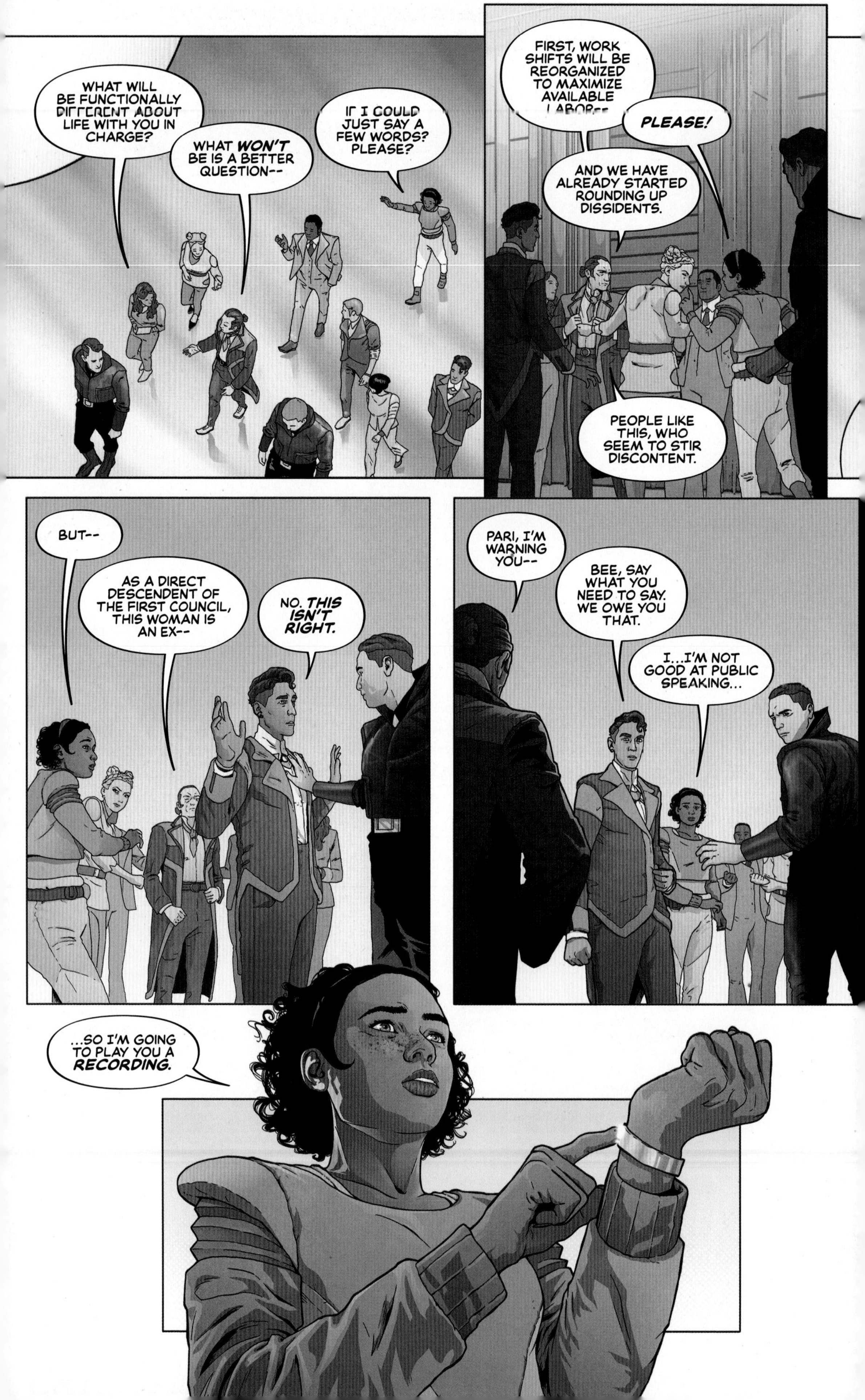
WHAT WILL BE FUNCTIONALLY DIFFERENT ABOUT LIFE WITH YOU IN CHARGE?
WHAT WON'T BE IS A BETTER QUESTION--
IF I COULD JUST SAY A FEW WORDS? PLEASE?
FIRST, WORK SHIFTS WILL BE REORGANIZED TO MAXIMIZE AVAILABLE LABOR--
PLEASE!
AND WE HAVE ALREADY STARTED ROUNDING UP DISSIDENTS.
PEOPLE LIKE THIS, WHO SEEM TO STIR DISCONTENT.
BUT--
AS A DIRECT DESCENDENT OF THE FIRST COUNCIL, THIS WOMAN IS AN EX--
NO. THIS ISN'T RIGHT.
PARI, I'M WARNING YOU--
BEE, SAY WHAT YOU NEED TO SAY. WE OWE YOU THAT.
I...I'M NOT GOOD AT PUBLIC SPEAKING...
...SO I'M GOING TO PLAY YOU A RECORDING.

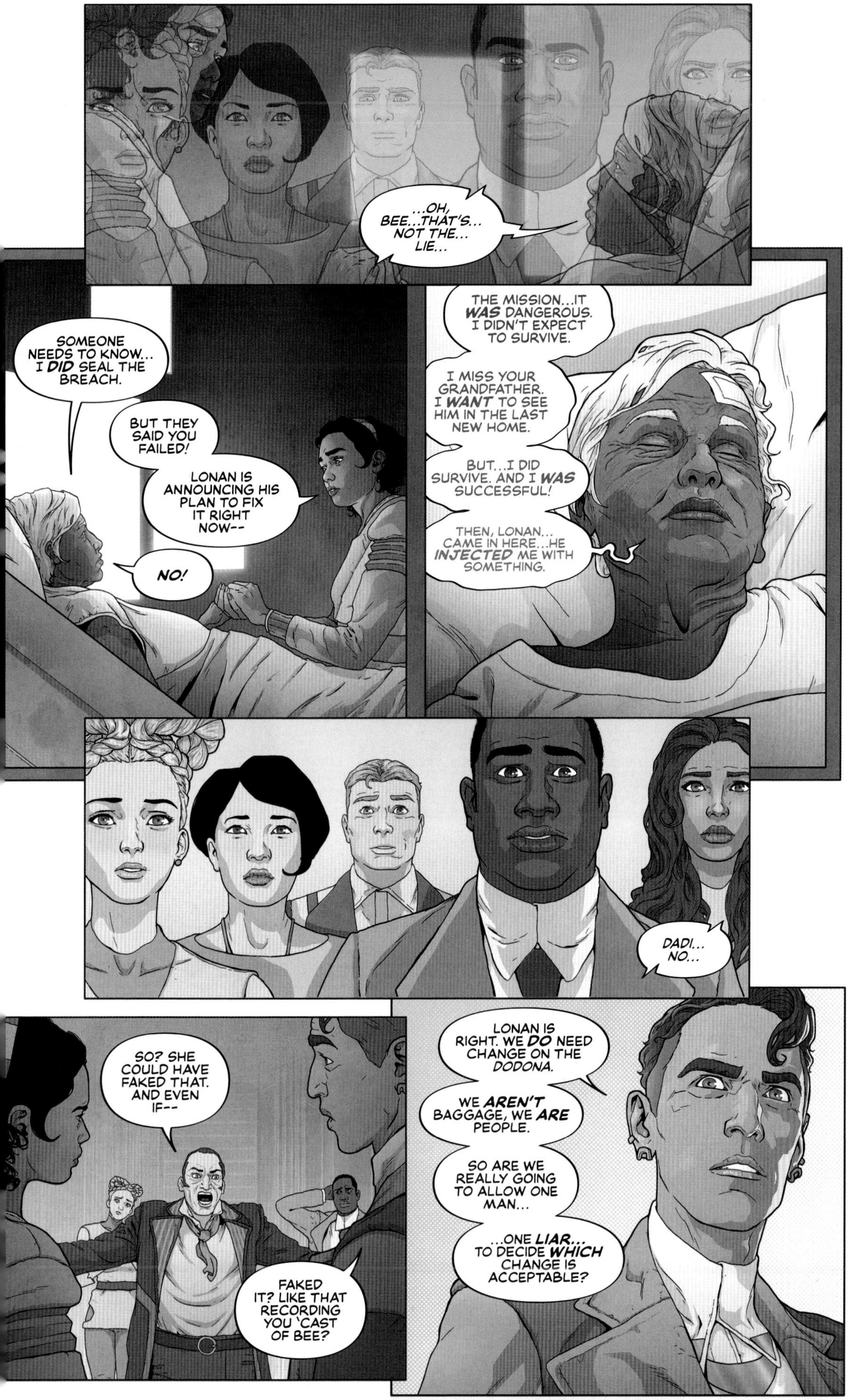
...OH, BEE...THAT'S... NOT THE... LIE...
SOMEONE NEEDS TO KNOW... I DID SEAL THE BREACH.
BUT THEY SAID YOU FAILED!
LONAN IS ANNOUNCING HIS PLAN TO FIX IT RIGHT NOW--
NO!
THE MISSION...IT WAS DANGEROUS. I DIDN'T EXPECT TO SURVIVE.
I MISS YOUR GRANDFATHER. I WANT TO SEE HIM IN THE LAST NEW HOME.
BUT...I DID SURVIVE. AND I WAS SUCCESSFUL!
THEN, LONAN... CAME IN HERE...HE INJECTED ME WITH SOMETHING.
DADI... NO...
SO? SHE COULD HAVE FAKED THAT. AND EVEN IF--
FAKED IT? LIKE THAT RECORDING YOU 'CAST OF BEE?
LONAN IS RIGHT. WE DO NEED CHANGE ON THE DODONA.
WE AREN'T BAGGAGE, WE ARE PEOPLE.
SO ARE WE REALLY GOING TO ALLOW ONE MAN...
...ONE LIAR... TO DECIDE WHICH CHANGE IS ACCEPTABLE?

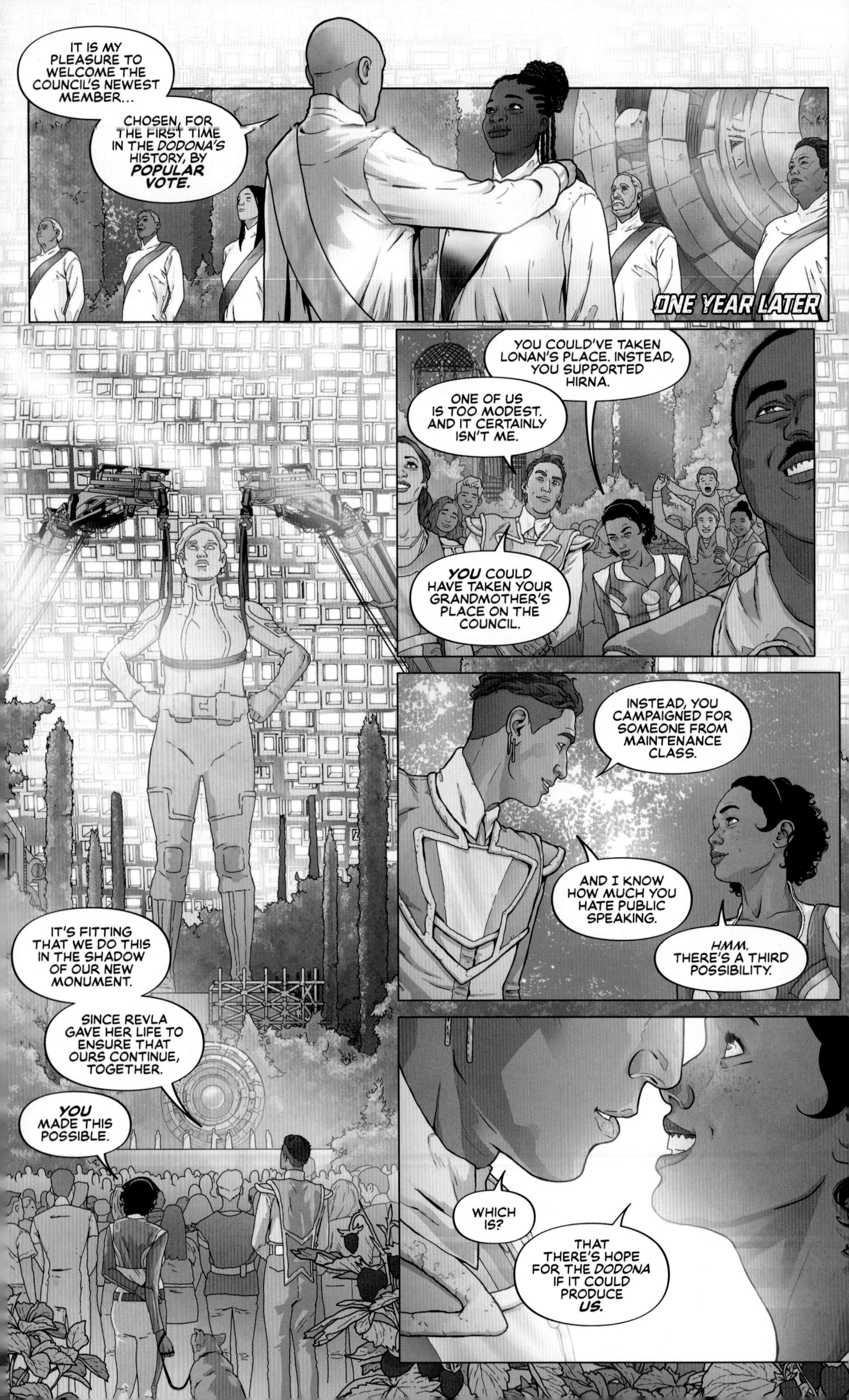

IT IS MY PLEASURE TO WELCOME THE COUNCIL'S NEWEST MEMBER...
CHOSEN, FOR THE FIRST TIME IN THE *DODONA'S* HISTORY, BY **POPULAR VOTE.**
ONE YEAR LATER
IT'S FITTING THAT WE DO THIS IN THE SHADOW OF OUR NEW MONUMENT.
SINCE REVLA GAVE HER LIFE TO ENSURE THAT OURS CONTINUE, TOGETHER.
YOU MADE THIS POSSIBLE.
YOU COULD'VE TAKEN LONAN'S PLACE. INSTEAD, YOU SUPPORTED HIRNA.
ONE OF US IS TOO MODEST. AND IT CERTAINLY ISN'T ME.
YOU COULD HAVE TAKEN YOUR GRANDMOTHER'S PLACE ON THE COUNCIL.
INSTEAD, YOU CAMPAIGNED FOR SOMEONE FROM MAINTENANCE CLASS.
AND I KNOW HOW MUCH YOU HATE PUBLIC SPEAKING.
HMM. THERE'S A THIRD POSSIBILITY.
WHICH IS?
THAT THERE'S HOPE FOR THE *DODONA* IF IT COULD PRODUCE ***US.***

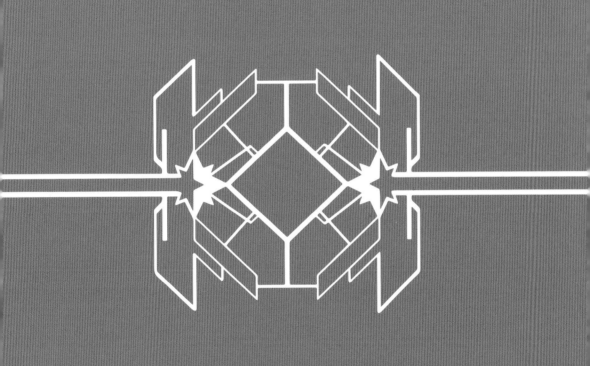

CHAPTER
THREE

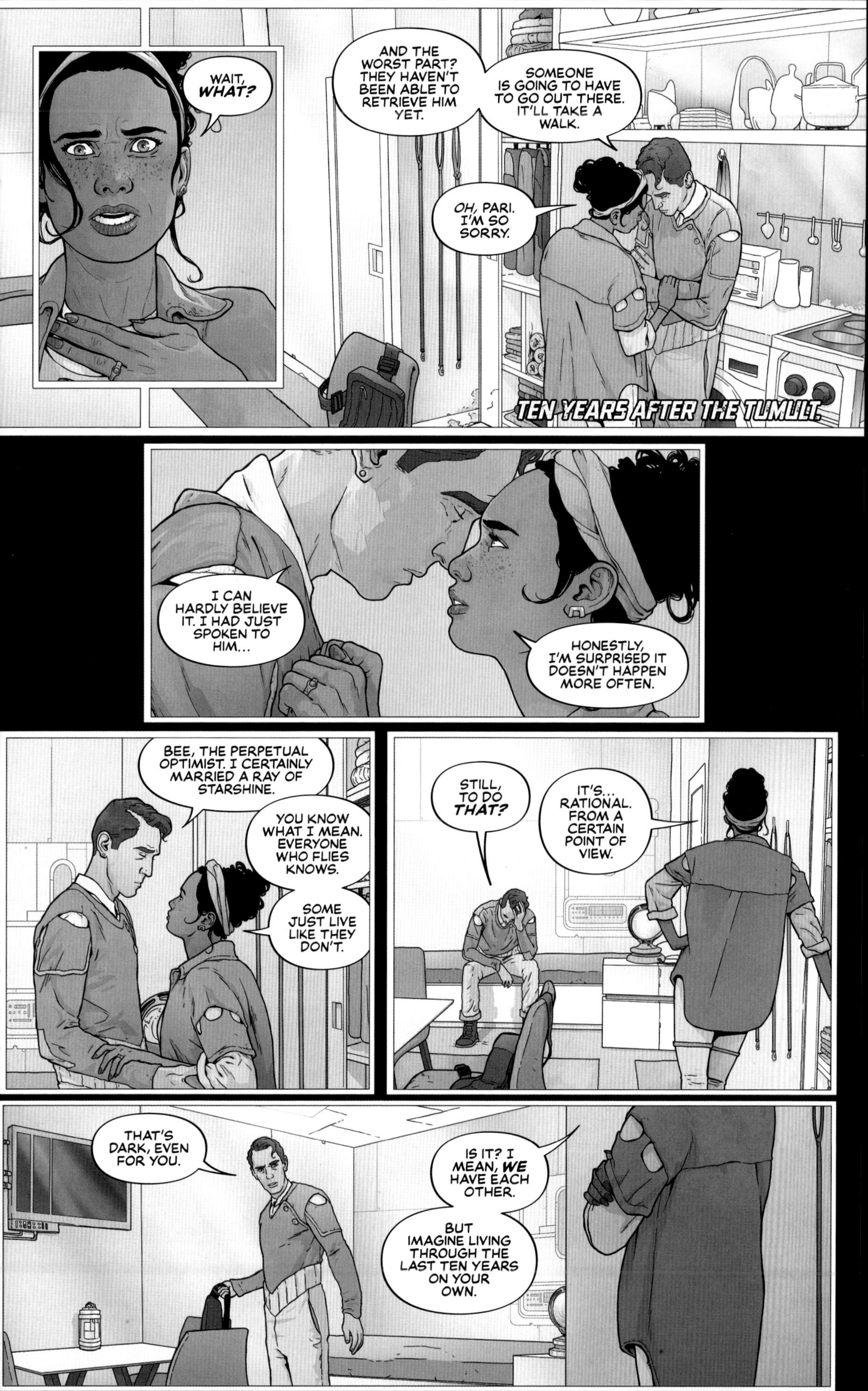
WAIT, WHAT?
AND THE WORST PART? THEY HAVEN'T BEEN ABLE TO RETRIEVE HIM YET.
SOMEONE IS GOING TO HAVE TO GO OUT THERE. IT'LL TAKE A WALK.
OH, PARI. I'M SO SORRY.
TEN YEARS AFTER THE TUMULT.
I CAN HARDLY BELIEVE IT. I HAD JUST SPOKEN TO HIM...
HONESTLY, I'M SURPRISED IT DOESN'T HAPPEN MORE OFTEN.
BEE, THE PERPETUAL OPTIMIST. I CERTAINLY MARRIED A RAY OF STARSHINE.
YOU KNOW WHAT I MEAN. EVERYONE WHO FLIES KNOWS.
SOME JUST LIVE LIKE THEY DON'T.
STILL, TO DO THAT?
IT'S... RATIONAL. FROM A CERTAIN POINT OF VIEW.
THAT'S DARK, EVEN FOR YOU.
IS IT? I MEAN, WE HAVE EACH OTHER.
BUT IMAGINE LIVING THROUGH THE LAST TEN YEARS ON YOUR OWN.

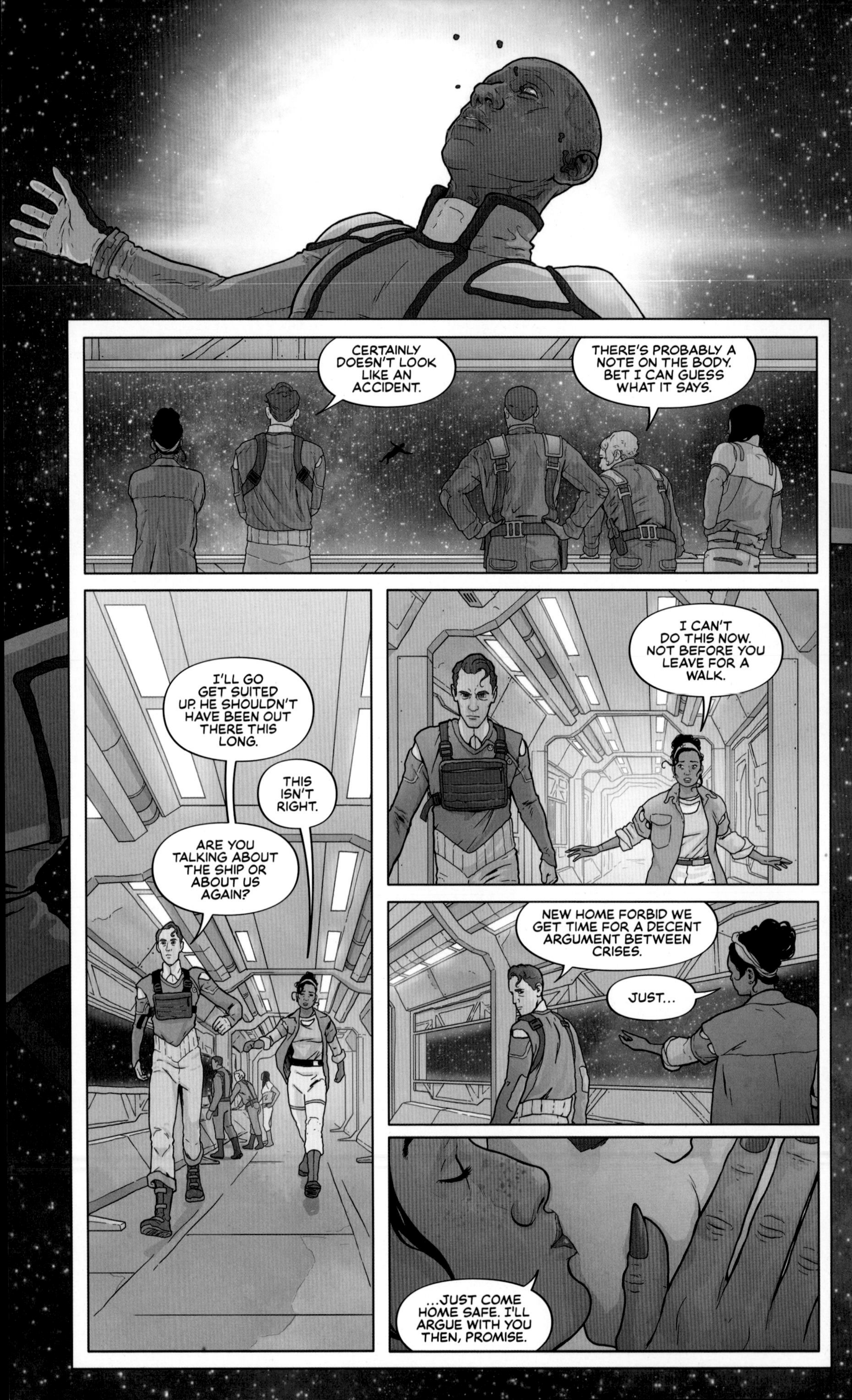
CERTAINLY DOESN'T LOOK LIKE AN ACCIDENT.
THERE'S PROBABLY A NOTE ON THE BODY. BET I CAN GUESS WHAT IT SAYS.
I'LL GO GET SUITED UP. HE SHOULDN'T HAVE BEEN OUT THERE THIS LONG.
THIS ISN'T RIGHT.
ARE YOU TALKING ABOUT THE SHIP OR ABOUT US AGAIN?
I CAN'T DO THIS NOW. NOT BEFORE YOU LEAVE FOR A WALK.
NEW HOME FORBID WE GET TIME FOR A DECENT ARGUMENT BETWEEN CRISES.
JUST...
...JUST COME HOME SAFE. I'LL ARGUE WITH YOU THEN, PROMISE.

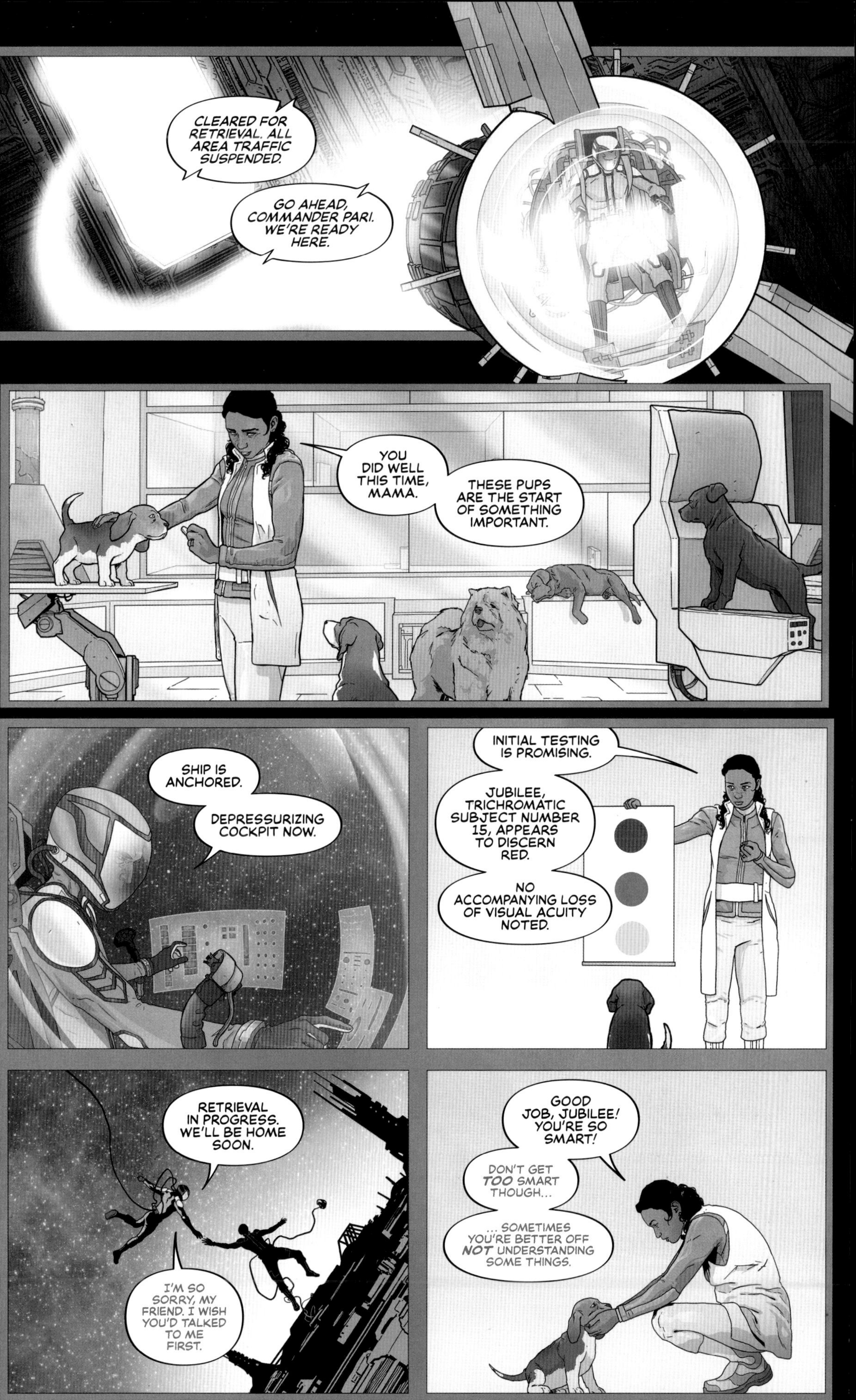
CLEARED FOR RETRIEVAL. ALL AREA TRAFFIC SUSPENDED.
GO AHEAD, COMMANDER PARI. WE'RE READY HERE.
YOU DID WELL THIS TIME, MAMA.
THESE PUPS ARE THE START OF SOMETHING IMPORTANT.
SHIP IS ANCHORED.
DEPRESSURIZING COCKPIT NOW.
INITIAL TESTING IS PROMISING.
JUBILEE, TRICHROMATIC SUBJECT NUMBER 15, APPEARS TO DISCERN RED.
NO ACCOMPANYING LOSS OF VISUAL ACUITY NOTED.
RETRIEVAL IN PROGRESS. WE'LL BE HOME SOON.
I'M SO SORRY, MY FRIEND. I WISH YOU'D TALKED TO ME FIRST.
GOOD JOB, JUBILEE! YOU'RE SO SMART!
DON'T GET *TOO* SMART THOUGH...
... SOMETIMES YOU'RE BETTER OFF *NOT* UNDERSTANDING SOME THINGS.

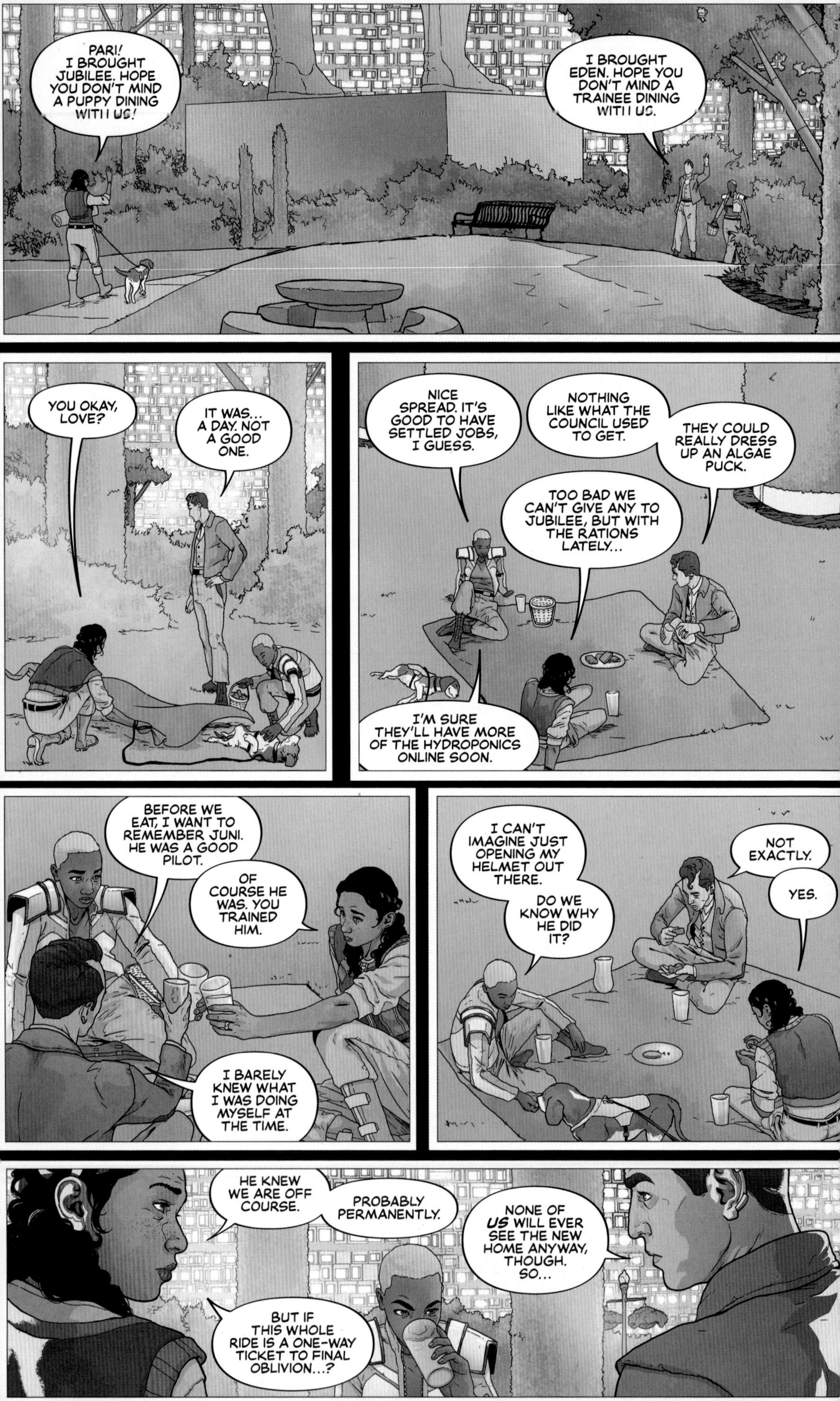
PARI! I BROUGHT JUBILEE. HOPE YOU DON'T MIND A PUPPY DINING WITH US!
I BROUGHT EDEN. HOPE YOU DON'T MIND A TRAINEE DINING WITH US.
YOU OKAY, LOVE?
IT WAS... A DAY. NOT A GOOD ONE.
NICE SPREAD. IT'S GOOD TO HAVE SETTLED JOBS, I GUESS.
NOTHING LIKE WHAT THE COUNCIL USED TO GET.
THEY COULD REALLY DRESS UP AN ALGAE PUCK.
TOO BAD WE CAN'T GIVE ANY TO JUBILEE, BUT WITH THE RATIONS LATELY...
I'M SURE THEY'LL HAVE MORE OF THE HYDROPONICS ONLINE SOON.
BEFORE WE EAT, I WANT TO REMEMBER JUNI. HE WAS A GOOD PILOT.
OF COURSE HE WAS. YOU TRAINED HIM.
I BARELY KNEW WHAT I WAS DOING MYSELF AT THE TIME.
I CAN'T IMAGINE JUST OPENING MY HELMET OUT THERE.
DO WE KNOW WHY HE DID IT?
NOT EXACTLY.
YES.
HE KNEW WE ARE OFF COURSE.
PROBABLY PERMANENTLY.
NONE OF *US* WILL EVER SEE THE NEW HOME ANYWAY, THOUGH. SO...
BUT IF THIS WHOLE RIDE IS A ONE-WAY TICKET TO FINAL OBLIVION...?

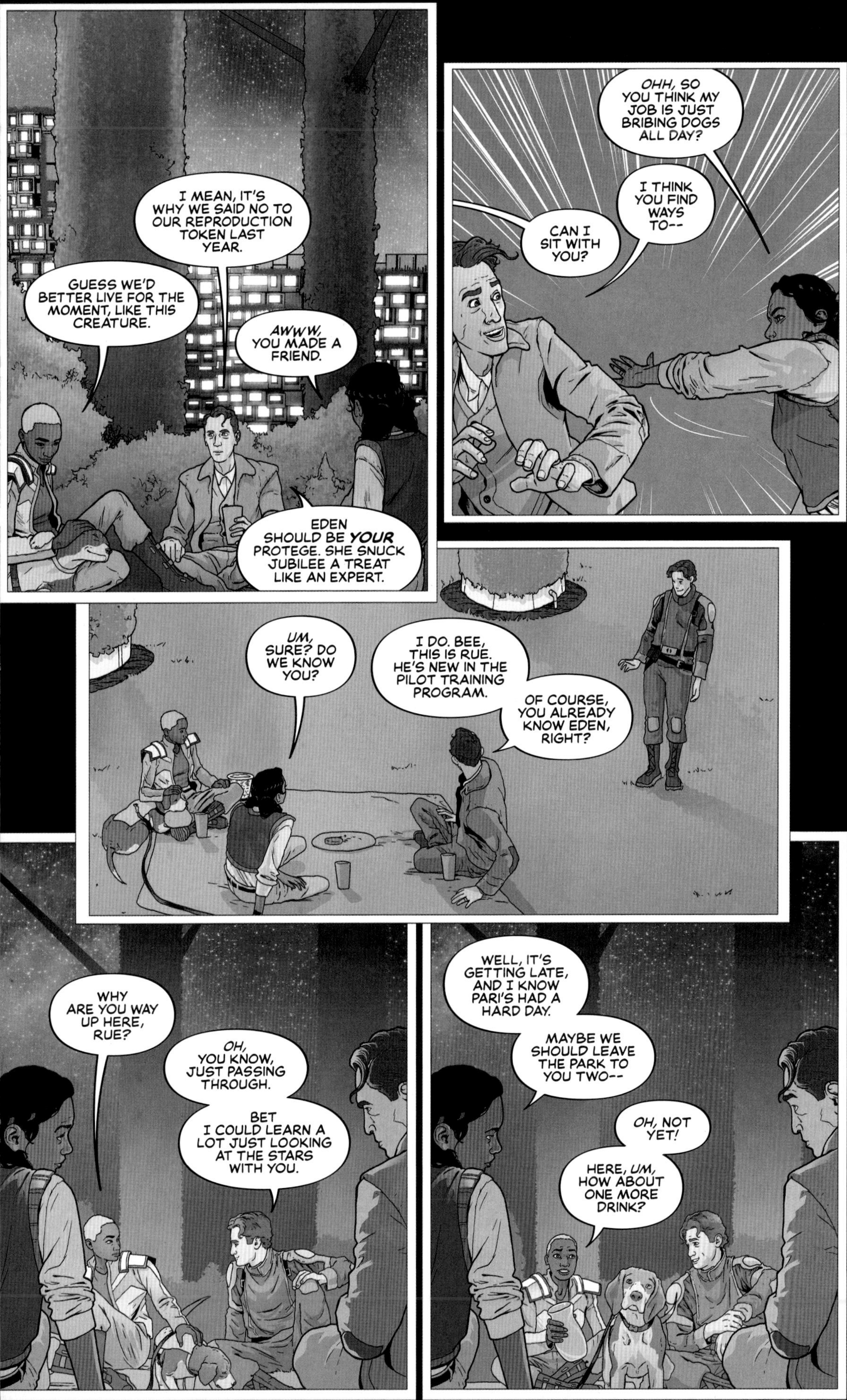

I MEAN, IT'S WHY WE SAID NO TO OUR REPRODUCTION TOKEN LAST YEAR.
GUESS WE'D BETTER LIVE FOR THE MOMENT, LIKE THIS CREATURE.
AWWW, YOU MADE A FRIEND.
EDEN SHOULD BE ***YOUR*** PROTEGE. SHE SNUCK JUBILEE A TREAT LIKE AN EXPERT.
OHH, SO YOU THINK MY JOB IS JUST BRIBING DOGS ALL DAY?
I THINK YOU FIND WAYS TO--
CAN I SIT WITH YOU?
UM, SURE? DO WE KNOW YOU?
I DO. BEE, THIS IS RUE. HE'S NEW IN THE PILOT TRAINING PROGRAM.
OF COURSE, YOU ALREADY KNOW EDEN, RIGHT?
WHY ARE YOU WAY UP HERE, RUE?
OH, YOU KNOW, JUST PASSING THROUGH.
BET I COULD LEARN A LOT JUST LOOKING AT THE STARS WITH YOU.
WELL, IT'S GETTING LATE, AND I KNOW PARI'S HAD A HARD DAY.
MAYBE WE SHOULD LEAVE THE PARK TO YOU TWO--
OH, NOT YET!
HERE, *UM,* HOW ABOUT ONE MORE DRINK?

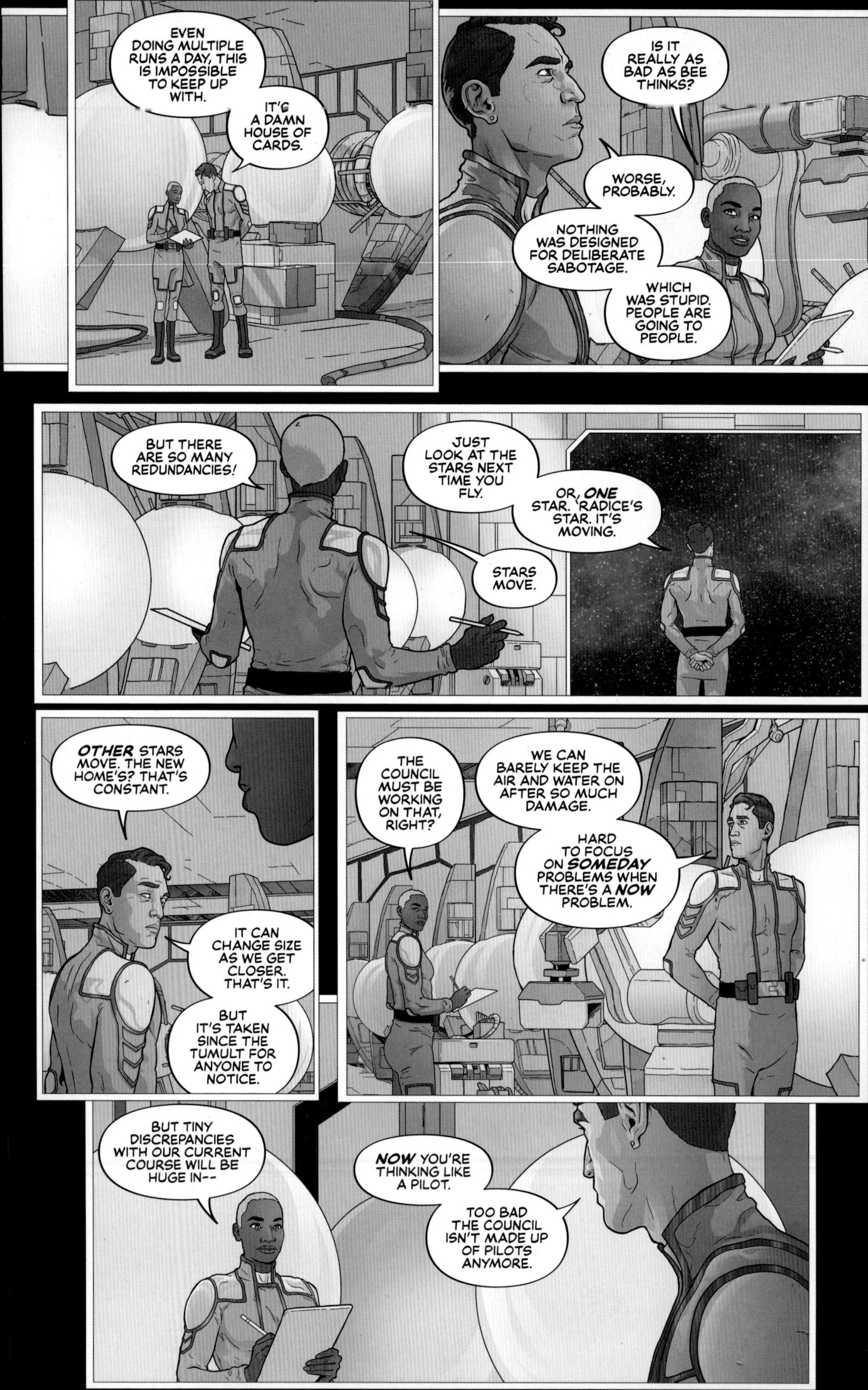
EVEN DOING MULTIPLE RUNS A DAY, THIS IS IMPOSSIBLE TO KEEP UP WITH.
IT'S A DAMN HOUSE OF CARDS.
IS IT REALLY AS BAD AS BEE THINKS?
WORSE, PROBABLY.
NOTHING WAS DESIGNED FOR DELIBERATE SABOTAGE.
WHICH WAS STUPID. PEOPLE ARE GOING TO PEOPLE.
BUT THERE ARE SO MANY REDUNDANCIES!
JUST LOOK AT THE STARS NEXT TIME YOU FLY.
STARS MOVE.
OR, ONE STAR. 'RADICE'S STAR. IT'S MOVING.
OTHER STARS MOVE. THE NEW HOME'S? THAT'S CONSTANT.
IT CAN CHANGE SIZE AS WE GET CLOSER. THAT'S IT.
BUT IT'S TAKEN SINCE THE TUMULT FOR ANYONE TO NOTICE.
THE COUNCIL MUST BE WORKING ON THAT, RIGHT?
WE CAN BARELY KEEP THE AIR AND WATER ON AFTER SO MUCH DAMAGE.
HARD TO FOCUS ON SOMEDAY PROBLEMS WHEN THERE'S A NOW PROBLEM.
BUT TINY DISCREPANCIES WITH OUR CURRENT COURSE WILL BE HUGE IN--
NOW YOU'RE THINKING LIKE A PILOT.
TOO BAD THE COUNCIL ISN'T MADE UP OF PILOTS ANYMORE.

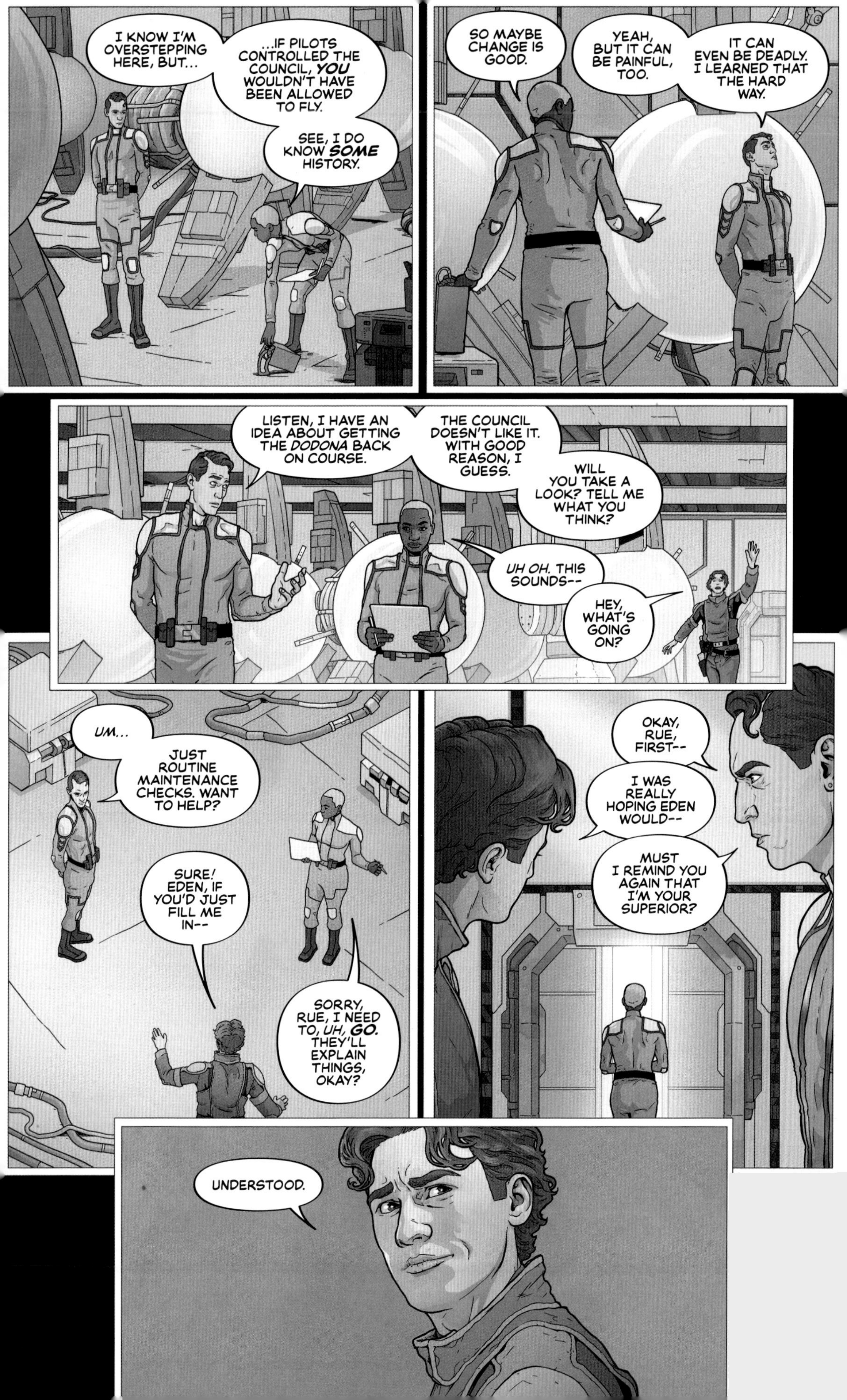
I KNOW I'M OVERSTEPPING HERE, BUT...
...IF PILOTS CONTROLLED THE COUNCIL, ***YOU*** WOULDN'T HAVE BEEN ALLOWED TO FLY.
SEE, I DO KNOW ***SOME*** HISTORY.
SO MAYBE CHANGE IS GOOD.
YEAH, BUT IT CAN BE PAINFUL, TOO.
IT CAN EVEN BE DEADLY. I LEARNED THAT THE HARD WAY.
LISTEN, I HAVE AN IDEA ABOUT GETTING THE *DODONA* BACK ON COURSE.
THE COUNCIL DOESN'T LIKE IT. WITH GOOD REASON, I GUESS.
WILL YOU TAKE A LOOK? TELL ME WHAT YOU THINK?
UH OH. THIS SOUNDS--
HEY, WHAT'S GOING ON?
UM...
JUST ROUTINE MAINTENANCE CHECKS. WANT TO HELP?
SURE! EDEN, IF YOU'D JUST FILL ME IN--
SORRY, RUE, I NEED TO, *UH*, ***GO***. THEY'LL EXPLAIN THINGS, OKAY?
OKAY, RUE, FIRST--
I WAS REALLY HOPING EDEN WOULD--
MUST I REMIND YOU AGAIN THAT I'M YOUR SUPERIOR?
UNDERSTOOD.

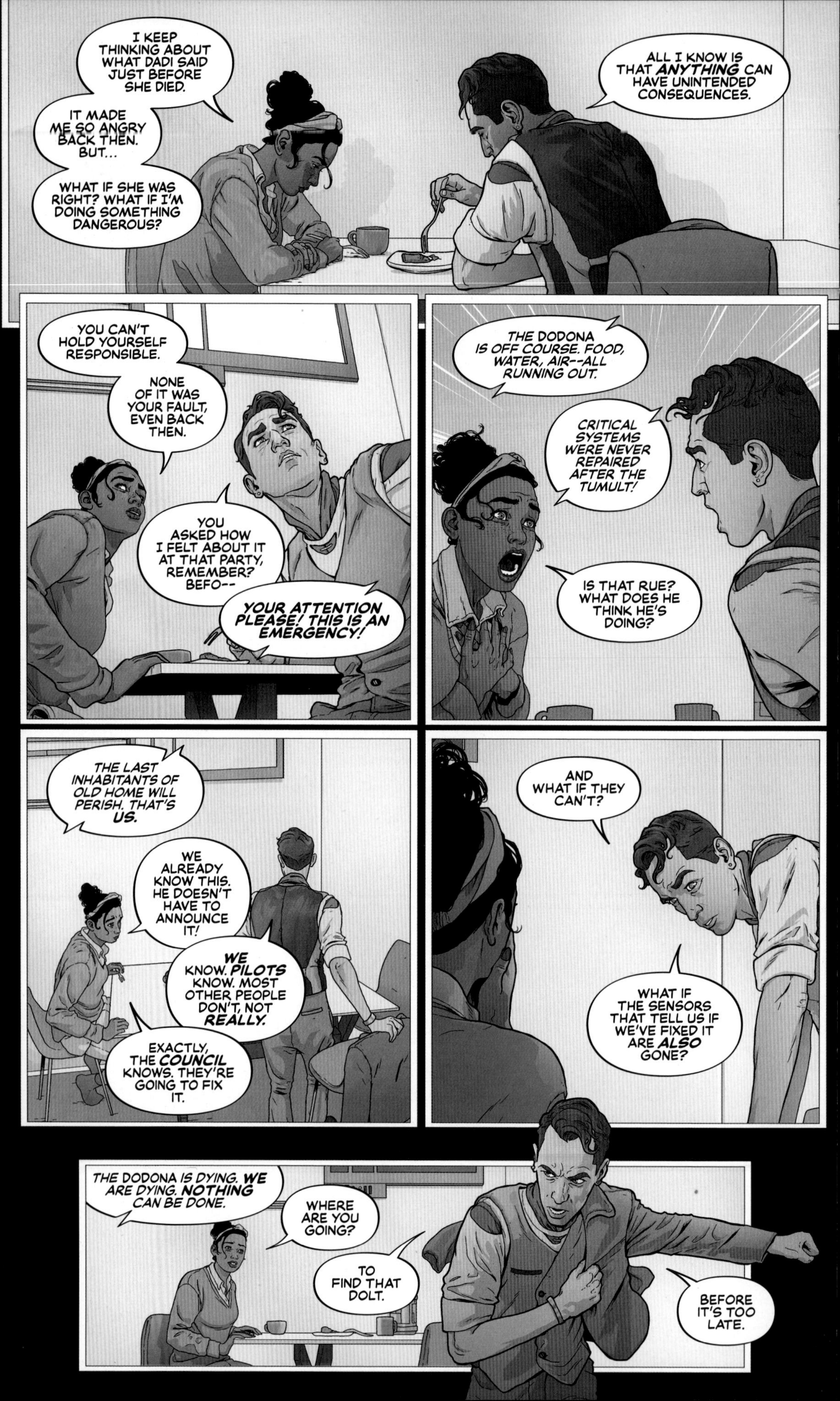
I KEEP THINKING ABOUT WHAT DADI SAID JUST BEFORE SHE DIED.
IT MADE ME SO ANGRY BACK THEN. BUT...
WHAT IF SHE WAS RIGHT? WHAT IF I'M DOING SOMETHING DANGEROUS?
ALL I KNOW IS THAT ANYTHING CAN HAVE UNINTENDED CONSEQUENCES.
YOU CAN'T HOLD YOURSELF RESPONSIBLE.
NONE OF IT WAS YOUR FAULT, EVEN BACK THEN.
YOU ASKED HOW I FELT ABOUT IT AT THAT PARTY, REMEMBER? BEFO--
YOUR ATTENTION PLEASE! THIS IS AN EMERGENCY!
THE DODONA IS OFF COURSE. FOOD, WATER, AIR--ALL RUNNING OUT.
CRITICAL SYSTEMS WERE NEVER REPAIRED AFTER THE TUMULT!
IS THAT RUE? WHAT DOES HE THINK HE'S DOING?
THE LAST INHABITANTS OF OLD HOME WILL PERISH. THAT'S US.
WE ALREADY KNOW THIS. HE DOESN'T HAVE TO ANNOUNCE IT!
WE KNOW. PILOTS KNOW. MOST OTHER PEOPLE DON'T, NOT REALLY.
EXACTLY, THE COUNCIL KNOWS. THEY'RE GOING TO FIX IT.
AND WHAT IF THEY CAN'T?
WHAT IF THE SENSORS THAT TELL US IF WE'VE FIXED IT ARE ALSO GONE?
THE DODONA IS DYING. WE ARE DYING. NOTHING CAN BE DONE.
WHERE ARE YOU GOING?
TO FIND THAT DOLT.
BEFORE IT'S TOO LATE.

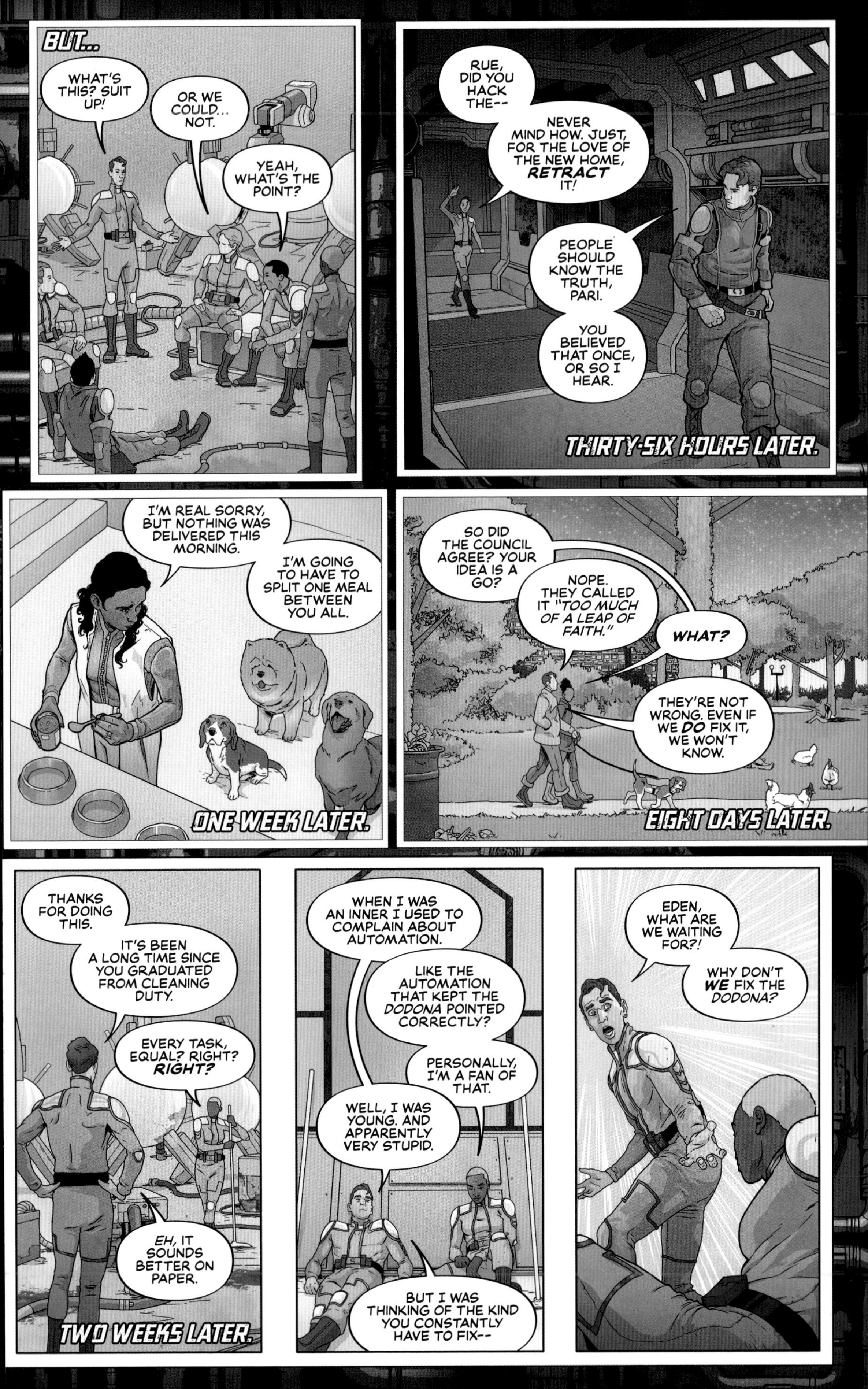
BUT...
WHAT'S THIS? SUIT UP!
OR WE COULD... NOT.
YEAH, WHAT'S THE POINT?
RUE, DID YOU HACK THE--
NEVER MIND HOW. JUST, FOR THE LOVE OF THE NEW HOME, RETRACT IT!
PEOPLE SHOULD KNOW THE TRUTH, PARI.
YOU BELIEVED THAT ONCE, OR SO I HEAR.
THIRTY-SIX HOURS LATER.
I'M REAL SORRY, BUT NOTHING WAS DELIVERED THIS MORNING.
I'M GOING TO HAVE TO SPLIT ONE MEAL BETWEEN YOU ALL.
ONE WEEK LATER.
SO DID THE COUNCIL AGREE? YOUR IDEA IS A GO?
NOPE. THEY CALLED IT "TOO MUCH OF A LEAP OF FAITH."
WHAT?
THEY'RE NOT WRONG. EVEN IF WE DO FIX IT, WE WON'T KNOW.
EIGHT DAYS LATER.
THANKS FOR DOING THIS.
IT'S BEEN A LONG TIME SINCE YOU GRADUATED FROM CLEANING DUTY.
EVERY TASK, EQUAL? RIGHT? RIGHT?
EH, IT SOUNDS BETTER ON PAPER.
TWO WEEKS LATER.
WHEN I WAS AN INNER I USED TO COMPLAIN ABOUT AUTOMATION.
LIKE THE AUTOMATION THAT KEPT THE DODONA POINTED CORRECTLY?
PERSONALLY, I'M A FAN OF THAT.
WELL, I WAS YOUNG. AND APPARENTLY VERY STUPID.
BUT I WAS THINKING OF THE KIND YOU CONSTANTLY HAVE TO FIX--
EDEN, WHAT ARE WE WAITING FOR?!
WHY DON'T WE FIX THE DODONA?

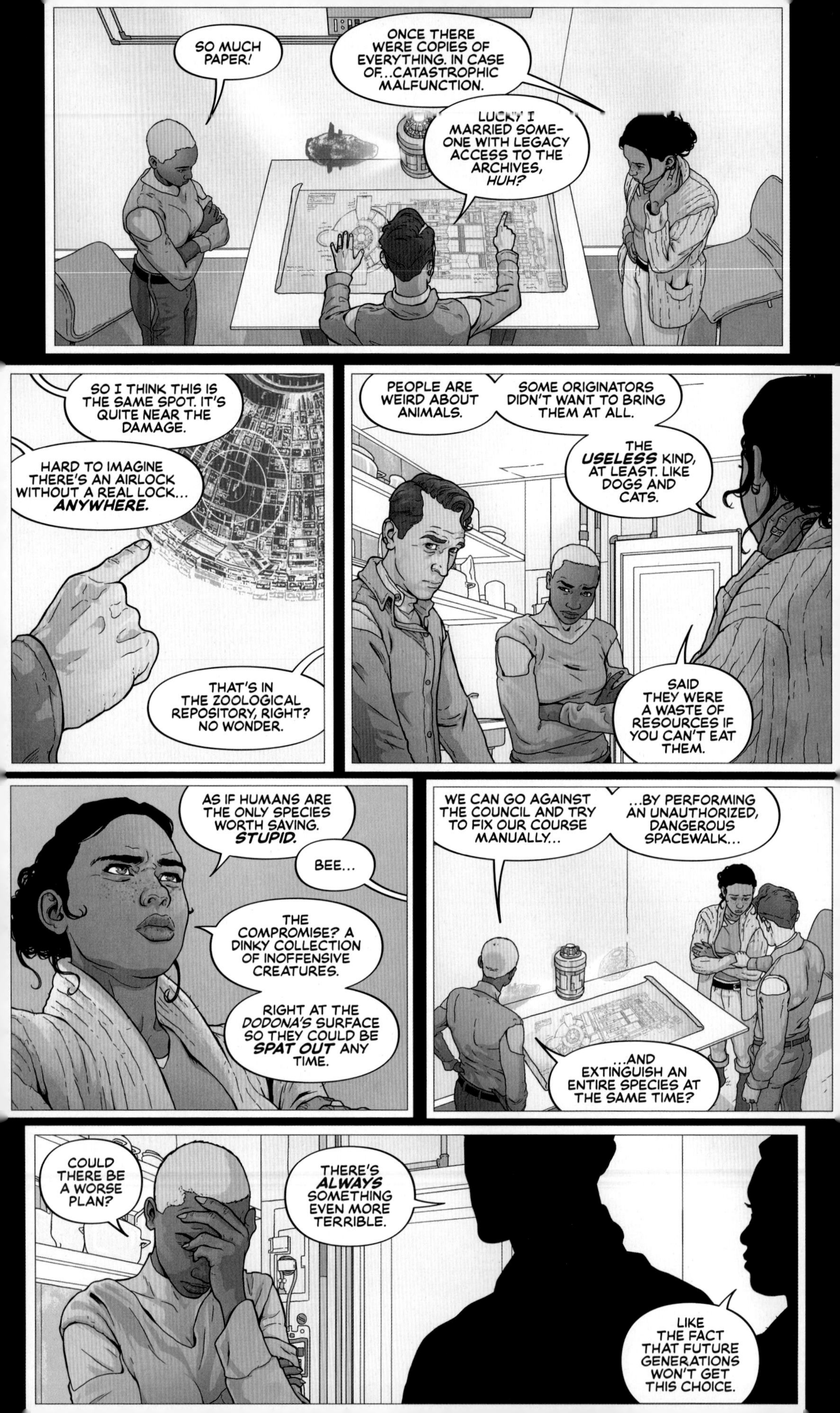
SO MUCH PAPER!
ONCE THERE WERE COPIES OF EVERYTHING. IN CASE OF...CATASTROPHIC MALFUNCTION.
LUCKY I MARRIED SOMEONE WITH LEGACY ACCESS TO THE ARCHIVES, *HUH?*
SO I THINK THIS IS THE SAME SPOT. IT'S QUITE NEAR THE DAMAGE.
HARD TO IMAGINE THERE'S AN AIRLOCK WITHOUT A REAL LOCK... ***ANYWHERE.***
THAT'S IN THE ZOOLOGICAL REPOSITORY, RIGHT? NO WONDER.
PEOPLE ARE WEIRD ABOUT ANIMALS.
SOME ORIGINATORS DIDN'T WANT TO BRING THEM AT ALL.
THE ***USELESS*** KIND, AT LEAST. LIKE DOGS AND CATS.
SAID THEY WERE A WASTE OF RESOURCES IF YOU CAN'T EAT THEM.
AS IF HUMANS ARE THE ONLY SPECIES WORTH SAVING. ***STUPID.***
BEE...
THE COMPROMISE? A DINKY COLLECTION OF INOFFENSIVE CREATURES.
RIGHT AT THE *DODONA'S* SURFACE SO THEY COULD BE ***SPAT OUT*** ANY TIME.
WE CAN GO AGAINST THE COUNCIL AND TRY TO FIX OUR COURSE MANUALLY...
...BY PERFORMING AN UNAUTHORIZED, DANGEROUS SPACEWALK...
...AND EXTINGUISH AN ENTIRE SPECIES AT THE SAME TIME?
COULD THERE BE A WORSE PLAN?
THERE'S ***ALWAYS*** SOMETHING EVEN MORE TERRIBLE.
LIKE THE FACT THAT FUTURE GENERATIONS WON'T GET THIS CHOICE.

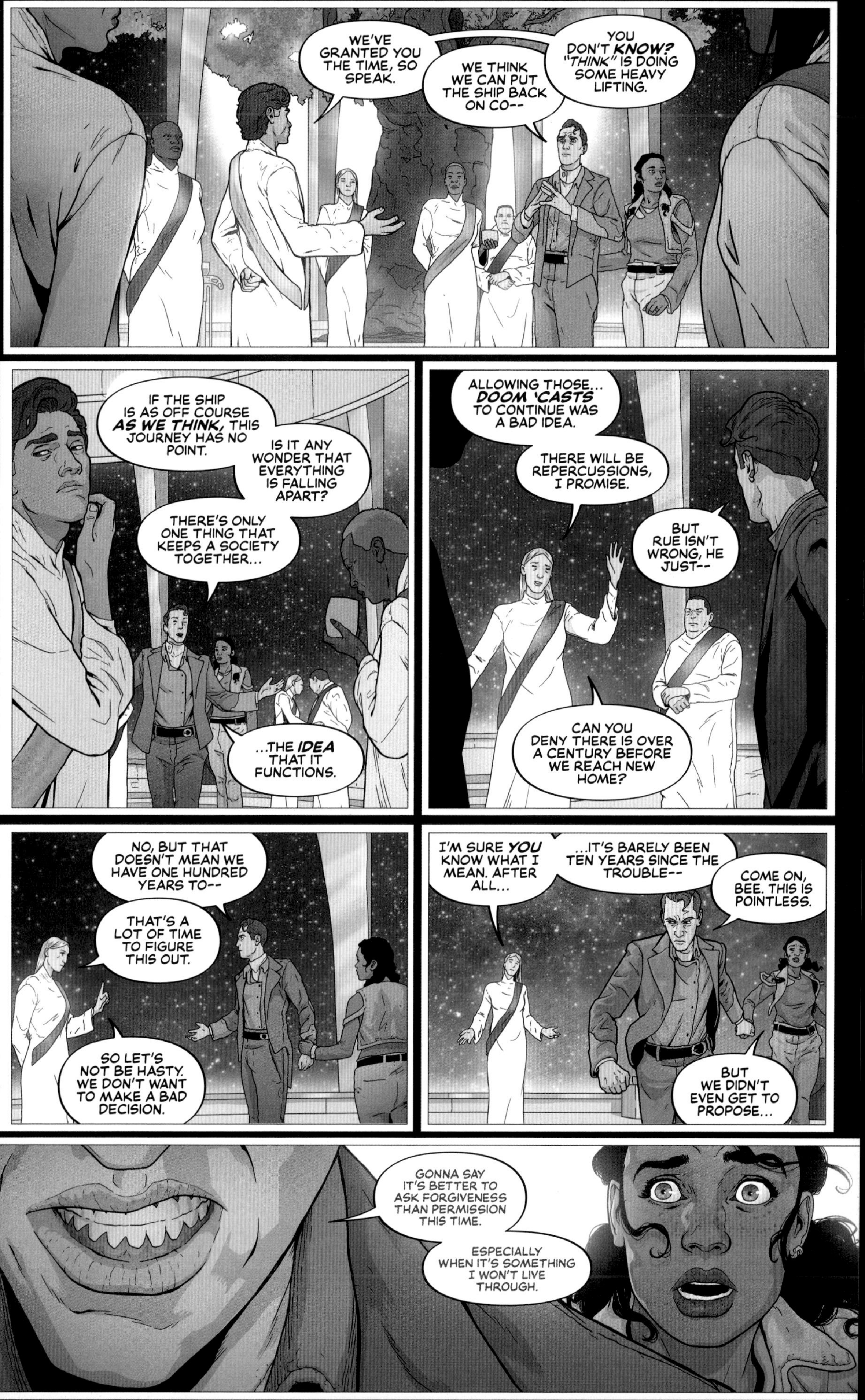
WE'VE GRANTED YOU THE TIME, SO SPEAK.
WE THINK WE CAN PUT THE SHIP BACK ON CO--
YOU DON'T *KNOW?* "*THINK*" IS DOING SOME HEAVY LIFTING.
IF THE SHIP IS AS OFF COURSE *AS WE THINK,* THIS JOURNEY HAS NO POINT.
IS IT ANY WONDER THAT EVERYTHING IS FALLING APART?
THERE'S ONLY ONE THING THAT KEEPS A SOCIETY TOGETHER...
...THE *IDEA* THAT IT FUNCTIONS.
ALLOWING THOSE... *DOOM 'CASTS* TO CONTINUE WAS A BAD IDEA.
THERE WILL BE REPERCUSSIONS, I PROMISE.
BUT RUE ISN'T WRONG, HE JUST--
CAN YOU DENY THERE IS OVER A CENTURY BEFORE WE REACH NEW HOME?
NO, BUT THAT DOESN'T MEAN WE HAVE ONE HUNDRED YEARS TO--
THAT'S A LOT OF TIME TO FIGURE THIS OUT.
SO LET'S NOT BE HASTY. WE DON'T WANT TO MAKE A BAD DECISION.
I'M SURE *YOU* KNOW WHAT I MEAN. AFTER ALL...
...IT'S BARELY BEEN TEN YEARS SINCE THE TROUBLE--
COME ON, BEE. THIS IS POINTLESS.
BUT WE DIDN'T EVEN GET TO PROPOSE...
GONNA SAY IT'S BETTER TO ASK FORGIVENESS THAN PERMISSION THIS TIME.
ESPECIALLY WHEN IT'S SOMETHING I WON'T LIVE THROUGH.

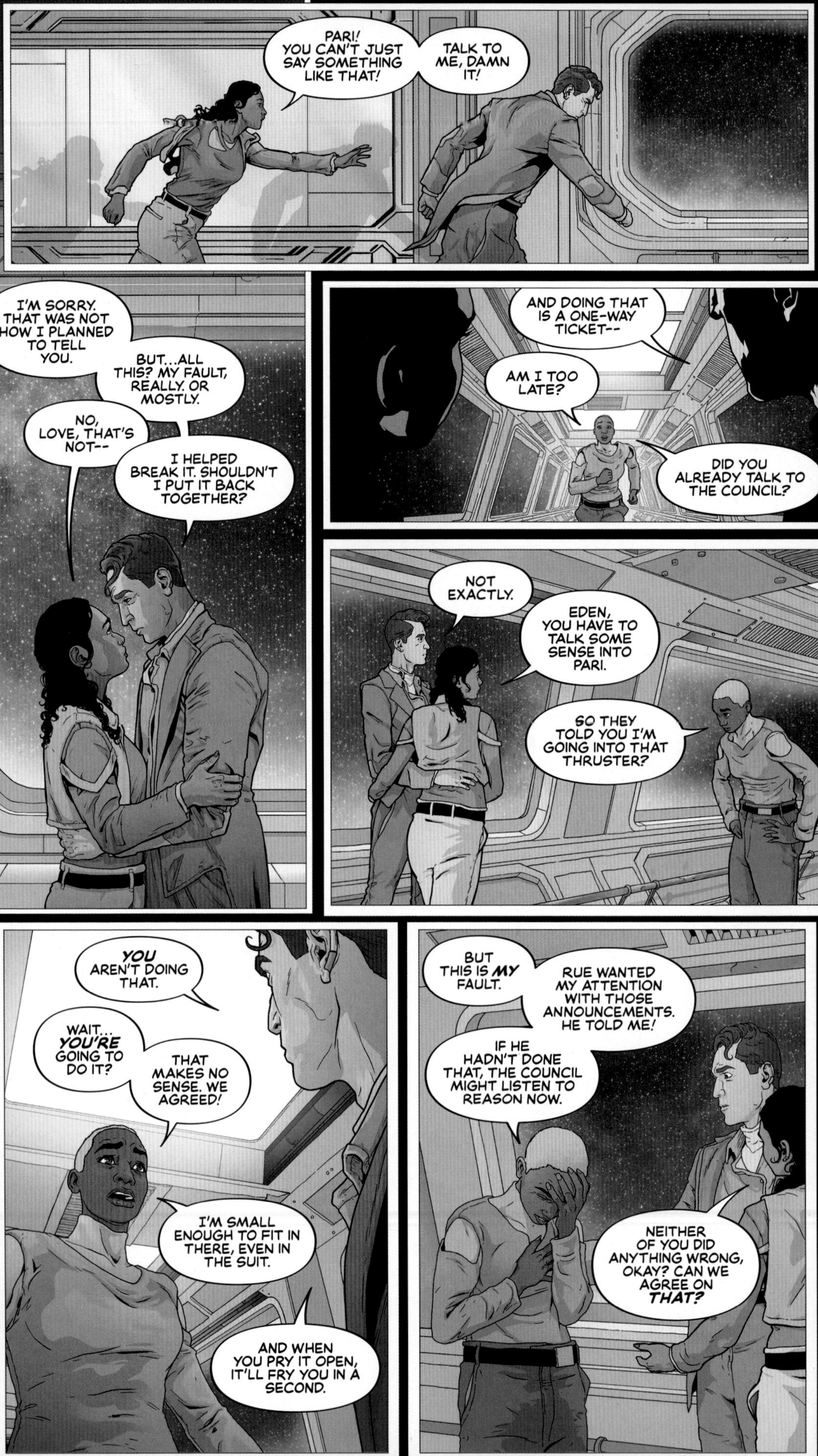
PARI! YOU CAN'T JUST SAY SOMETHING LIKE THAT!
TALK TO ME, DAMN IT!
I'M SORRY. THAT WAS NOT HOW I PLANNED TO TELL YOU.
BUT...ALL THIS? MY FAULT, REALLY. OR MOSTLY.
NO, LOVE, THAT'S NOT--
I HELPED BREAK IT. SHOULDN'T I PUT IT BACK TOGETHER?
AND DOING THAT IS A ONE-WAY TICKET--
AM I TOO LATE?
DID YOU ALREADY TALK TO THE COUNCIL?
NOT EXACTLY.
EDEN, YOU HAVE TO TALK SOME SENSE INTO PARI.
SO THEY TOLD YOU I'M GOING INTO THAT THRUSTER?
YOU AREN'T DOING THAT.
WAIT... YOU'RE GOING TO DO IT?
THAT MAKES NO SENSE. WE AGREED!
I'M SMALL ENOUGH TO FIT IN THERE, EVEN IN THE SUIT.
AND WHEN YOU PRY IT OPEN, IT'LL FRY YOU IN A SECOND.
BUT THIS IS MY FAULT.
RUE WANTED MY ATTENTION WITH THOSE ANNOUNCEMENTS. HE TOLD ME!
IF HE HADN'T DONE THAT, THE COUNCIL MIGHT LISTEN TO REASON NOW.
NEITHER OF YOU DID ANYTHING WRONG, OKAY? CAN WE AGREE ON THAT?

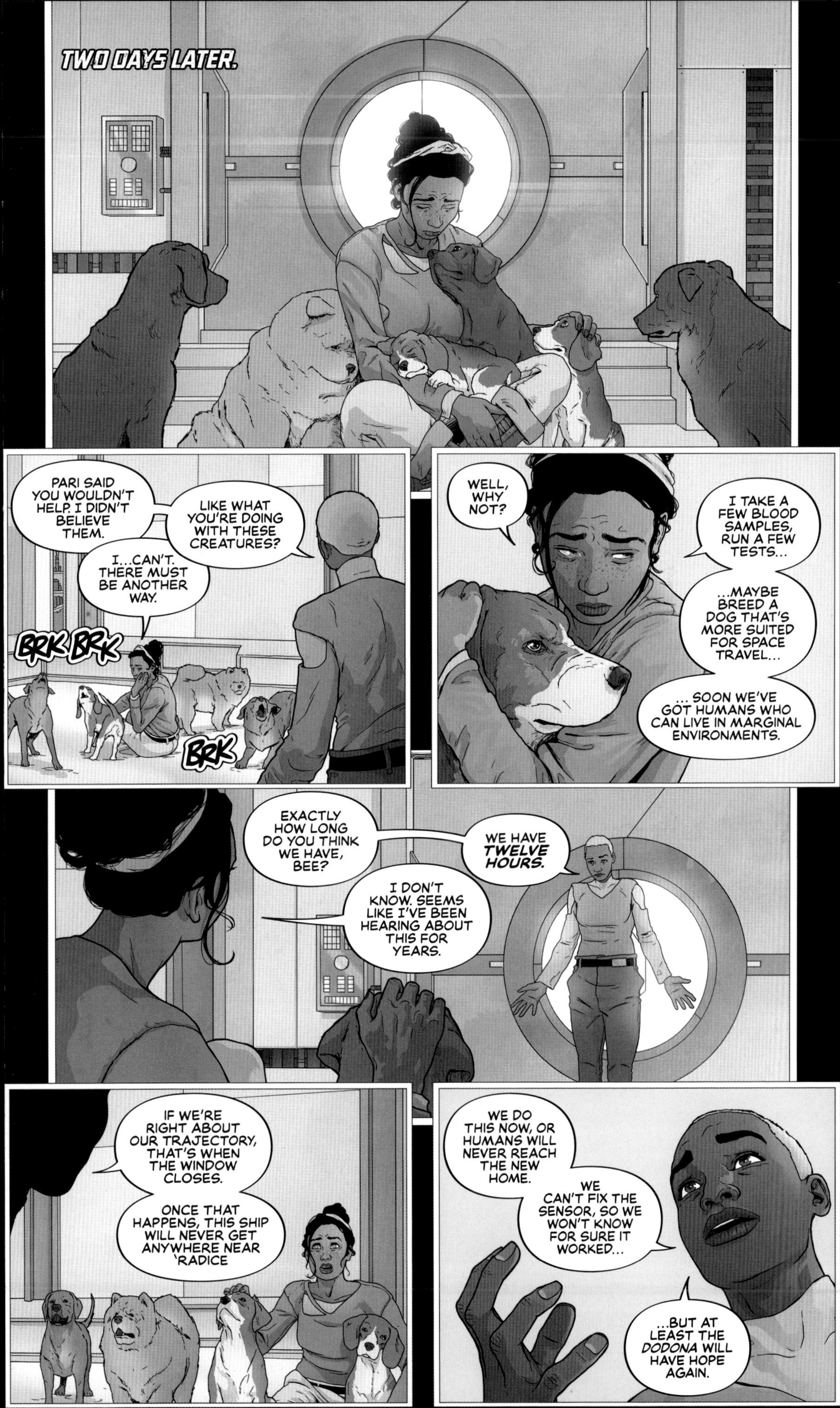
TWO DAYS LATER.
PARI SAID YOU WOULDN'T HELP. I DIDN'T BELIEVE THEM.
LIKE WHAT YOU'RE DOING WITH THESE CREATURES?
I...CAN'T. THERE MUST BE ANOTHER WAY.
BRK BRK
BRK
WELL, WHY NOT?
I TAKE A FEW BLOOD SAMPLES, RUN A FEW TESTS...
...MAYBE BREED A DOG THAT'S MORE SUITED FOR SPACE TRAVEL...
... SOON WE'VE GOT HUMANS WHO CAN LIVE IN MARGINAL ENVIRONMENTS.
EXACTLY HOW LONG DO YOU THINK WE HAVE, BEE?
WE HAVE *TWELVE HOURS.*
I DON'T KNOW. SEEMS LIKE I'VE BEEN HEARING ABOUT THIS FOR YEARS.
IF WE'RE RIGHT ABOUT OUR TRAJECTORY, THAT'S WHEN THE WINDOW CLOSES.
ONCE THAT HAPPENS, THIS SHIP WILL NEVER GET ANYWHERE NEAR 'RADICE
WE DO THIS NOW, OR HUMANS WILL NEVER REACH THE NEW HOME.
WE CAN'T FIX THE SENSOR, SO WE WON'T KNOW FOR SURE IT WORKED...
...BUT AT LEAST THE *DODONA* WILL HAVE HOPE AGAIN.

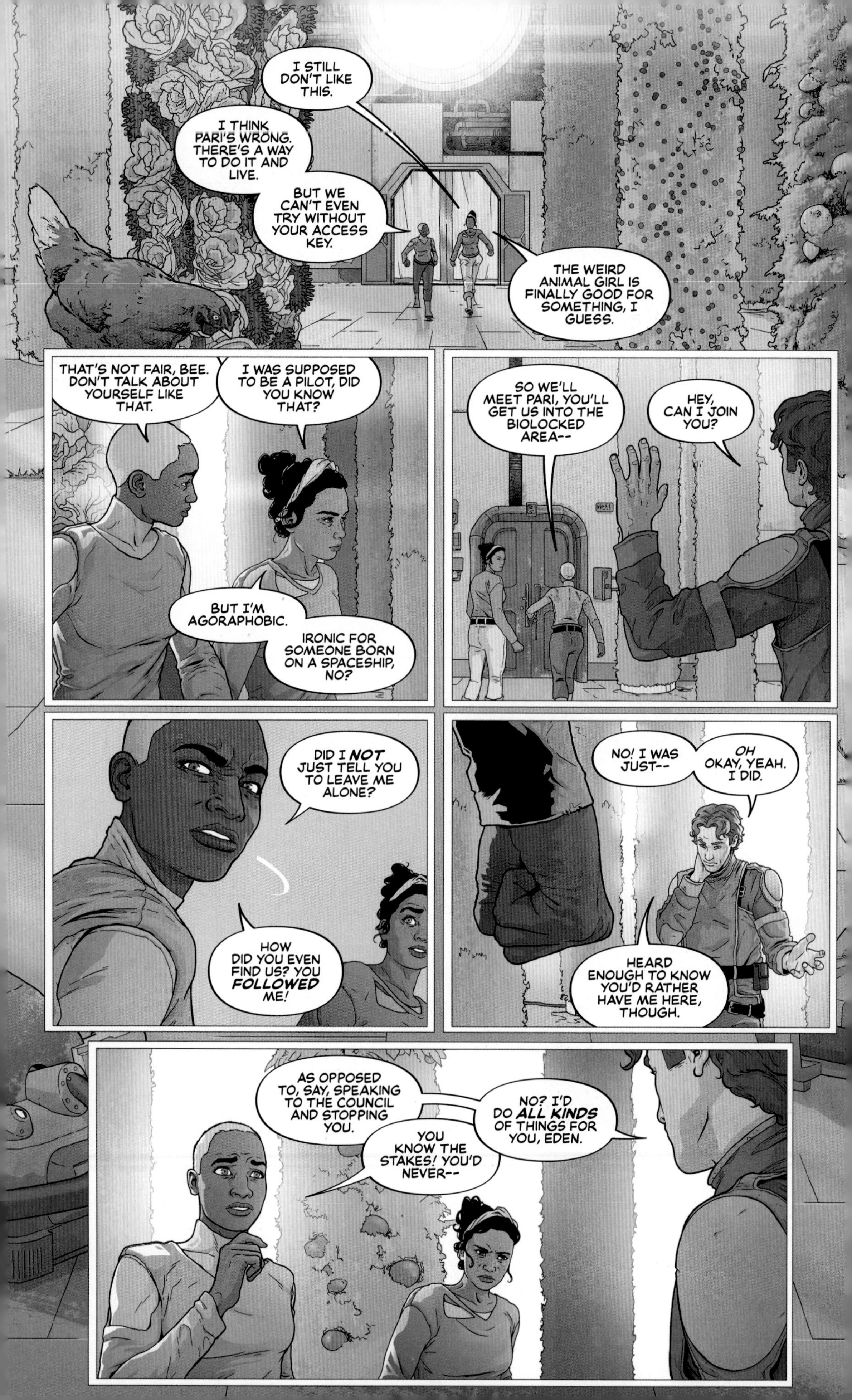
I STILL DON'T LIKE THIS.
I THINK PARI'S WRONG. THERE'S A WAY TO DO IT AND LIVE.
BUT WE CAN'T EVEN TRY WITHOUT YOUR ACCESS KEY.
THE WEIRD ANIMAL GIRL IS FINALLY GOOD FOR SOMETHING, I GUESS.
THAT'S NOT FAIR, BEE. DON'T TALK ABOUT YOURSELF LIKE THAT.
I WAS SUPPOSED TO BE A PILOT, DID YOU KNOW THAT?
BUT I'M AGORAPHOBIC.
IRONIC FOR SOMEONE BORN ON A SPACESHIP, NO?
SO WE'LL MEET PARI, YOU'LL GET US INTO THE BIOLOCKED AREA--
HEY, CAN I JOIN YOU?
DID I ***NOT*** JUST TELL YOU TO LEAVE ME ALONE?
HOW DID YOU EVEN FIND US? YOU ***FOLLOWED*** ME!
NO! I WAS JUST--
OH OKAY, YEAH. I DID.
HEARD ENOUGH TO KNOW YOU'D RATHER HAVE ME HERE, THOUGH.
AS OPPOSED TO, SAY, SPEAKING TO THE COUNCIL AND STOPPING YOU.
YOU KNOW THE STAKES! YOU'D NEVER--
NO? I'D DO ***ALL KINDS*** OF THINGS FOR YOU, EDEN.

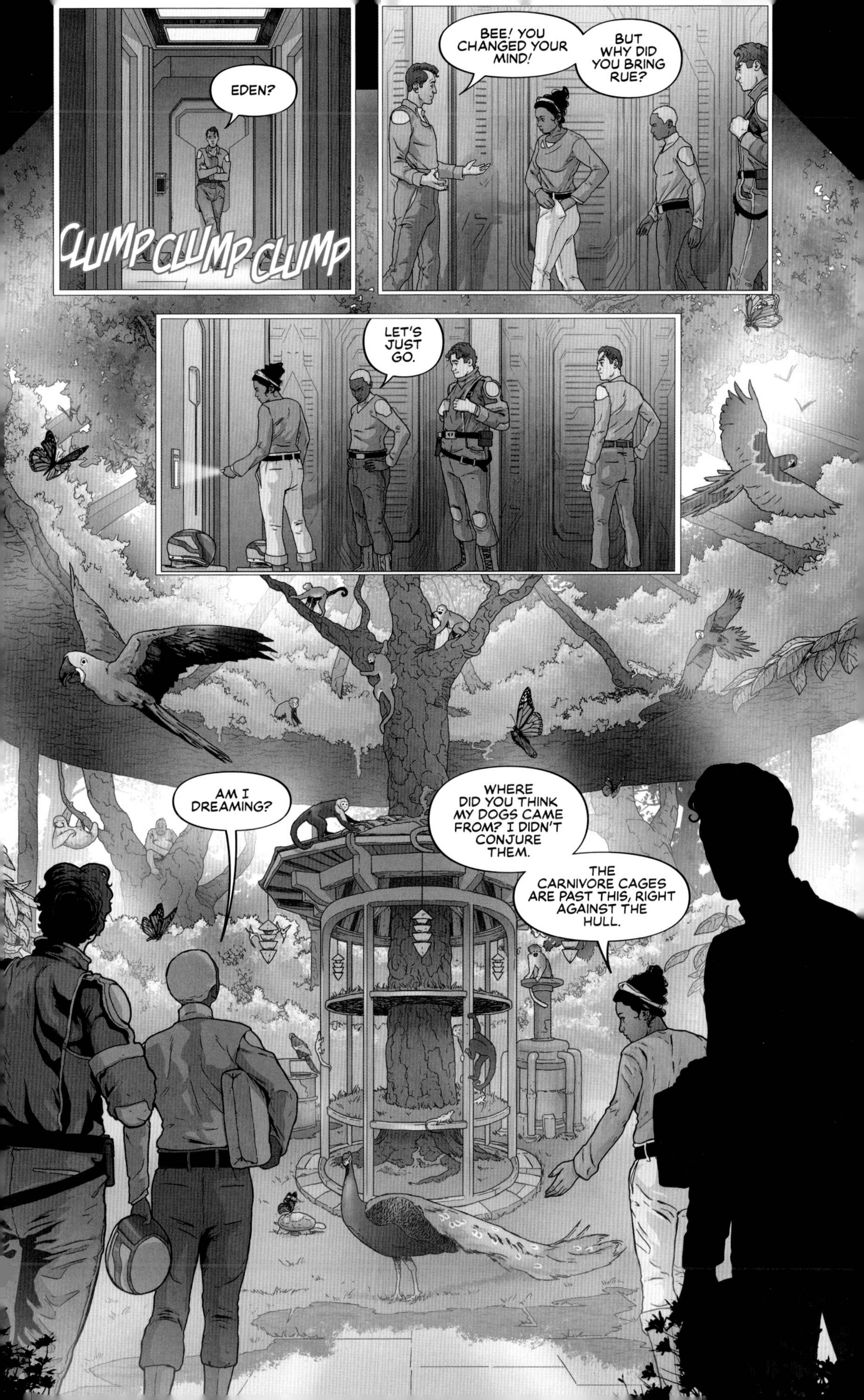
EDEN?
CLUMP CLUMP CLUMP
BEE! YOU CHANGED YOUR MIND!
BUT WHY DID YOU BRING RUE?
LET'S JUST GO.
AM I DREAMING?
WHERE DID YOU THINK MY DOGS CAME FROM? I DIDN'T CONJURE THEM.
THE CARNIVORE CAGES ARE PAST THIS, RIGHT AGAINST THE HULL.

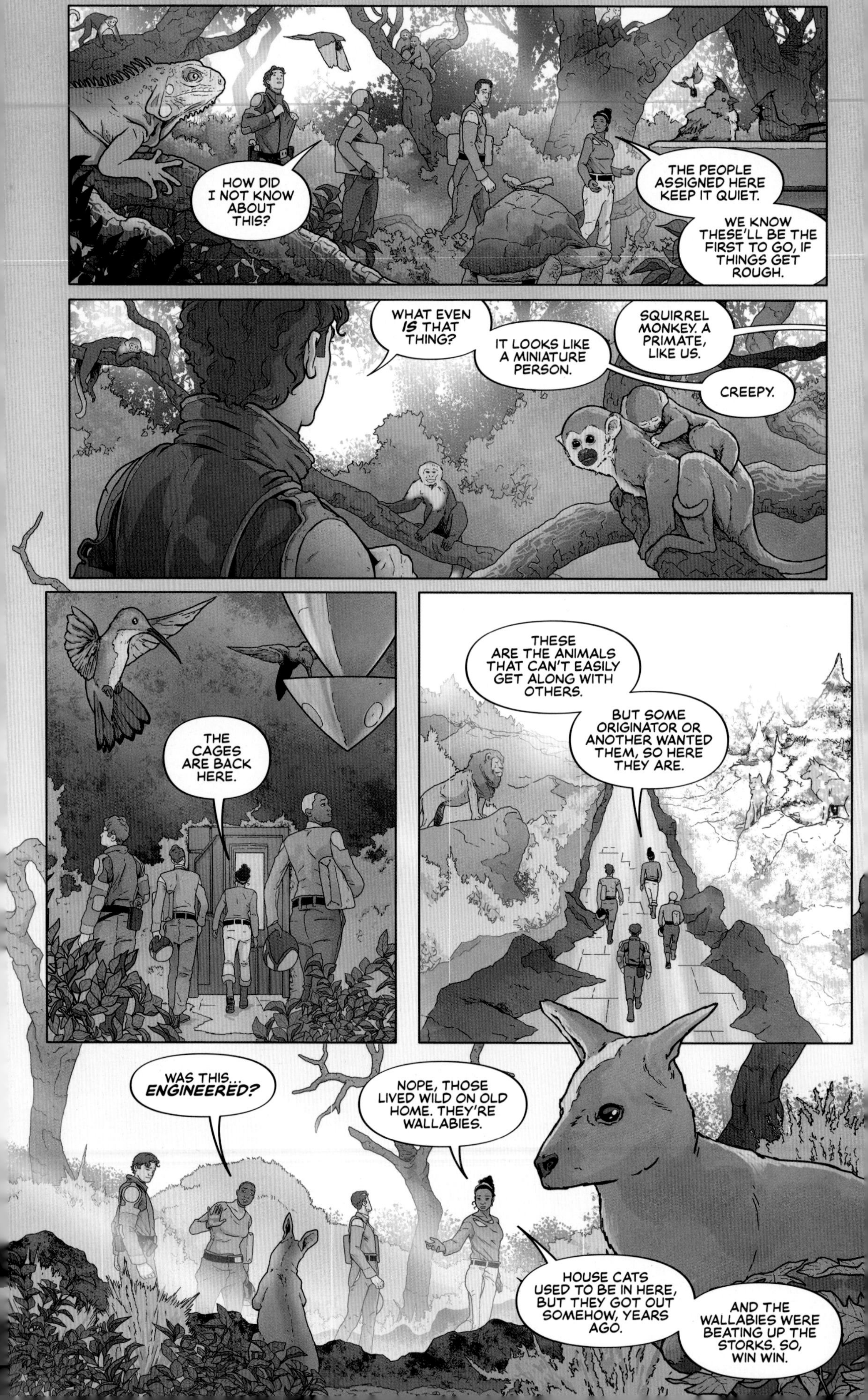
HOW DID I NOT KNOW ABOUT THIS?
THE PEOPLE ASSIGNED HERE KEEP IT QUIET.
WE KNOW THESE'LL BE THE FIRST TO GO, IF THINGS GET ROUGH.
WHAT EVEN IS THAT THING?
IT LOOKS LIKE A MINIATURE PERSON.
SQUIRREL MONKEY. A PRIMATE, LIKE US.
CREEPY.
THE CAGES ARE BACK HERE.
THESE ARE THE ANIMALS THAT CAN'T EASILY GET ALONG WITH OTHERS.
BUT SOME ORIGINATOR OR ANOTHER WANTED THEM, SO HERE THEY ARE.
WAS THIS... ENGINEERED?
NOPE, THOSE LIVED WILD ON OLD HOME. THEY'RE WALLABIES.
HOUSE CATS USED TO BE IN HERE, BUT THEY GOT OUT SOMEHOW, YEARS AGO.
AND THE WALLABIES WERE BEATING UP THE STORKS. SO, WIN WIN.

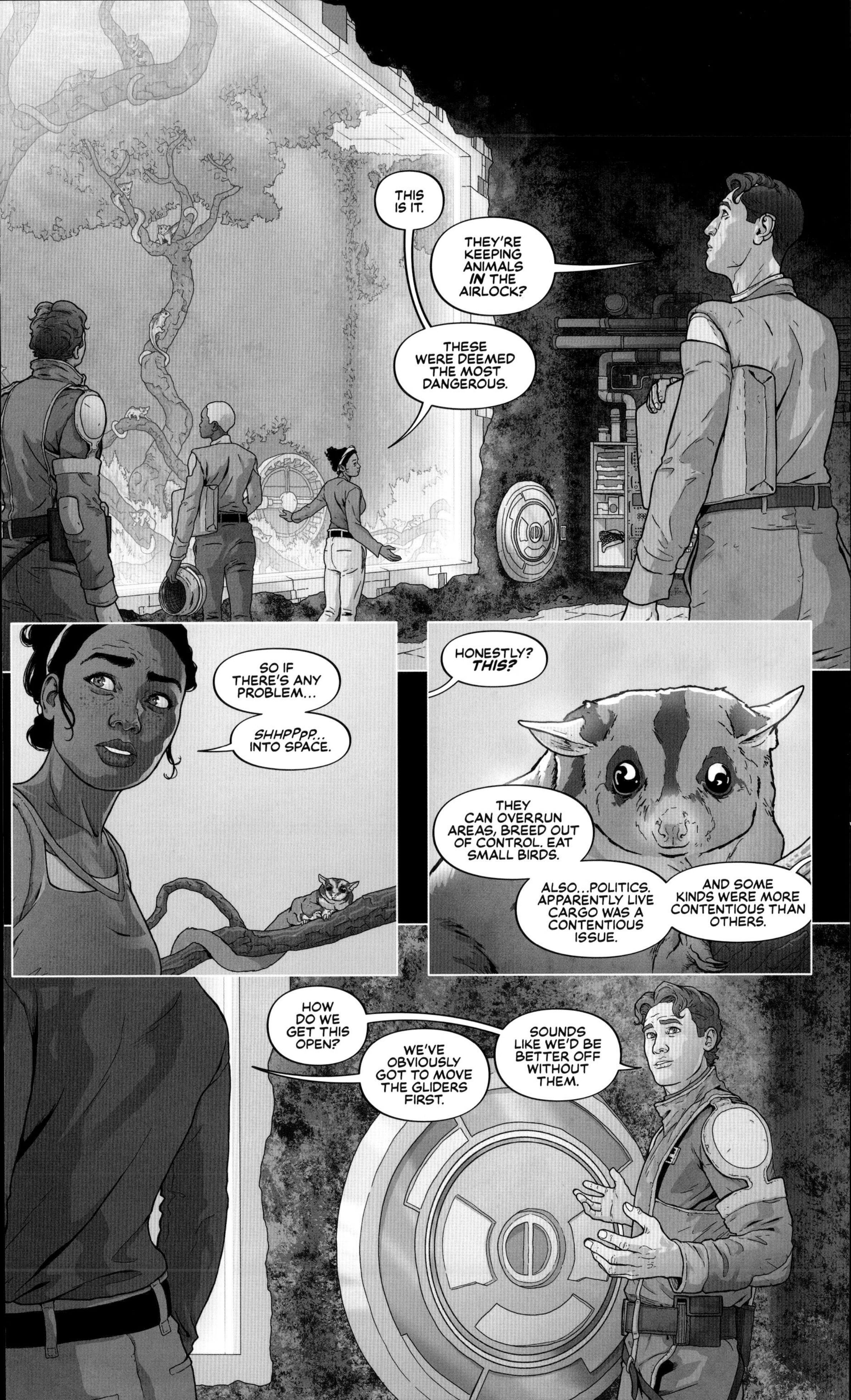

THIS IS IT.
THEY'RE KEEPING ANIMALS *IN* THE AIRLOCK?
THESE WERE DEEMED THE MOST DANGEROUS.
SO IF THERE'S ANY PROBLEM...
SHHPPpp... INTO SPACE.
HONESTLY? ***THIS?***
THEY CAN OVERRUN AREAS, BREED OUT OF CONTROL. EAT SMALL BIRDS.
ALSO...POLITICS. APPARENTLY LIVE CARGO WAS A CONTENTIOUS ISSUE.
AND SOME KINDS WERE MORE CONTENTIOUS THAN OTHERS.
HOW DO WE GET THIS OPEN?
SOUNDS LIKE WE'D BE BETTER OFF WITHOUT THEM.
WE'VE OBVIOUSLY GOT TO MOVE THE GLIDERS FIRST.

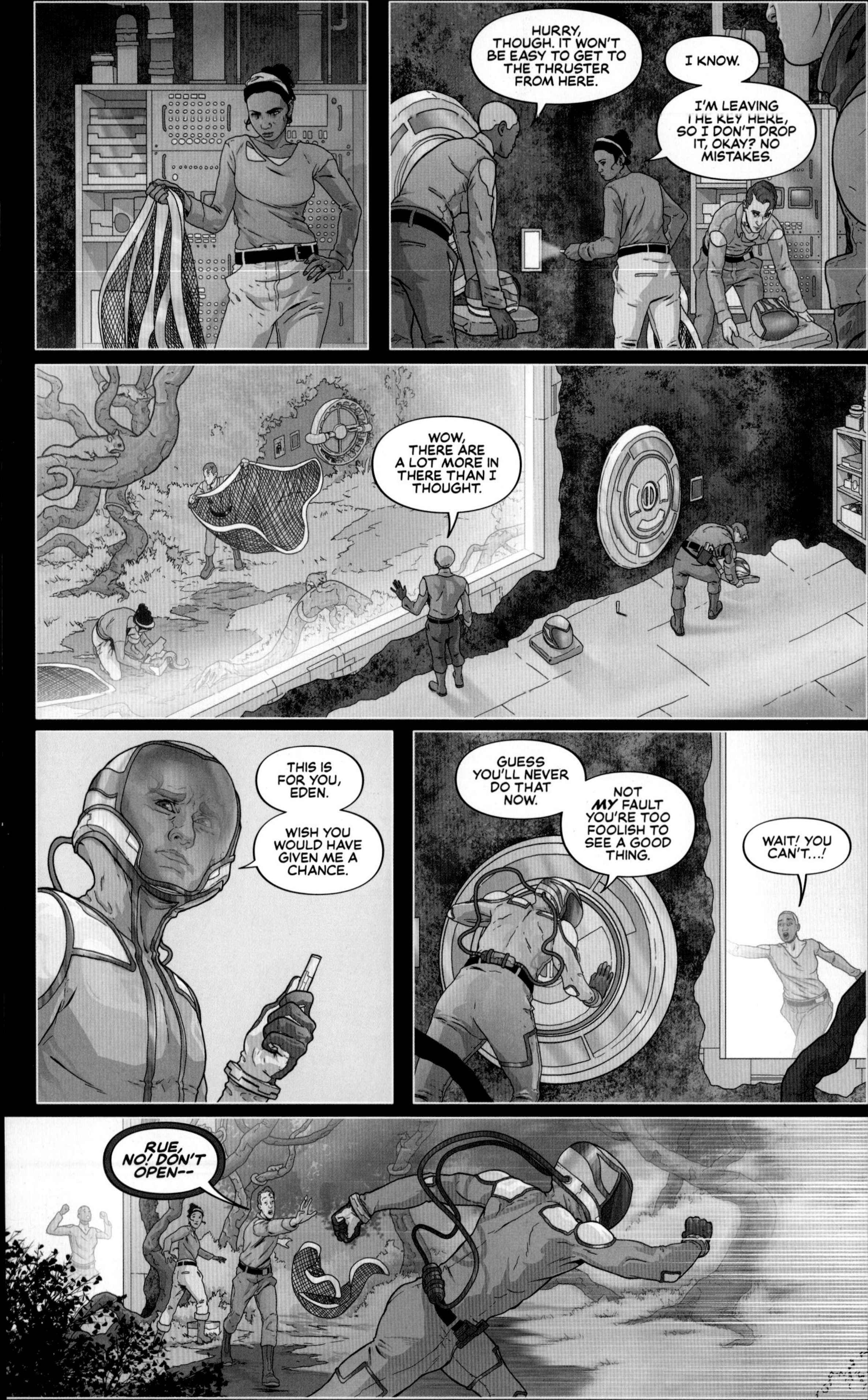
HURRY, THOUGH. IT WON'T BE EASY TO GET TO THE THRUSTER FROM HERE.
I KNOW.
I'M LEAVING THE KEY HERE, SO I DON'T DROP IT, OKAY? NO MISTAKES.
WOW, THERE ARE A LOT MORE IN THERE THAN I THOUGHT.
THIS IS FOR YOU, EDEN.
WISH YOU WOULD HAVE GIVEN ME A CHANCE.
GUESS YOU'LL NEVER DO THAT NOW.
NOT MY FAULT YOU'RE TOO FOOLISH TO SEE A GOOD THING.
WAIT! YOU CAN'T...!
RUE, NO! DON'T OPEN--

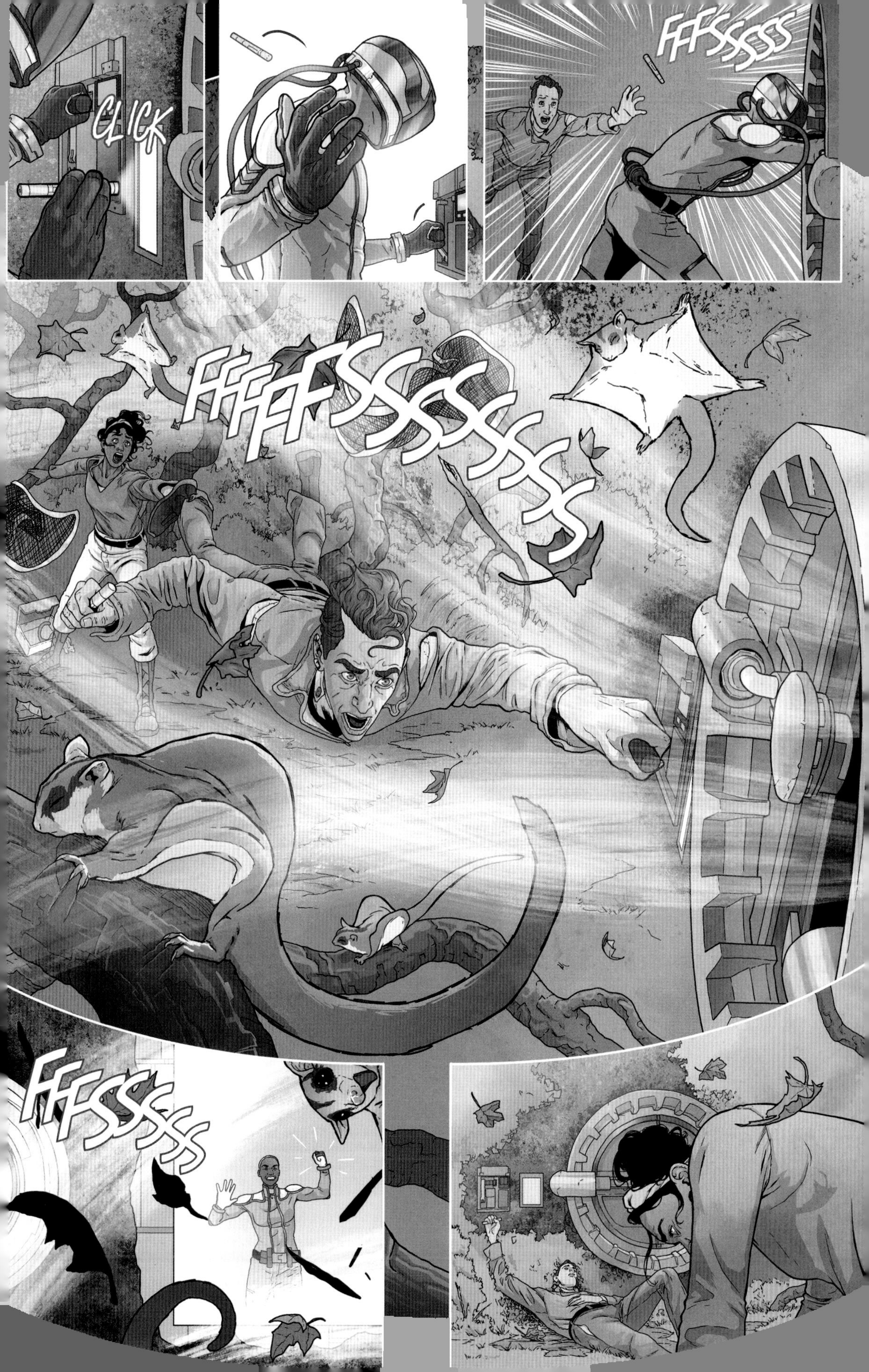
CLICK
FFFSSSSS
FFFFFSSSSSSSSS
FFFSSSSSS

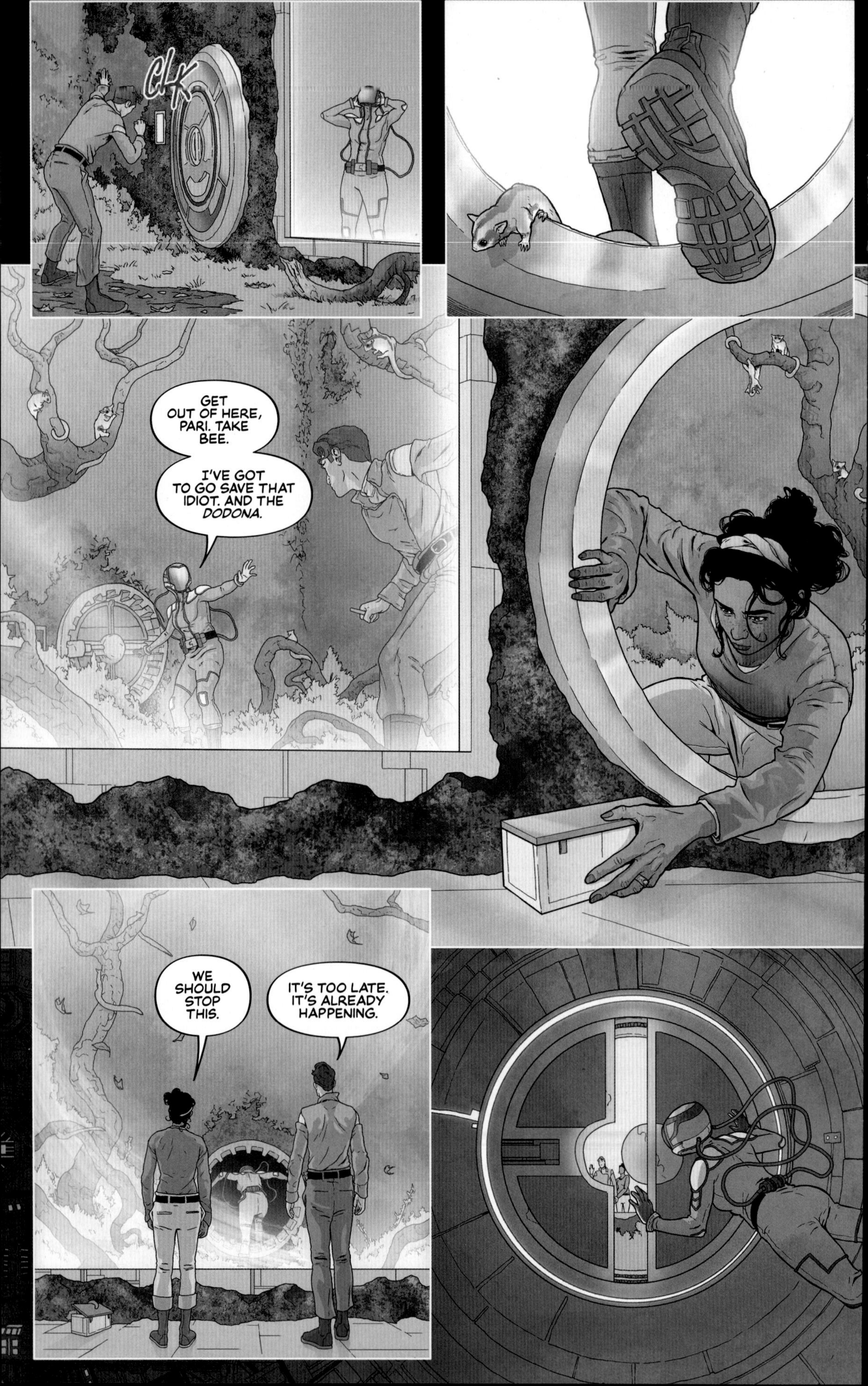
CLK
GET OUT OF HERE, PARI. TAKE BEE.
I'VE GOT TO GO SAVE THAT IDIOT. AND THE *DODONA*.
WE SHOULD STOP THIS.
IT'S TOO LATE. IT'S ALREADY HAPPENING.

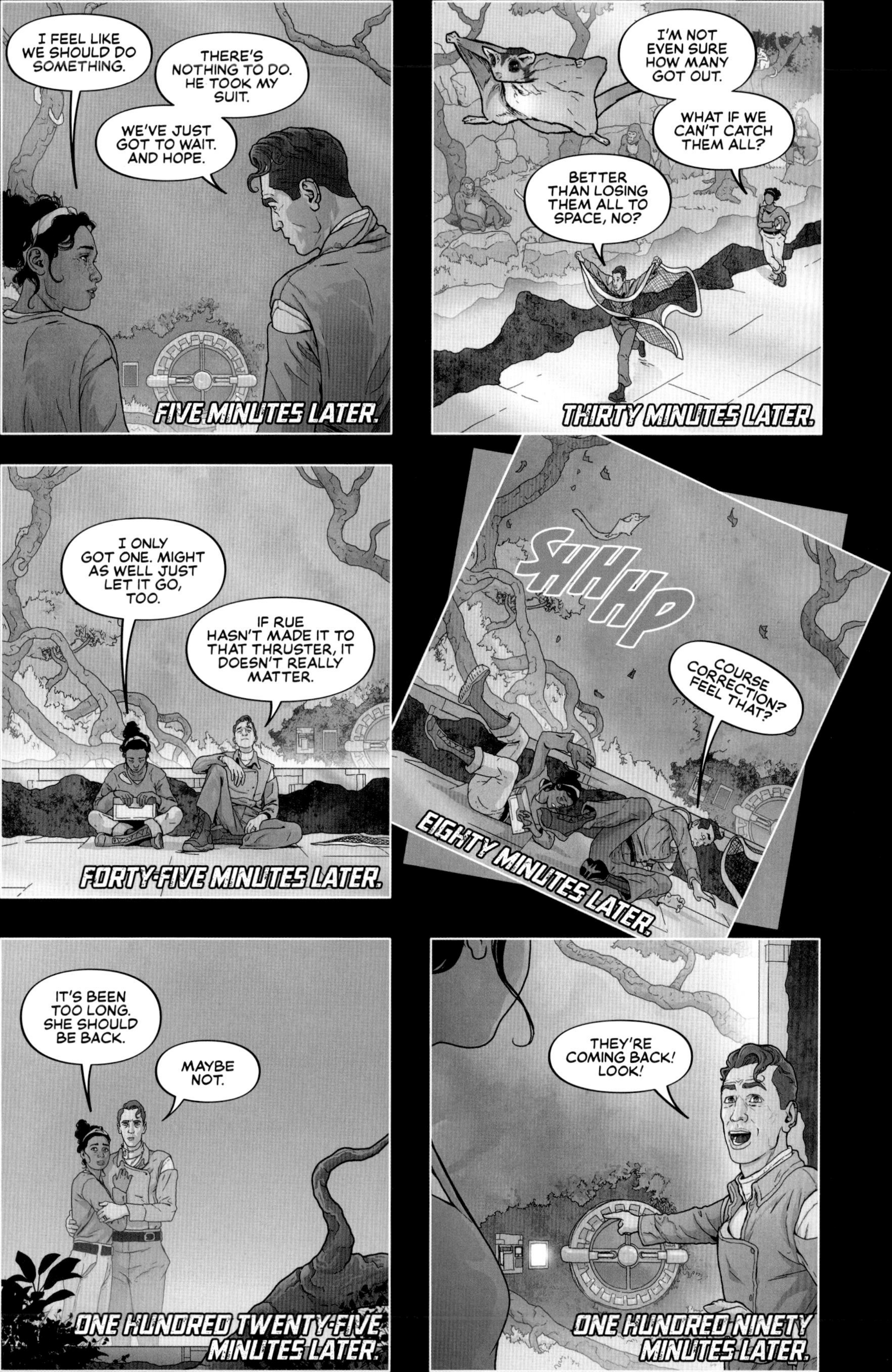
I FEEL LIKE WE SHOULD DO SOMETHING.
THERE'S NOTHING TO DO. HE TOOK MY SUIT.
WE'VE JUST GOT TO WAIT. AND HOPE.
FIVE MINUTES LATER.
I'M NOT EVEN SURE HOW MANY GOT OUT.
WHAT IF WE CAN'T CATCH THEM ALL?
BETTER THAN LOSING THEM ALL TO SPACE, NO?
THIRTY MINUTES LATER.
I ONLY GOT ONE. MIGHT AS WELL JUST LET IT GO, TOO.
IF RUE HASN'T MADE IT TO THAT THRUSTER, IT DOESN'T REALLY MATTER.
FORTY-FIVE MINUTES LATER.
SHHHP
COURSE CORRECTION? FEEL THAT?
EIGHTY MINUTES LATER.
IT'S BEEN TOO LONG. SHE SHOULD BE BACK.
MAYBE NOT.
ONE HUNDRED TWENTY-FIVE MINUTES LATER.
THEY'RE COMING BACK! LOOK!
ONE HUNDRED NINETY MINUTES LATER.

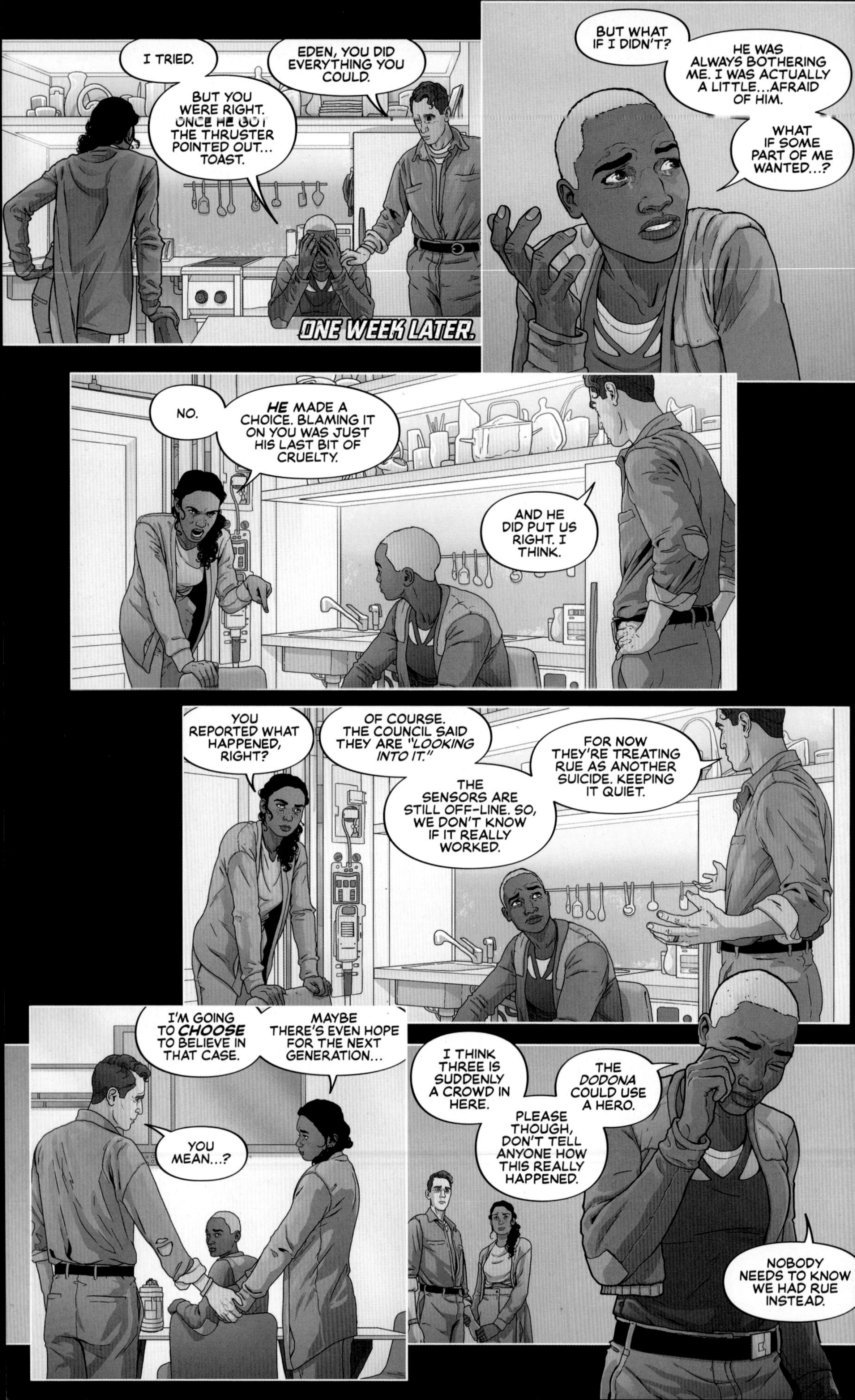
I TRIED.
EDEN, YOU DID EVERYTHING YOU COULD.
BUT YOU WERE RIGHT. ONCE HE GOT THE THRUSTER POINTED OUT... TOAST.
ONE WEEK LATER.
BUT WHAT IF I DIDN'T?
HE WAS ALWAYS BOTHERING ME. I WAS ACTUALLY A LITTLE...AFRAID OF HIM.
WHAT IF SOME PART OF ME WANTED...?
NO.
HE MADE A CHOICE. BLAMING IT ON YOU WAS JUST HIS LAST BIT OF CRUELTY.
AND HE DID PUT US RIGHT. I THINK.
YOU REPORTED WHAT HAPPENED, RIGHT?
OF COURSE. THE COUNCIL SAID THEY ARE "LOOKING INTO IT."
THE SENSORS ARE STILL OFF-LINE. SO, WE DON'T KNOW IF IT REALLY WORKED.
FOR NOW THEY'RE TREATING RUE AS ANOTHER SUICIDE. KEEPING IT QUIET.
I'M GOING TO CHOOSE TO BELIEVE IN THAT CASE.
MAYBE THERE'S EVEN HOPE FOR THE NEXT GENERATION...
YOU MEAN...?
I THINK THREE IS SUDDENLY A CROWD IN HERE.
THE DODONA COULD USE A HERO.
PLEASE THOUGH, DON'T TELL ANYONE HOW THIS REALLY HAPPENED.
NOBODY NEEDS TO KNOW WE HAD RUE INSTEAD.

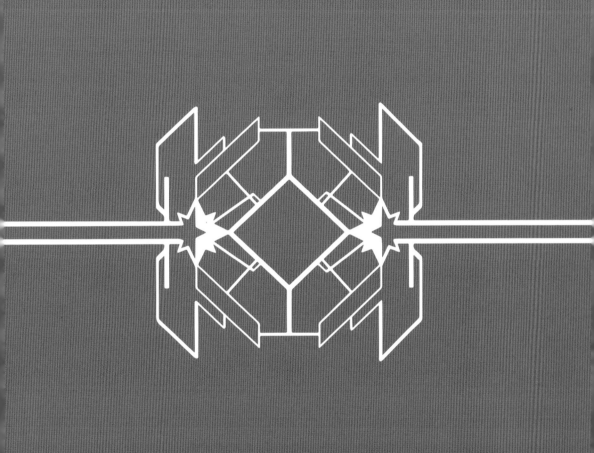

CHAPTER
FOUR

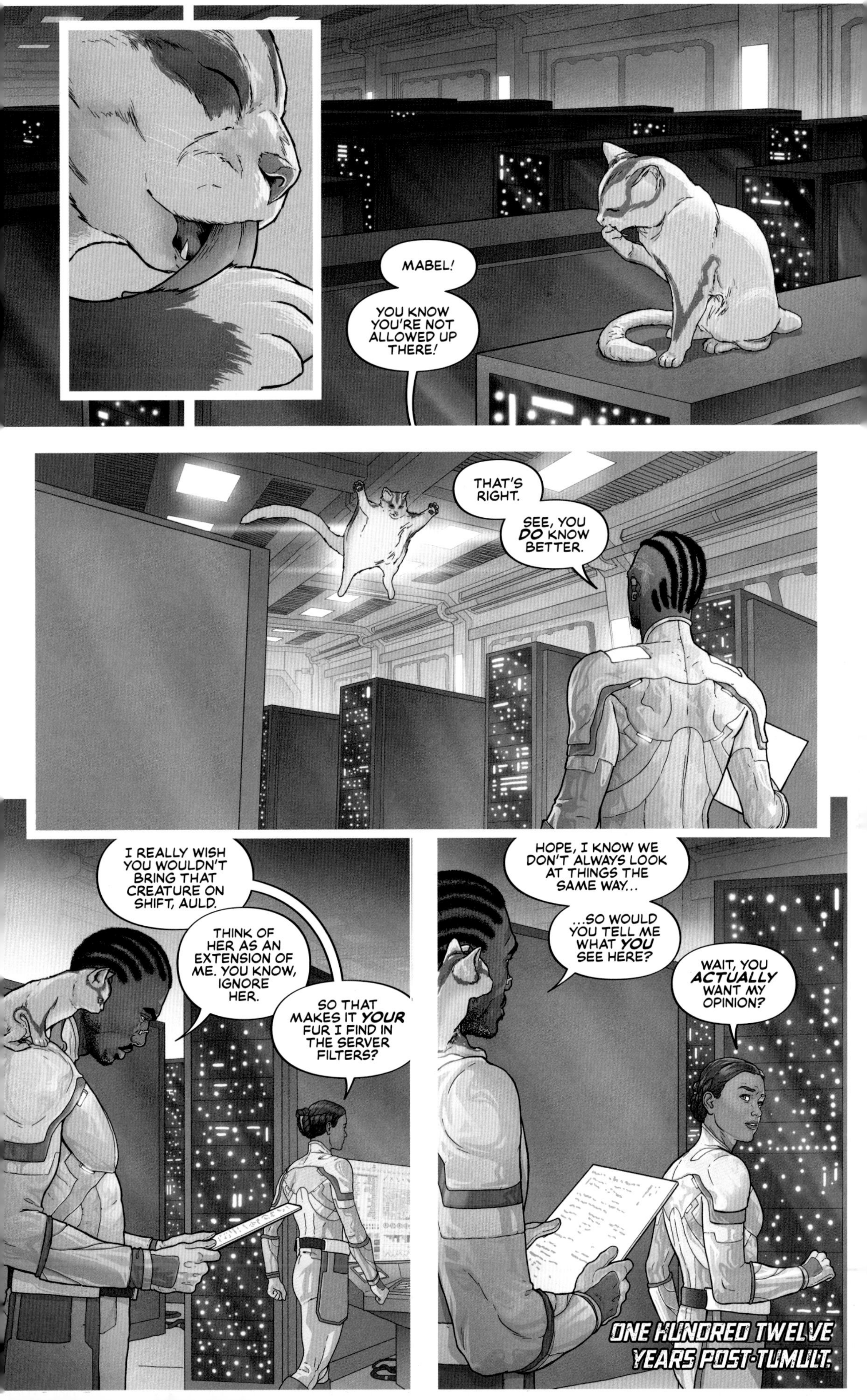
MABEL!
YOU KNOW YOU'RE NOT ALLOWED UP THERE!
THAT'S RIGHT.
SEE, YOU *DO* KNOW BETTER.
I REALLY WISH YOU WOULDN'T BRING THAT CREATURE ON SHIFT, AULD.
THINK OF HER AS AN EXTENSION OF ME. YOU KNOW, IGNORE HER.
SO THAT MAKES IT *YOUR* FUR I FIND IN THE SERVER FILTERS?
HOPE, I KNOW WE DON'T ALWAYS LOOK AT THINGS THE SAME WAY...
...SO WOULD YOU TELL ME WHAT *YOU* SEE HERE?
WAIT, YOU *ACTUALLY* WANT MY OPINION?
ONE HUNDRED TWELVE YEARS POST-TUMULT.

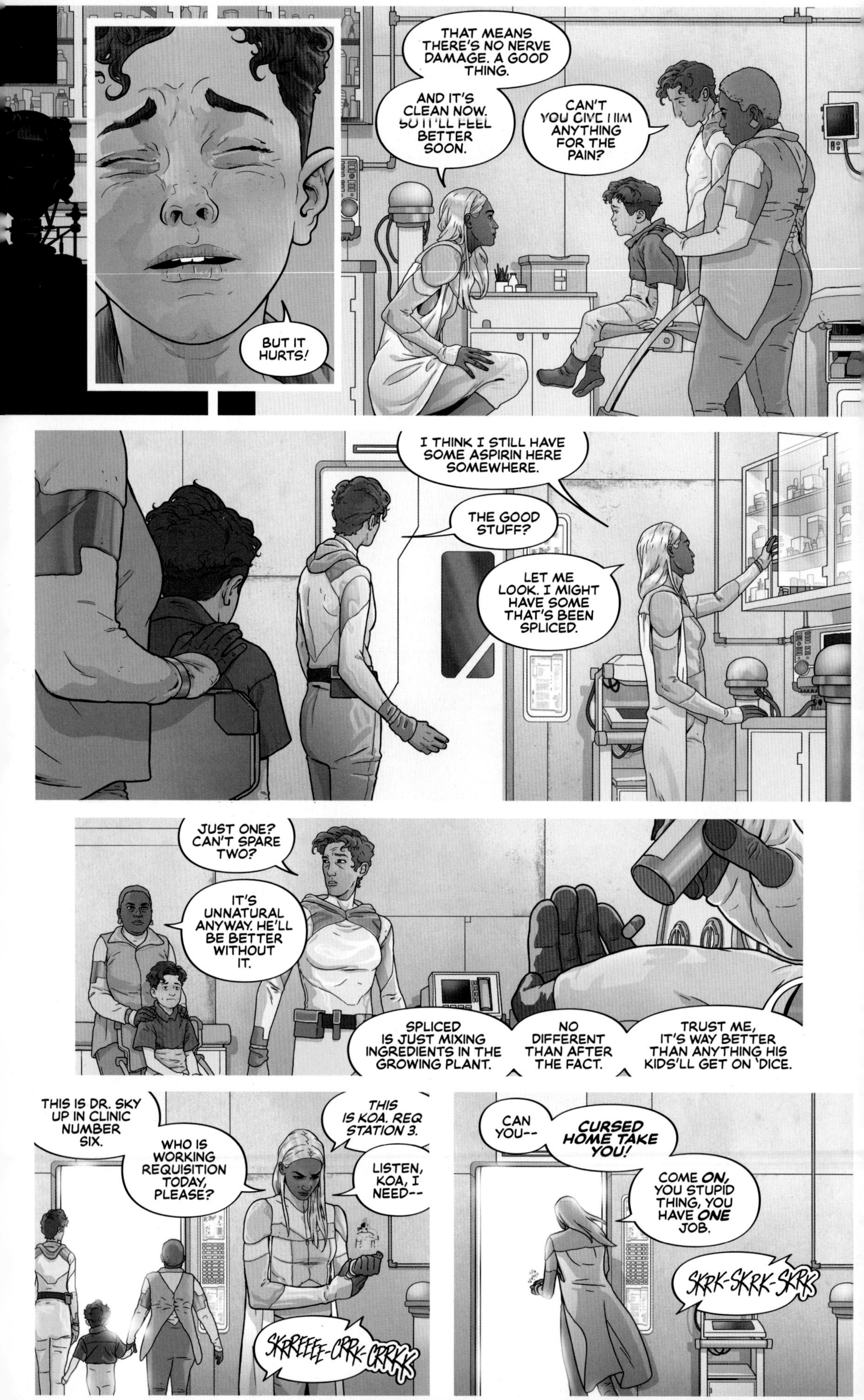
BUT IT HURTS!
THAT MEANS THERE'S NO NERVE DAMAGE. A GOOD THING.
AND IT'S CLEAN NOW. SO IT'LL FEEL BETTER SOON.
CAN'T YOU GIVE HIM ANYTHING FOR THE PAIN?
I THINK I STILL HAVE SOME ASPIRIN HERE SOMEWHERE.
THE GOOD STUFF?
LET ME LOOK. I MIGHT HAVE SOME THAT'S BEEN SPLICED.
JUST ONE? CAN'T SPARE TWO?
IT'S UNNATURAL ANYWAY. HE'LL BE BETTER WITHOUT IT.
SPLICED IS JUST MIXING INGREDIENTS IN THE GROWING PLANT.
NO DIFFERENT THAN AFTER THE FACT.
TRUST ME, IT'S WAY BETTER THAN ANYTHING HIS KIDS'LL GET ON 'DICE.
THIS IS DR. SKY UP IN CLINIC NUMBER SIX.
WHO IS WORKING REQUISITION TODAY, PLEASE?
THIS IS KOA. REQ STATION 3.
LISTEN, KOA, I NEED--
SKREEEEE-CRRK-CRRKK
CAN YOU--
CURSED HOME TAKE YOU!
COME ON, YOU STUPID THING, YOU HAVE ONE JOB.
SKRK-SKRK-SKRK

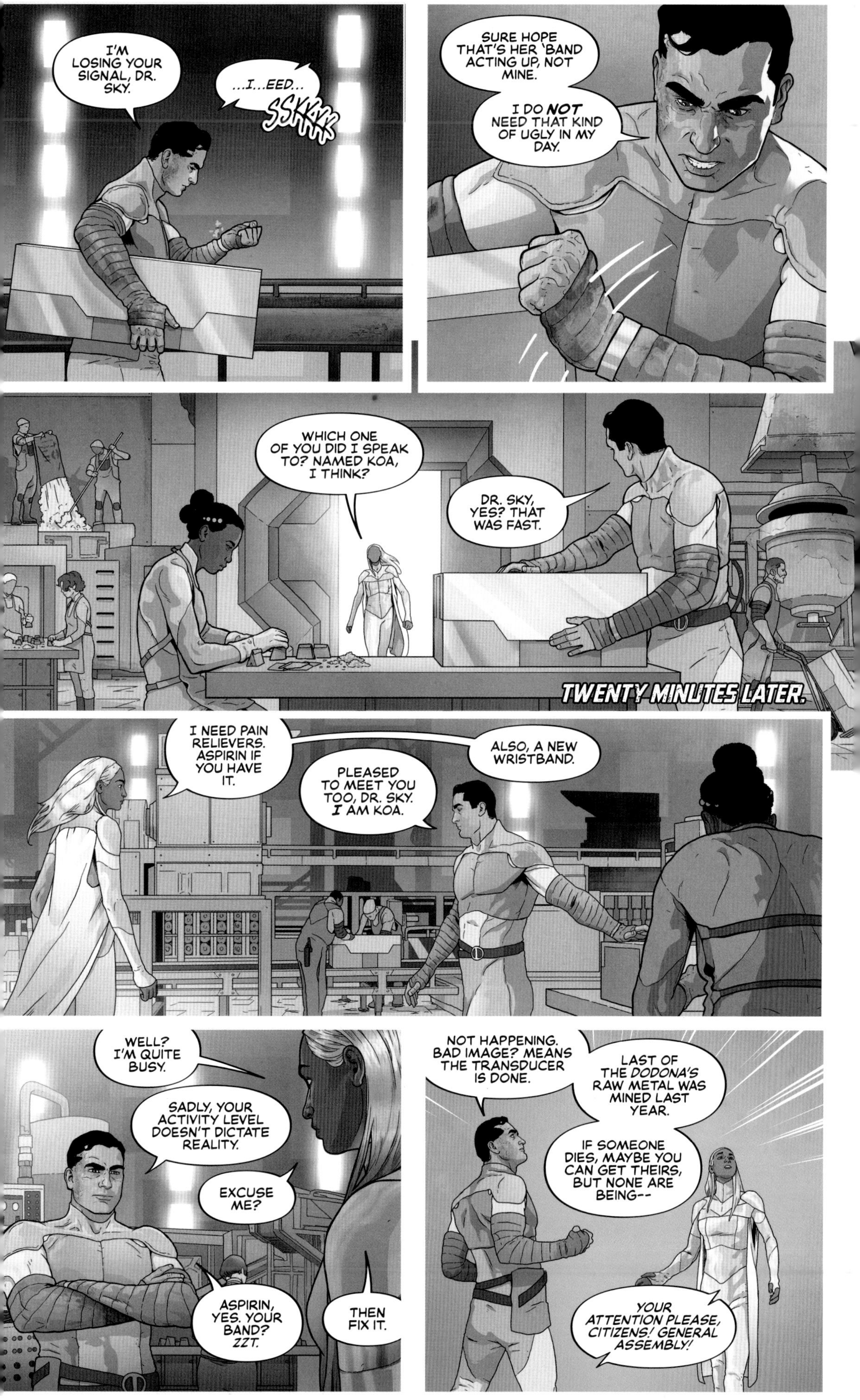
I'M LOSING YOUR SIGNAL, DR. SKY.
...I...EED...
SSKKKK
SURE HOPE THAT'S HER 'BAND ACTING UP, NOT MINE.
I DO NOT NEED THAT KIND OF UGLY IN MY DAY.
WHICH ONE OF YOU DID I SPEAK TO? NAMED KOA, I THINK?
DR. SKY, YES? THAT WAS FAST.
TWENTY MINUTES LATER.
I NEED PAIN RELIEVERS. ASPIRIN IF YOU HAVE IT.
ALSO, A NEW WRISTBAND.
PLEASED TO MEET YOU TOO, DR. SKY. I AM KOA.
WELL? I'M QUITE BUSY.
SADLY, YOUR ACTIVITY LEVEL DOESN'T DICTATE REALITY.
EXCUSE ME?
ASPIRIN, YES. YOUR BAND? ZZT.
THEN FIX IT.
NOT HAPPENING. BAD IMAGE? MEANS THE TRANSDUCER IS DONE.
LAST OF THE DODONA'S RAW METAL WAS MINED LAST YEAR.
IF SOMEONE DIES, MAYBE YOU CAN GET THEIRS, BUT NONE ARE BEING--
YOUR ATTENTION PLEASE, CITIZENS! GENERAL ASSEMBLY!

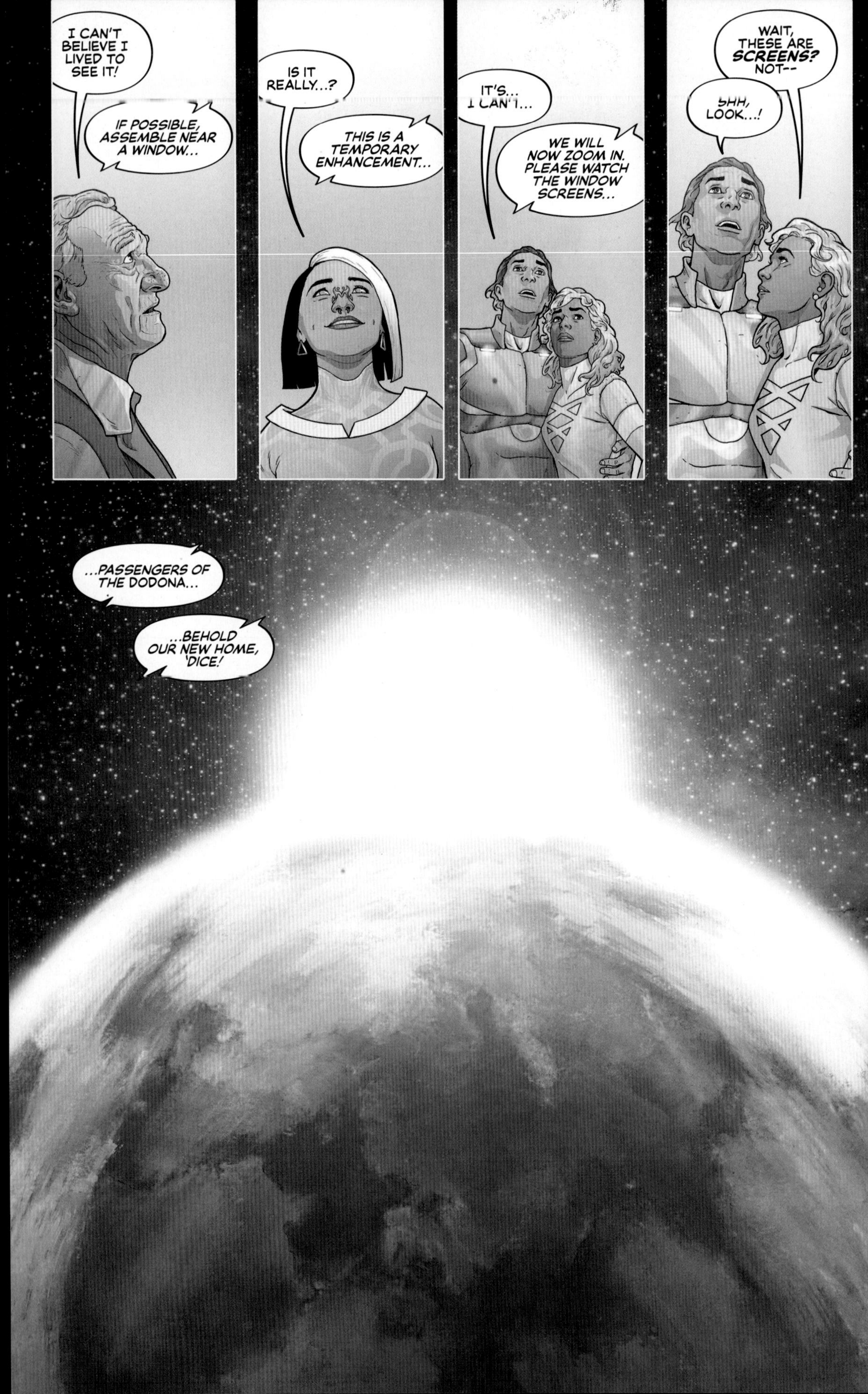
I CAN'T BELIEVE I LIVED TO SEE IT!
IF POSSIBLE, ASSEMBLE NEAR A WINDOW...
IS IT REALLY...?
THIS IS A TEMPORARY ENHANCEMENT...
IT'S... I CAN'T...
WE WILL NOW ZOOM IN. PLEASE WATCH THE WINDOW SCREENS...
WAIT, THESE ARE SCREENS? NOT--
SHH, LOOK...!
...PASSENGERS OF THE DODONA...
...BEHOLD OUR NEW HOME, 'DICE!

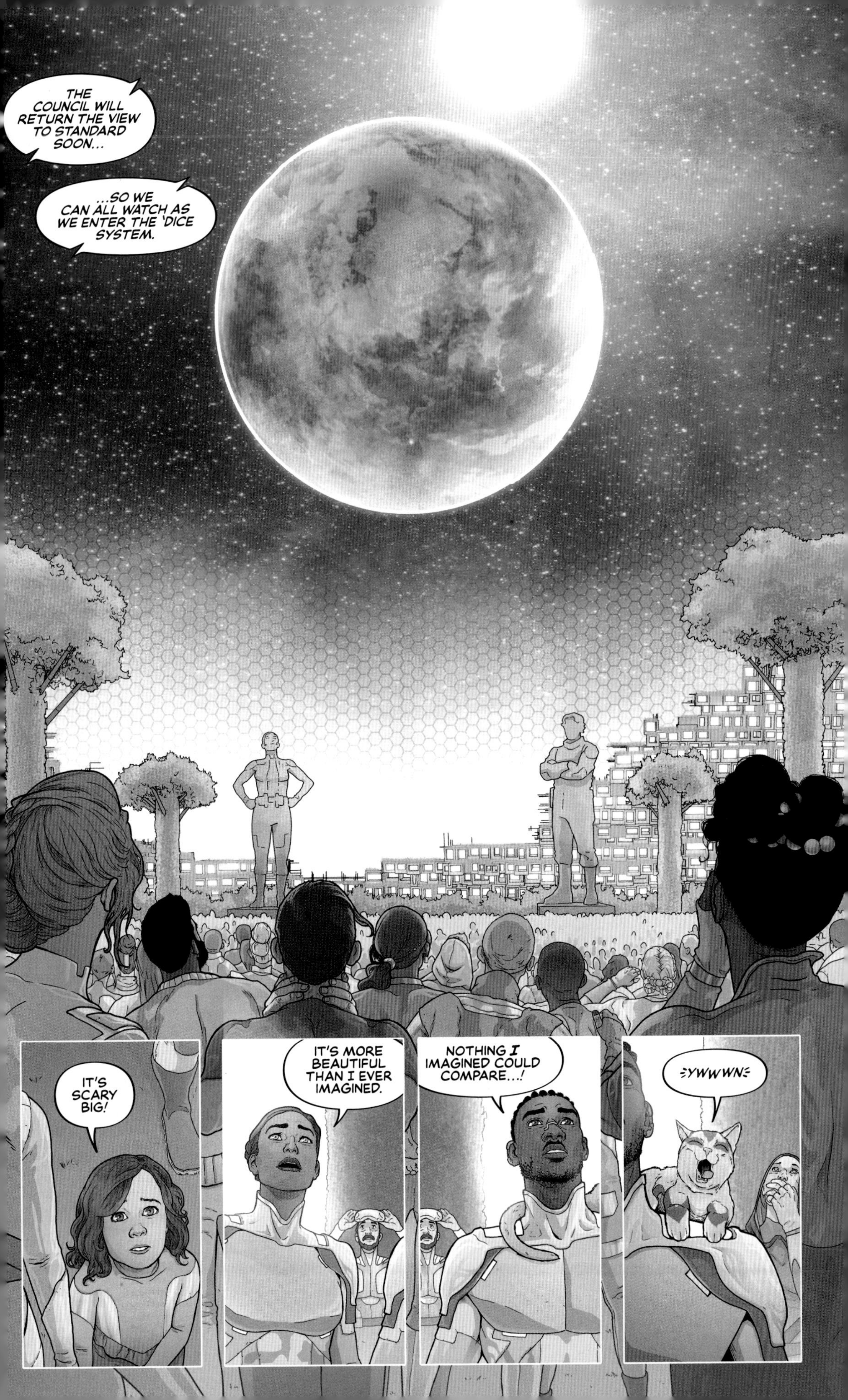
THE COUNCIL WILL RETURN THE VIEW TO STANDARD SOON...
...SO WE CAN ALL WATCH AS WE ENTER THE 'DICE SYSTEM.
IT'S SCARY BIG!
IT'S MORE BEAUTIFUL THAN I EVER IMAGINED.
NOTHING *I* IMAGINED COULD COMPARE...!
=YWWWN=

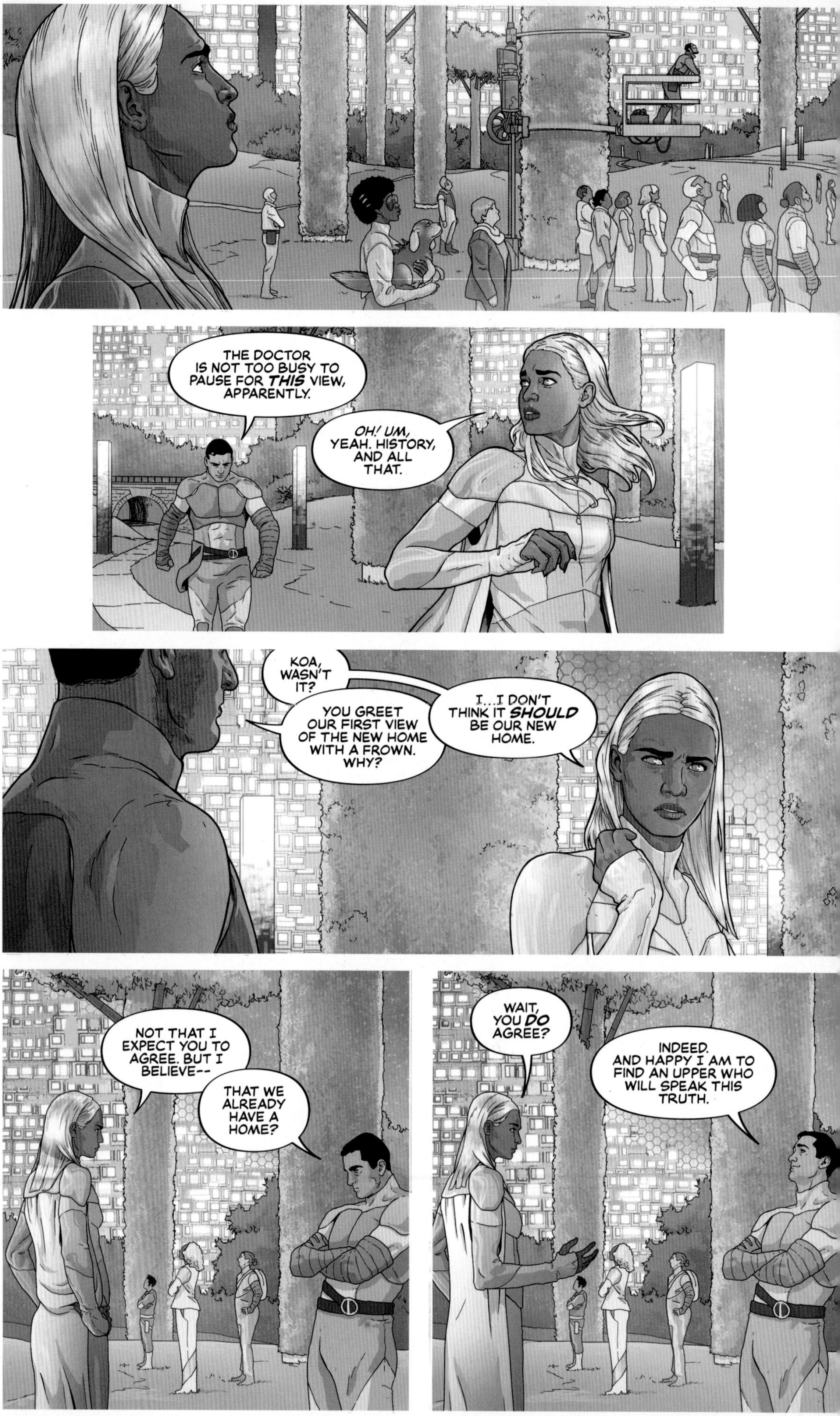
THE DOCTOR IS NOT TOO BUSY TO PAUSE FOR THIS VIEW, APPARENTLY.
OH! UM, YEAH. HISTORY, AND ALL THAT.
KOA, WASN'T IT?
YOU GREET OUR FIRST VIEW OF THE NEW HOME WITH A FROWN. WHY?
I...I DON'T THINK IT SHOULD BE OUR NEW HOME.
NOT THAT I EXPECT YOU TO AGREE. BUT I BELIEVE--
THAT WE ALREADY HAVE A HOME?
WAIT, YOU DO AGREE?
INDEED. AND HAPPY I AM TO FIND AN UPPER WHO WILL SPEAK THIS TRUTH.

I KNOW THERE ARE CHALLENGES TO MAKING THE *DODONA* PERMANENT.

HUMANITY HAS BESTED MANY CHALLENGES IN THE PAST.

EXACTLY!

YOU FEEL THIS STRONGLY.

DON'T YOU?

HUMANS ALWAYS FIND A WAY TO FIX SITUATIONS IN THE END. *ALWAYS.*

MANY BELIEVE SO.

GOOD, THAT'S VERY GOOD.

I THINK I SHOULD INTRODUCE YOU TO SOME OF MY PEOPLE.

WORKERS, LIKE YOU?

IF I AM NOT MISTAKEN, YOU ALSO WORK HARD.

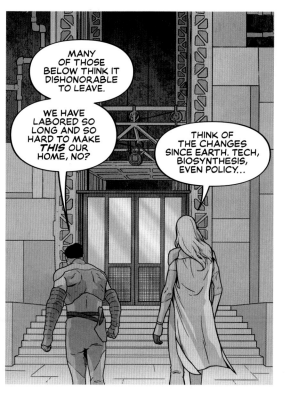

MANY OF THOSE BELOW THINK IT DISHONORABLE TO LEAVE.

WE HAVE LABORED SO LONG AND SO HARD TO MAKE *THIS* OUR HOME, NO?

THINK OF THE CHANGES SINCE EARTH. TECH, BIOSYNTHESIS, EVEN POLICY...

YES, THERE ARE SHORTAGES.

BUT WE HAVE CREATED WHOLE NEW SPECIES IN THE LAST CENTURY...

...SURELY BUILDING ON THAT IS BETTER THAN STARTING OVER ON 'DICE?

THESE ARE MOMENTOUS TIMES.
AT LAST, AFTER GENERATIONS...
...THE NEW HOME IS WITHIN REACH!
I'VE ASKED A PAIR OF NAVIGATORS HERE TO SPEAK TODAY.
WITHOUT THEIR SHARP EYES WE WOULDN'T HAVE THIS MUCH NOTICE.
HOPE, AULD, PLEASE TELL US MORE ABOUT WHAT YOU'VE DISCOVERED.
DO YOU WANT TO START...?
YOU WILL EXPLAIN IT BETTER. GO AHEAD.
WE'VE TRUSTED THE FIXES MADE AFTER THE TUMULT FOR A CENTURY.
BUT WE DIDN'T KNOW FOR CERTAIN UNTIL YESTERDAY.
AULD DID A MANUAL CALCULATION.
HE FIGURED OUT WE HAVE ONE CHANCE AT THIS.
WE'VE GOT TO FIRE EVERY RESERVE WE'VE GOT AT THE RIGHT TIME.
THAT'LL SLOW US ENOUGH FOR ORBITAL INSERTION. RIGHT?
IT WON'T BE EASY BUT IT'S DOABLE.
IF WE DON'T PREPARE, WE'LL SHOOT RIGHT THROUGH THE 'DICE SYSTEM--
SO?
SO, THE DODONA WOULD NEVER STOP--
AND OUR PEOPLE WON'T DIE IN A CRASH LANDING. SOUNDS A FAIR TRADE!

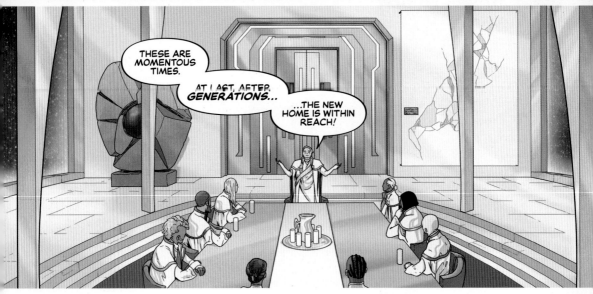

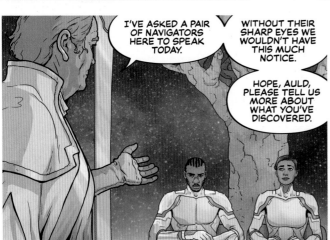

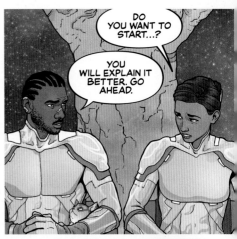

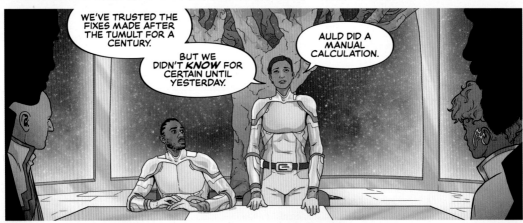

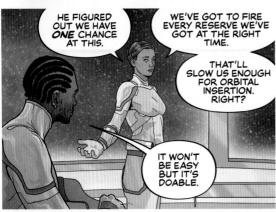

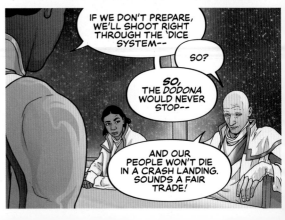

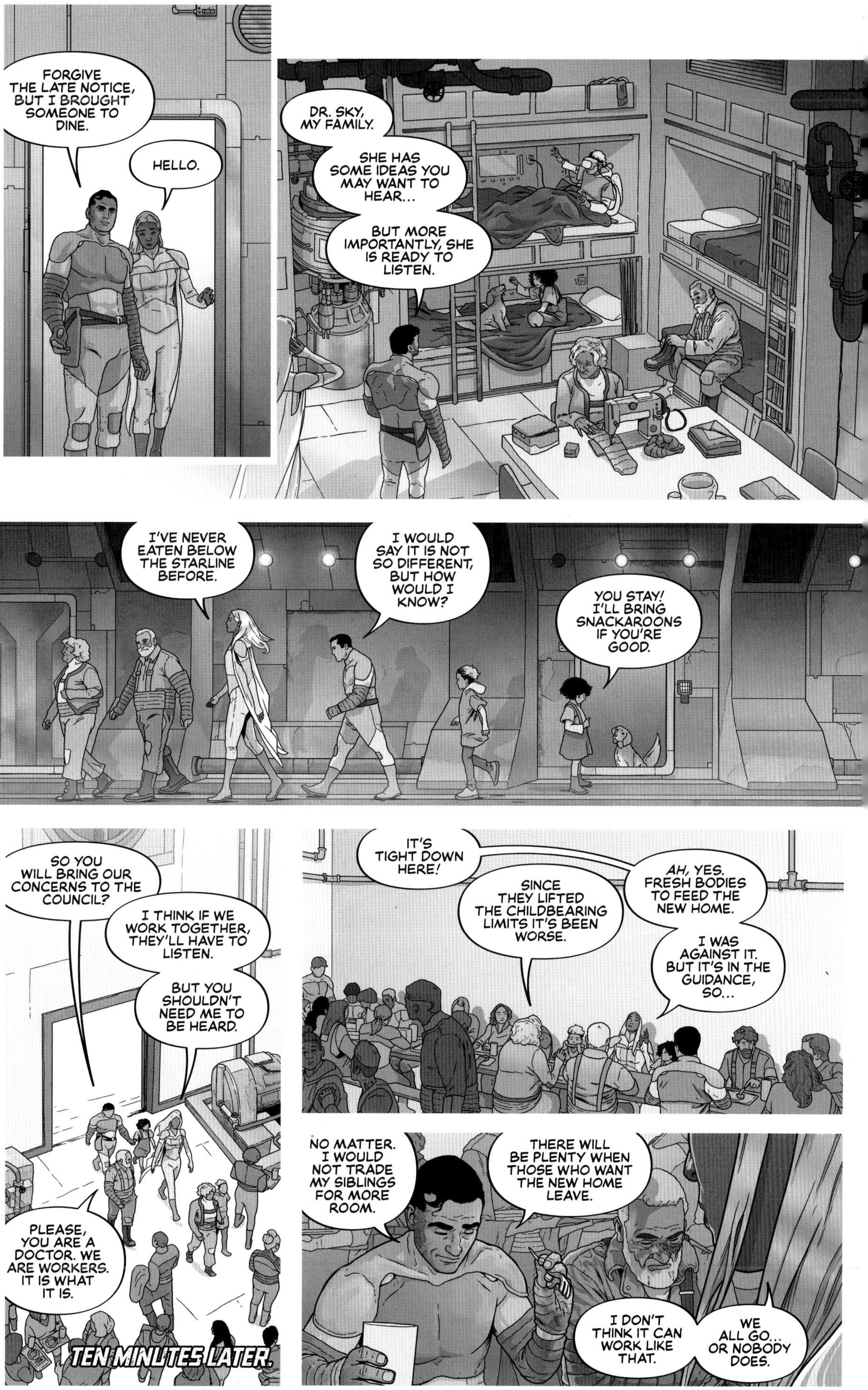
FORGIVE THE LATE NOTICE, BUT I BROUGHT SOMEONE TO DINE.
HELLO.
DR. SKY, MY FAMILY.
SHE HAS SOME IDEAS YOU MAY WANT TO HEAR...
BUT MORE IMPORTANTLY, SHE IS READY TO LISTEN.
I'VE NEVER EATEN BELOW THE STARLINE BEFORE.
I WOULD SAY IT IS NOT SO DIFFERENT, BUT HOW WOULD I KNOW?
YOU STAY! I'LL BRING SNACKAROONS IF YOU'RE GOOD.
SO YOU WILL BRING OUR CONCERNS TO THE COUNCIL?
I THINK IF WE WORK TOGETHER, THEY'LL HAVE TO LISTEN.
BUT YOU SHOULDN'T NEED ME TO BE HEARD.
PLEASE, YOU ARE A DOCTOR. WE ARE WORKERS. IT IS WHAT IT IS.
TEN MINUTES LATER.
IT'S TIGHT DOWN HERE!
SINCE THEY LIFTED THE CHILDBEARING LIMITS IT'S BEEN WORSE.
AH, YES. FRESH BODIES TO FEED THE NEW HOME.
I WAS AGAINST IT. BUT IT'S IN THE GUIDANCE, SO...
NO MATTER. I WOULD NOT TRADE MY SIBLINGS FOR MORE ROOM.
THERE WILL BE PLENTY WHEN THOSE WHO WANT THE NEW HOME LEAVE.
I DON'T THINK IT CAN WORK LIKE THAT.
WE ALL GO... OR NOBODY DOES.

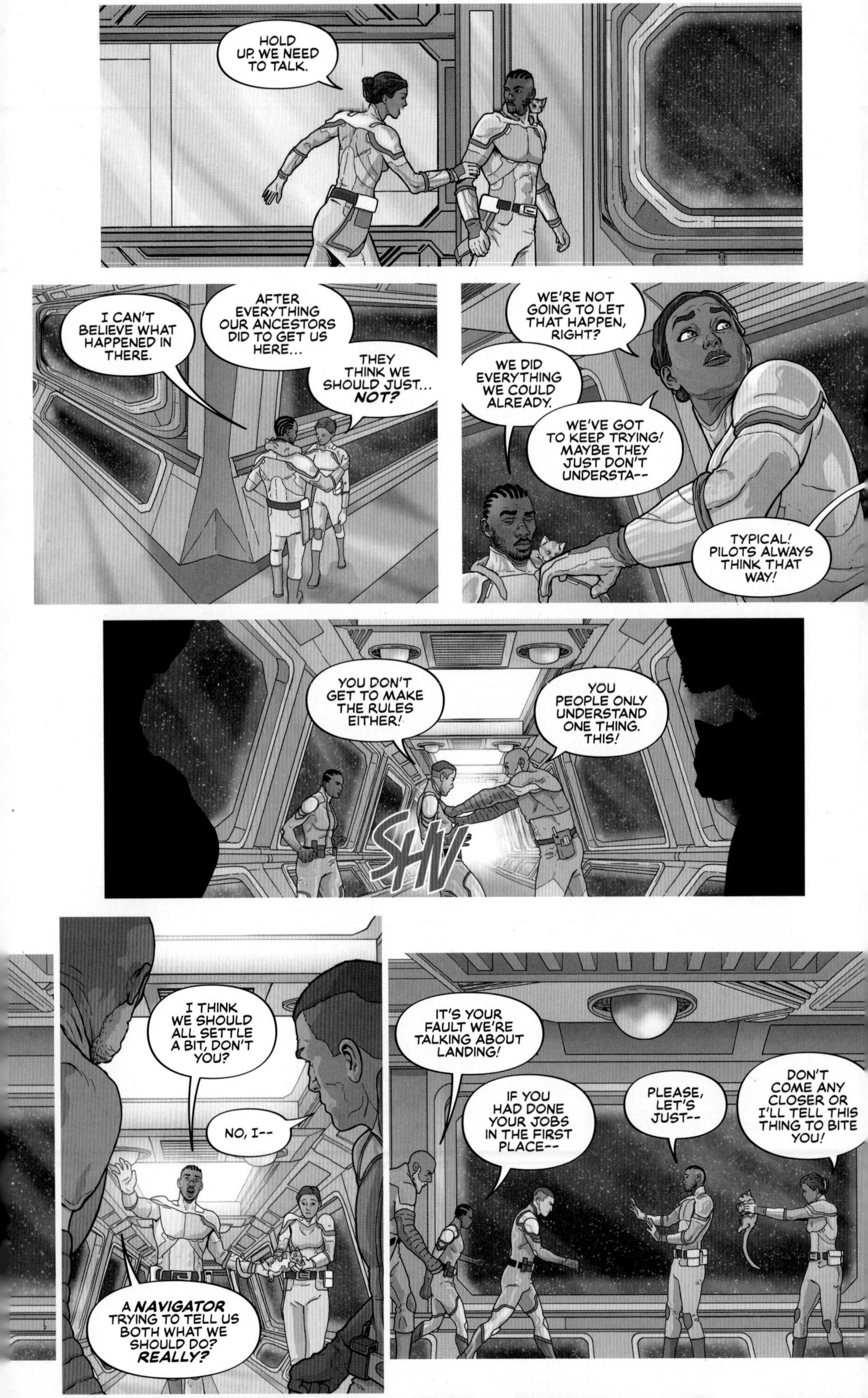
HOLD UP. WE NEED TO TALK.
I CAN'T BELIEVE WHAT HAPPENED IN THERE.
AFTER EVERYTHING OUR ANCESTORS DID TO GET US HERE...
THEY THINK WE SHOULD JUST... **NOT?**
WE'RE NOT GOING TO LET THAT HAPPEN, RIGHT?
WE DID EVERYTHING WE COULD ALREADY.
WE'VE GOT TO KEEP TRYING! MAYBE THEY JUST DON'T UNDERSTA--
TYPICAL! PILOTS ALWAYS THINK THAT WAY!
YOU DON'T GET TO MAKE THE RULES EITHER!
YOU PEOPLE ONLY UNDERSTAND ONE THING. THIS!
SHV
I THINK WE SHOULD ALL SETTLE A BIT, DON'T YOU?
NO, I--
A **NAVIGATOR** TRYING TO TELL US BOTH WHAT WE SHOULD DO? **REALLY?**
IT'S YOUR FAULT WE'RE TALKING ABOUT LANDING!
IF YOU HAD DONE YOUR JOBS IN THE FIRST PLACE--
PLEASE, LET'S JUST--
DON'T COME ANY CLOSER OR I'LL TELL THIS THING TO BITE YOU!

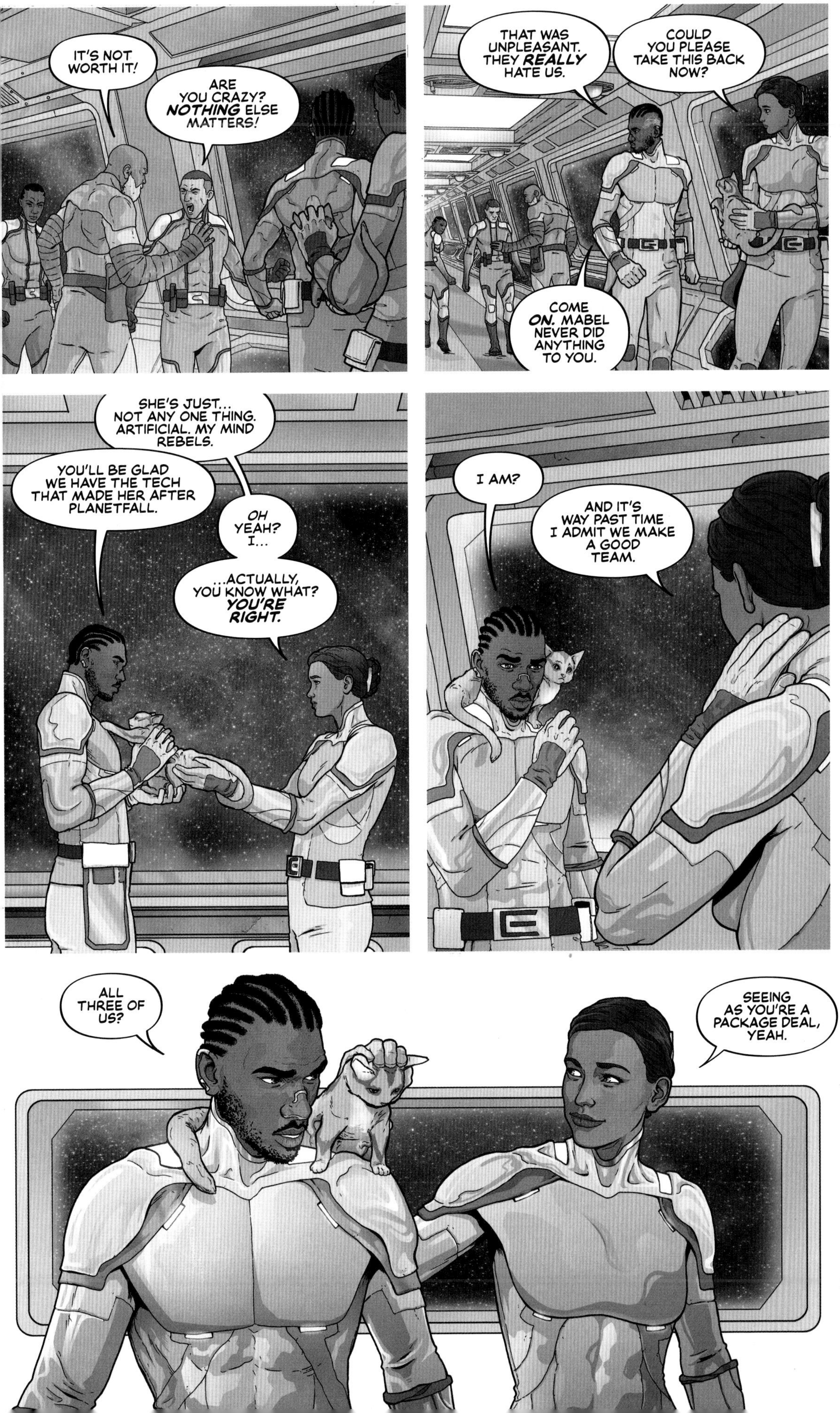
IT'S NOT WORTH IT!
ARE YOU CRAZY? NOTHING ELSE MATTERS!
THAT WAS UNPLEASANT. THEY REALLY HATE US.
COULD YOU PLEASE TAKE THIS BACK NOW?
COME ON. MABEL NEVER DID ANYTHING TO YOU.
SHE'S JUST... NOT ANY ONE THING. ARTIFICIAL. MY MIND REBELS.
YOU'LL BE GLAD WE HAVE THE TECH THAT MADE HER AFTER PLANETFALL.
OH YEAH? I...
...ACTUALLY, YOU KNOW WHAT? YOU'RE RIGHT.
I AM?
AND IT'S WAY PAST TIME I ADMIT WE MAKE A GOOD TEAM.
ALL THREE OF US?
SEEING AS YOU'RE A PACKAGE DEAL, YEAH.

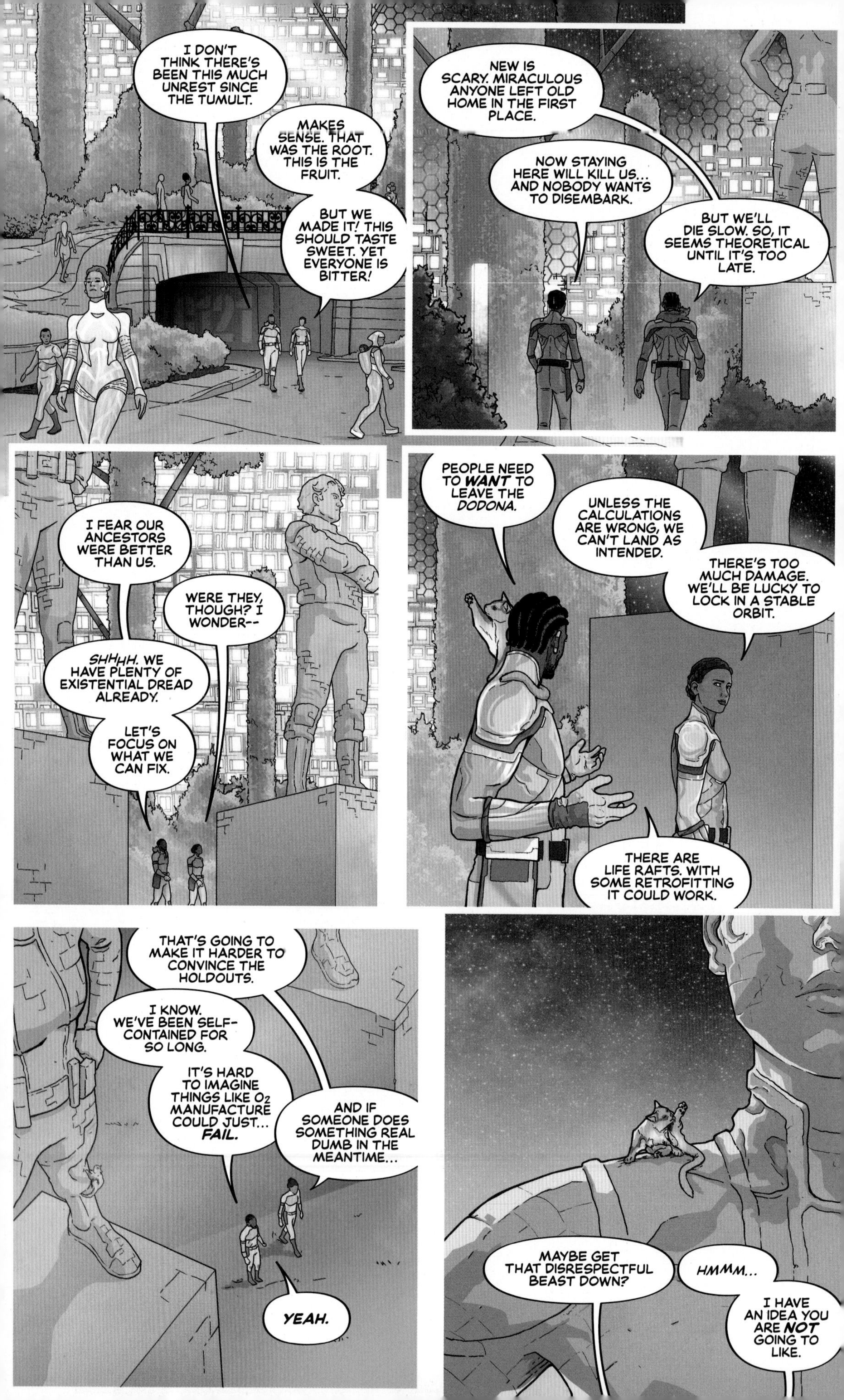

I DON'T THINK THERE'S BEEN THIS MUCH UNREST SINCE THE TUMULT.
MAKES SENSE. THAT WAS THE ROOT. THIS IS THE FRUIT.
BUT WE MADE IT! THIS SHOULD TASTE SWEET. YET EVERYONE IS BITTER!
NEW IS SCARY. MIRACULOUS ANYONE LEFT OLD HOME IN THE FIRST PLACE.
NOW STAYING HERE WILL KILL US... AND NOBODY WANTS TO DISEMBARK.
BUT WE'LL DIE SLOW. SO, IT SEEMS THEORETICAL UNTIL IT'S TOO LATE.
I FEAR OUR ANCESTORS WERE BETTER THAN US.
WERE THEY, THOUGH? I WONDER--
SHHHH. WE HAVE PLENTY OF EXISTENTIAL DREAD ALREADY.
LET'S FOCUS ON WHAT WE CAN FIX.
PEOPLE NEED TO **WANT** TO LEAVE THE *DODONA.*
UNLESS THE CALCULATIONS ARE WRONG, WE CAN'T LAND AS INTENDED.
THERE'S TOO MUCH DAMAGE. WE'LL BE LUCKY TO LOCK IN A STABLE ORBIT.
THERE ARE LIFE RAFTS. WITH SOME RETROFITTING IT COULD WORK.
THAT'S GOING TO MAKE IT HARDER TO CONVINCE THE HOLDOUTS.
I KNOW. WE'VE BEEN SELF-CONTAINED FOR SO LONG.
IT'S HARD TO IMAGINE THINGS LIKE O_2 MANUFACTURE COULD JUST... **FAIL.**
AND IF SOMEONE DOES SOMETHING REAL DUMB IN THE MEANTIME...
YEAH.
MAYBE GET THAT DISRESPECTFUL BEAST DOWN?
HMMM...
I HAVE AN IDEA YOU ARE **NOT** GOING TO LIKE.

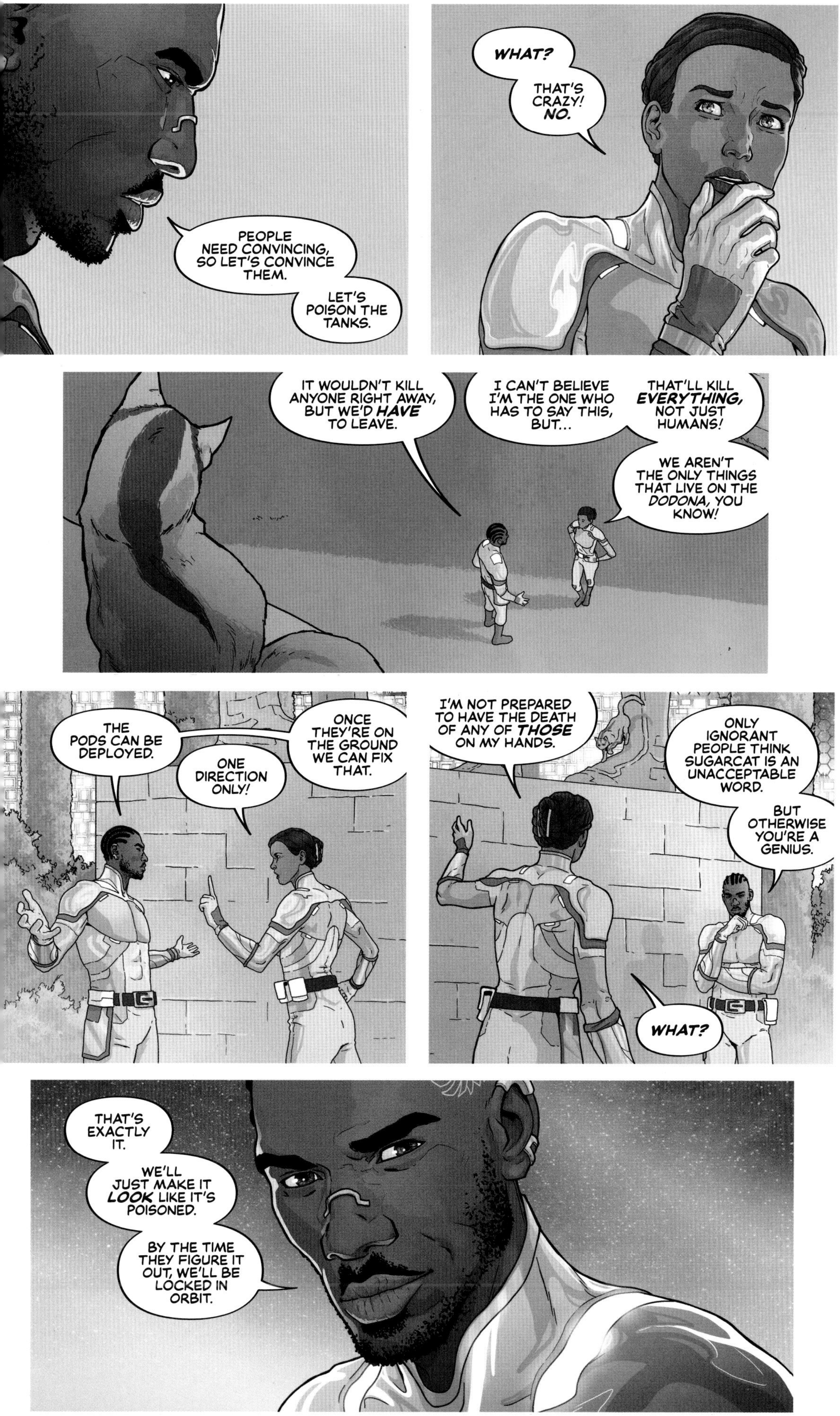

PEOPLE NEED CONVINCING, SO LET'S CONVINCE THEM.
LET'S POISON THE TANKS.
WHAT?
THAT'S CRAZY! *NO.*
IT WOULDN'T KILL ANYONE RIGHT AWAY, BUT WE'D *HAVE* TO LEAVE.
I CAN'T BELIEVE I'M THE ONE WHO HAS TO SAY THIS, BUT...
THAT'LL KILL *EVERYTHING,* NOT JUST HUMANS!
WE AREN'T THE ONLY THINGS THAT LIVE ON THE *DODONA,* YOU KNOW!
THE PODS CAN BE DEPLOYED.
ONE DIRECTION ONLY!
ONCE THEY'RE ON THE GROUND WE CAN FIX THAT.
I'M NOT PREPARED TO HAVE THE DEATH OF ANY OF *THOSE* ON MY HANDS.
ONLY IGNORANT PEOPLE THINK SUGARCAT IS AN UNACCEPTABLE WORD.
BUT OTHERWISE YOU'RE A GENIUS.
WHAT?
THAT'S EXACTLY IT.
WE'LL JUST MAKE IT *LOOK* LIKE IT'S POISONED.
BY THE TIME THEY FIGURE IT OUT, WE'LL BE LOCKED IN ORBIT.

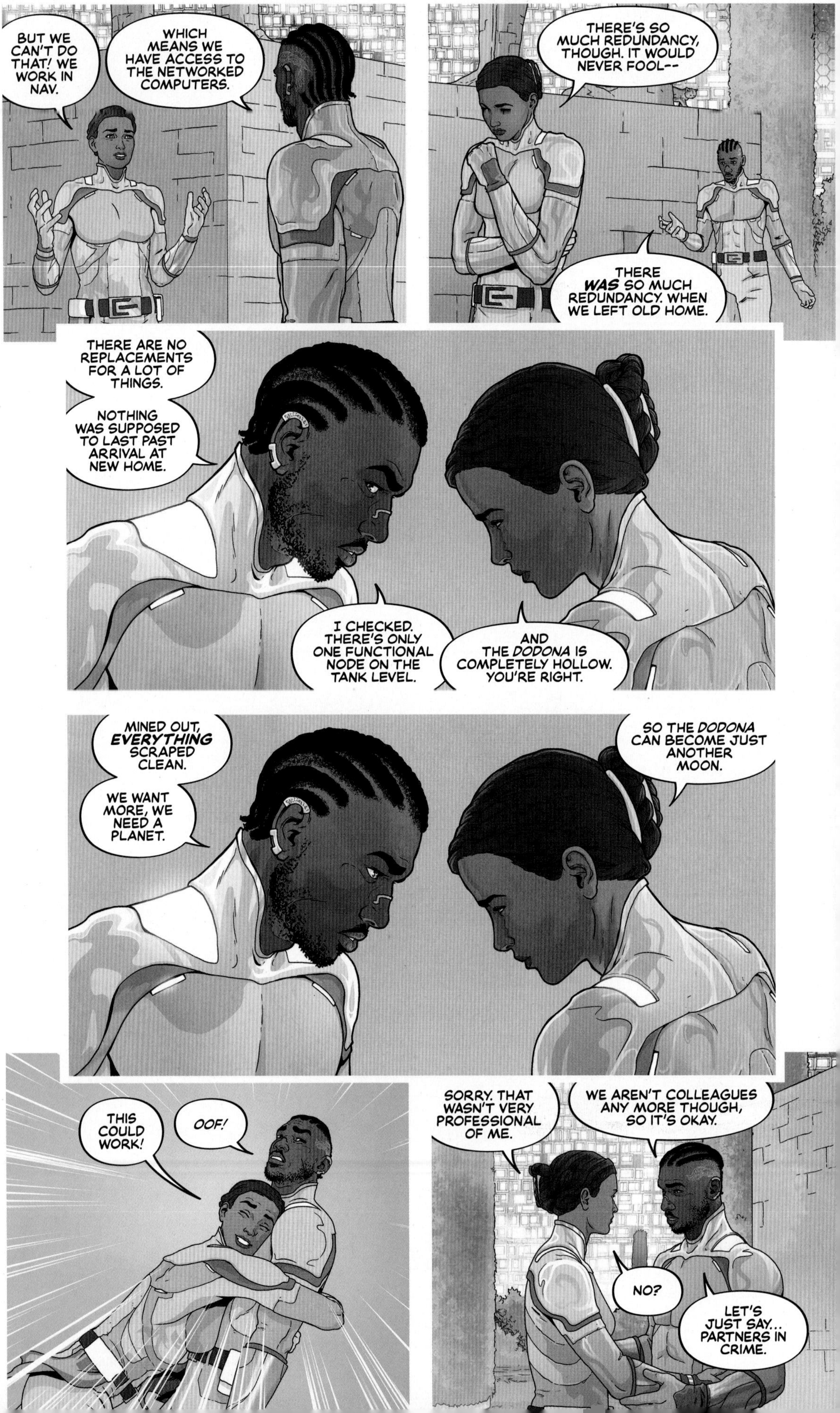
BUT WE CAN'T DO THAT! WE WORK IN NAV.
WHICH MEANS WE HAVE ACCESS TO THE NETWORKED COMPUTERS.
THERE'S SO MUCH REDUNDANCY, THOUGH. IT WOULD NEVER FOOL--
THERE *WAS* SO MUCH REDUNDANCY. WHEN WE LEFT OLD HOME.
THERE ARE NO REPLACEMENTS FOR A LOT OF THINGS.
NOTHING WAS SUPPOSED TO LAST PAST ARRIVAL AT NEW HOME.
I CHECKED. THERE'S ONLY ONE FUNCTIONAL NODE ON THE TANK LEVEL.
AND THE *DODONA* IS COMPLETELY HOLLOW. YOU'RE RIGHT.
MINED OUT, ***EVERYTHING*** SCRAPED CLEAN.
WE WANT MORE, WE NEED A PLANET.
SO THE *DODONA* CAN BECOME JUST ANOTHER MOON.
THIS COULD WORK!
OOF!
SORRY. THAT WASN'T VERY PROFESSIONAL OF ME.
WE AREN'T COLLEAGUES ANY MORE THOUGH, SO IT'S OKAY.
NO?
LET'S JUST SAY... PARTNERS IN CRIME.

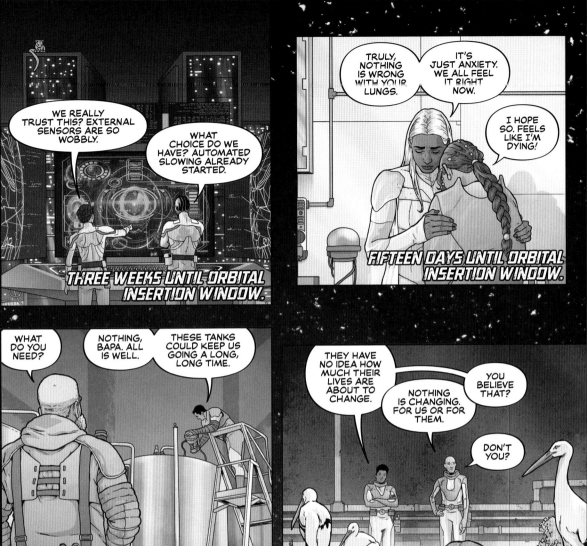

WE REALLY TRUST THIS? EXTERNAL SENSORS ARE SO WOBBLY.

WHAT CHOICE DO WE HAVE? AUTOMATED SLOWING ALREADY STARTED.

THREE WEEKS UNTIL ORBITAL INSERTION WINDOW.

TRULY, NOTHING IS WRONG WITH YOUR LUNGS.

IT'S JUST ANXIETY. WE ALL FEEL IT RIGHT NOW.

I HOPE SO. FEELS LIKE I'M DYING!

FIFTEEN DAYS UNTIL ORBITAL INSERTION WINDOW.

WHAT DO YOU NEED?

NOTHING, BAPA. ALL IS WELL.

THESE TANKS COULD KEEP US GOING A LONG, LONG TIME.

ELEVEN DAYS UNTIL ORBITAL INSERTION WINDOW.

THEY HAVE NO IDEA HOW MUCH THEIR LIVES ARE ABOUT TO CHANGE.

NOTHING IS CHANGING. FOR US OR FOR THEM.

YOU BELIEVE THAT?

DON'T YOU?

NINE DAYS BEFORE ORBITAL INSERTION WINDOW.

THEY SHOULD SHOW IT FOR REAL. I'M SICK OF SEEING IT MAGNIFIED.

THEY QUIT DOING THAT DAYS AGO!

BUT... IT...

I CAN'T WRAP MY HEAD AROUND IT, EITHER.

FIVE DAYS UNTIL ORBITAL INSERTION WINDOW.

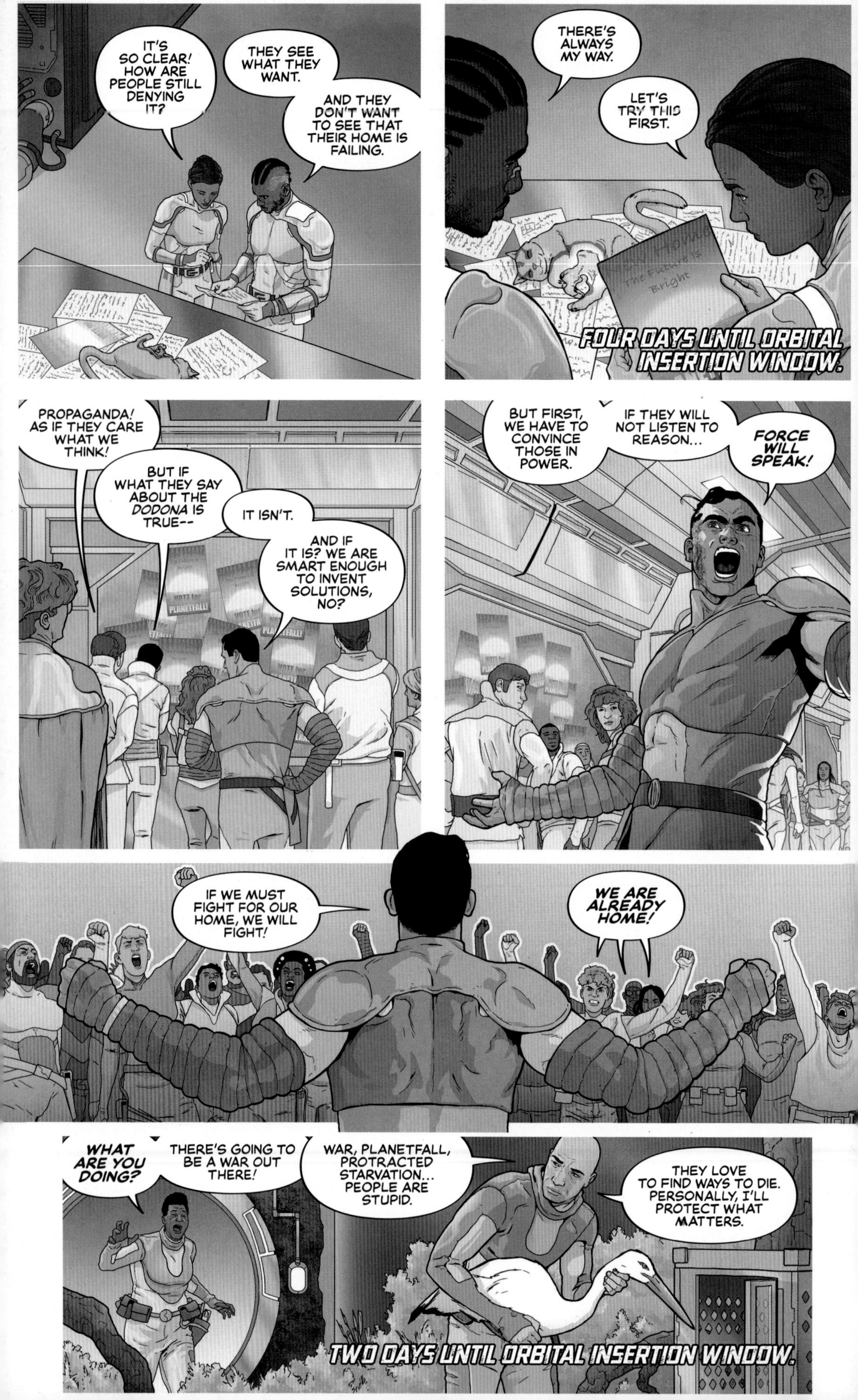
IT'S SO CLEAR! HOW ARE PEOPLE STILL DENYING IT?
THEY SEE WHAT THEY WANT.
AND THEY DON'T WANT TO SEE THAT THEIR HOME IS FAILING.
THERE'S ALWAYS MY WAY.
LET'S TRY THIS FIRST.
The Future Is Bright
FOUR DAYS UNTIL ORBITAL INSERTION WINDOW.
PROPAGANDA! AS IF THEY CARE WHAT WE THINK!
BUT IF WHAT THEY SAY ABOUT THE *DODONA* IS TRUE--
IT ISN'T.
AND IF IT IS? WE ARE SMART ENOUGH TO INVENT SOLUTIONS, NO?
VOTE for PLANETFALL!
BUT FIRST, WE HAVE TO CONVINCE THOSE IN POWER.
IF THEY WILL NOT LISTEN TO REASON...
FORCE WILL SPEAK!
IF WE MUST FIGHT FOR OUR HOME, WE WILL FIGHT!
WE ARE ALREADY HOME!
WHAT ARE YOU DOING?
THERE'S GOING TO BE A WAR OUT THERE!
WAR, PLANETFALL, PROTRACTED STARVATION... PEOPLE ARE STUPID.
THEY LOVE TO FIND WAYS TO DIE. PERSONALLY, I'LL PROTECT WHAT MATTERS.
TWO DAYS UNTIL ORBITAL INSERTION WINDOW.

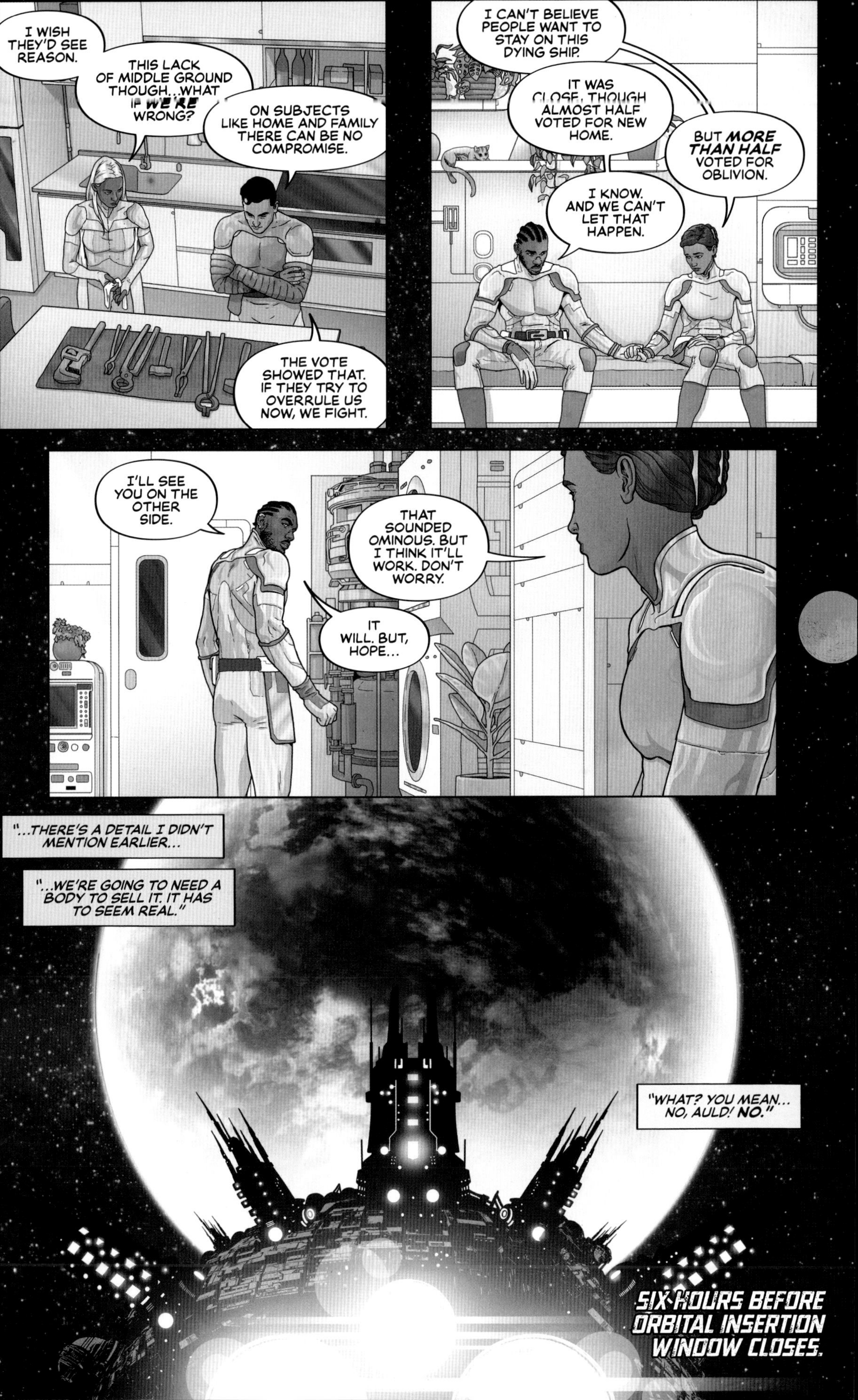
I WISH THEY'D SEE REASON.
THIS LACK OF MIDDLE GROUND THOUGH...WHAT IF ***WE'RE*** WRONG?
ON SUBJECTS LIKE HOME AND FAMILY THERE CAN BE NO COMPROMISE.
THE VOTE SHOWED THAT. IF THEY TRY TO OVERRULE US NOW, WE FIGHT.
I CAN'T BELIEVE PEOPLE WANT TO STAY ON THIS DYING SHIP.
IT WAS CLOSE, THOUGH. ALMOST HALF VOTED FOR NEW HOME.
BUT ***MORE THAN HALF*** VOTED FOR OBLIVION.
I KNOW. AND WE CAN'T LET THAT HAPPEN.
I'LL SEE YOU ON THE OTHER SIDE.
THAT SOUNDED OMINOUS. BUT I THINK IT'LL WORK. DON'T WORRY.
IT WILL. BUT, HOPE...
"...THERE'S A DETAIL I DIDN'T MENTION EARLIER...
"...WE'RE GOING TO NEED A BODY TO SELL IT. IT HAS TO SEEM REAL."
"WHAT? YOU MEAN... NO, AULD! **NO.**"
SIX HOURS BEFORE ORBITAL INSERTION WINDOW CLOSES.

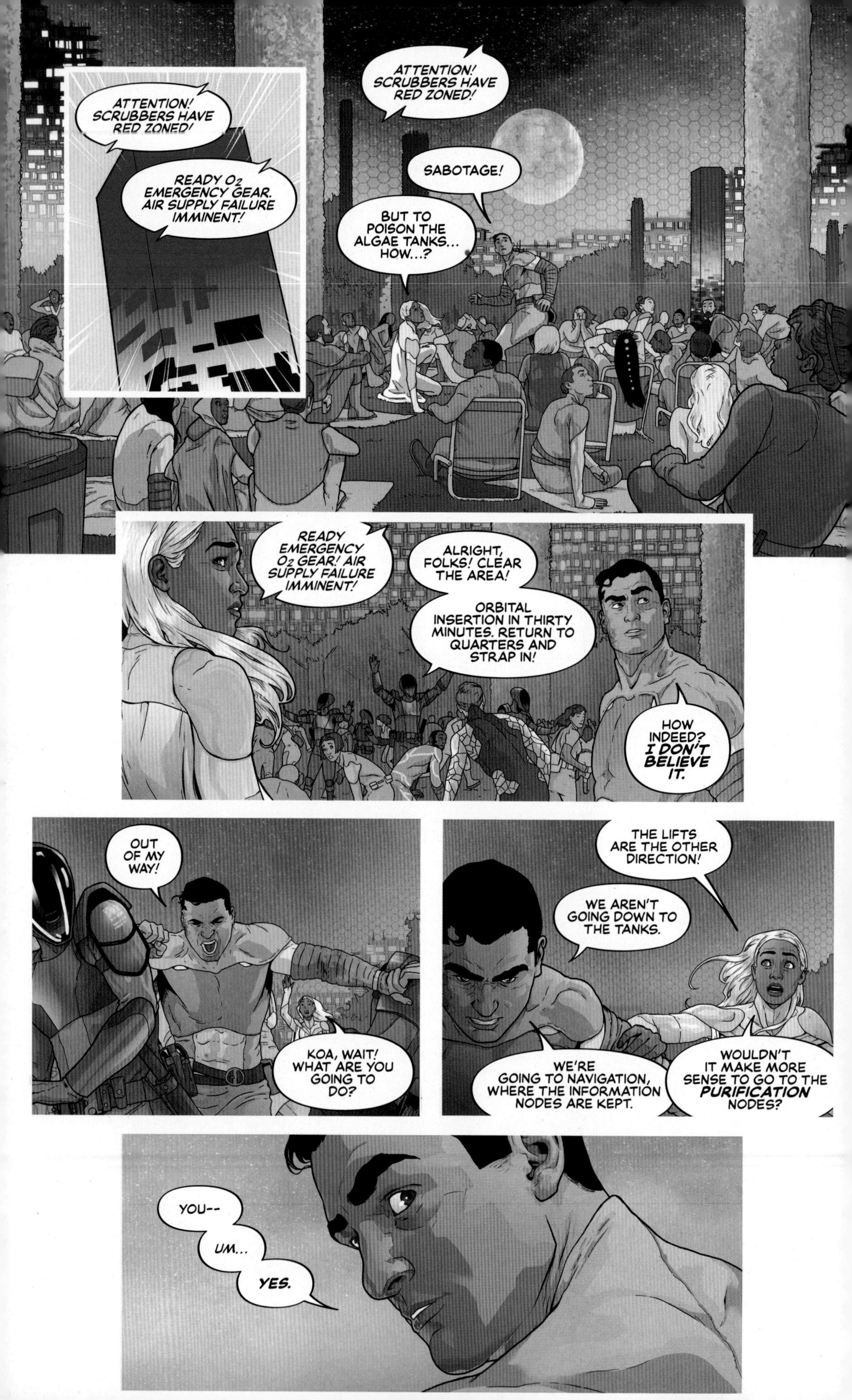
ATTENTION! SCRUBBERS HAVE RED ZONED!
READY O_2 EMERGENCY GEAR. AIR SUPPLY FAILURE IMMINENT!
ATTENTION! SCRUBBERS HAVE RED ZONED!
SABOTAGE!
BUT TO POISON THE ALGAE TANKS... HOW...?
READY EMERGENCY O_2 GEAR! AIR SUPPLY FAILURE IMMINENT!
ALRIGHT, FOLKS! CLEAR THE AREA!
ORBITAL INSERTION IN THIRTY MINUTES. RETURN TO QUARTERS AND STRAP IN!
HOW INDEED? I DON'T BELIEVE IT.
OUT OF MY WAY!
KOA, WAIT! WHAT ARE YOU GOING TO DO?
THE LIFTS ARE THE OTHER DIRECTION!
WE AREN'T GOING DOWN TO THE TANKS.
WE'RE GOING TO NAVIGATION, WHERE THE INFORMATION NODES ARE KEPT.
WOULDN'T IT MAKE MORE SENSE TO GO TO THE PURIFICATION NODES?
YOU--
UM...
YES.

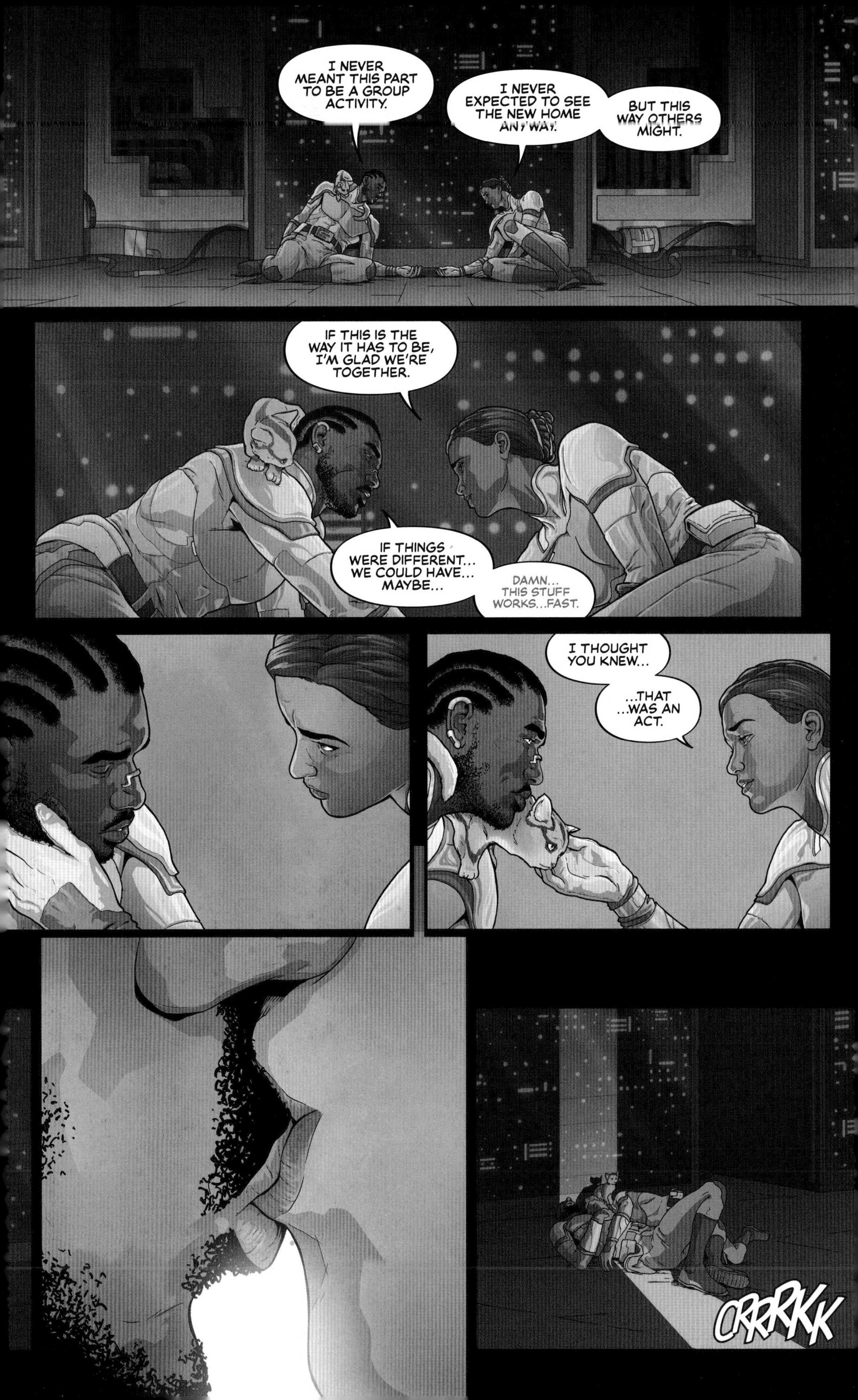
I NEVER MEANT THIS PART TO BE A GROUP ACTIVITY.
I NEVER EXPECTED TO SEE THE NEW HOME ANYWAY.
BUT THIS WAY OTHERS MIGHT.
IF THIS IS THE WAY IT HAS TO BE, I'M GLAD WE'RE TOGETHER.
IF THINGS WERE DIFFERENT... WE COULD HAVE... MAYBE...
DAMN... THIS STUFF WORKS...FAST.
I THOUGHT YOU KNEW...
...THAT ...WAS AN ACT.
CRRRKK

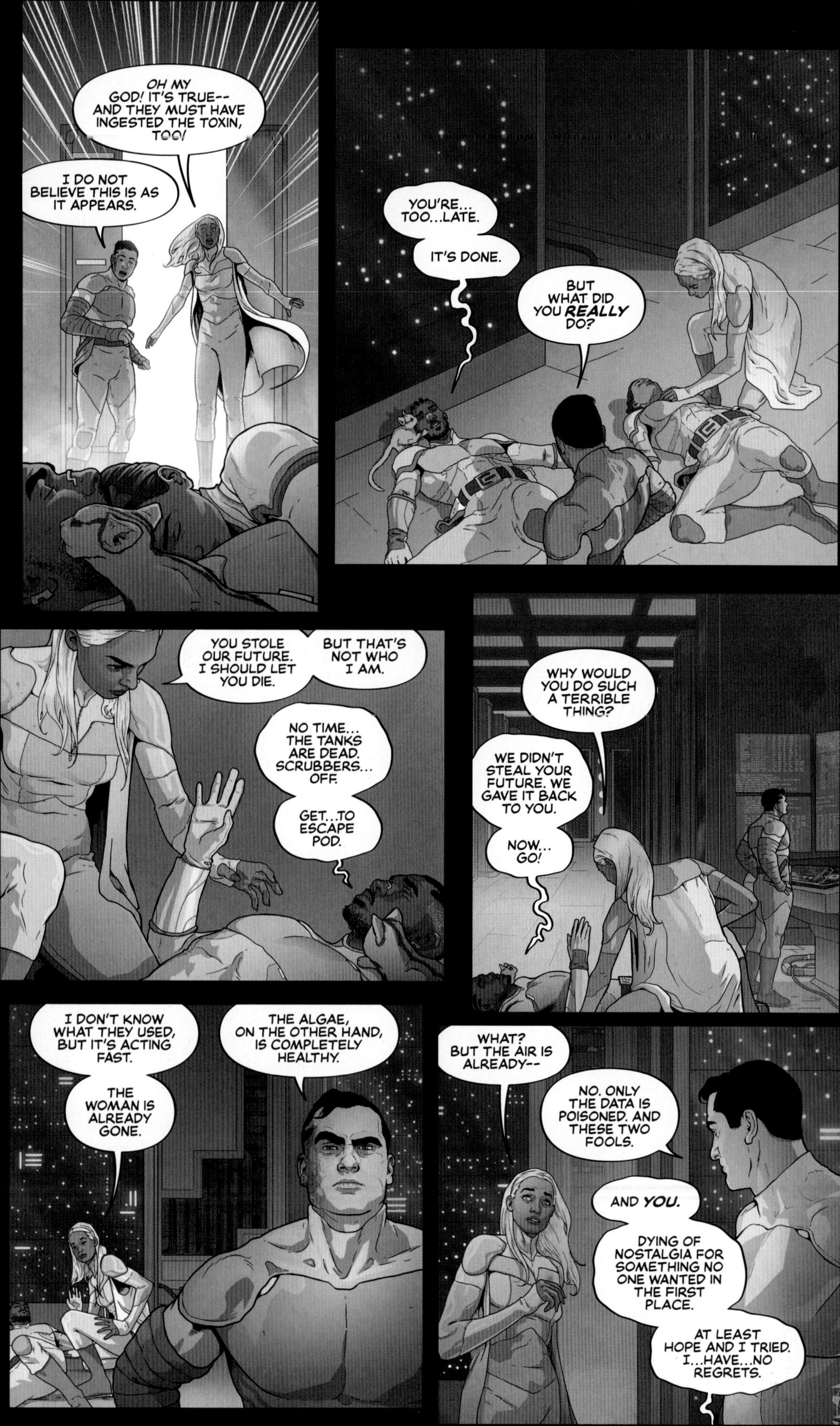
OH MY GOD! IT'S TRUE-- AND THEY MUST HAVE INGESTED THE TOXIN, TOO!
I DO NOT BELIEVE THIS IS AS IT APPEARS.
YOU'RE... TOO...LATE.
IT'S DONE.
BUT WHAT DID YOU *REALLY* DO?
YOU STOLE OUR FUTURE. I SHOULD LET YOU DIE.
BUT THAT'S NOT WHO I AM.
NO TIME... THE TANKS ARE DEAD. SCRUBBERS... OFF.
GET...TO ESCAPE POD.
WHY WOULD YOU DO SUCH A TERRIBLE THING?
WE DIDN'T STEAL YOUR FUTURE. WE GAVE IT BACK TO YOU.
NOW... GO!
I DON'T KNOW WHAT THEY USED, BUT IT'S ACTING FAST.
THE WOMAN IS ALREADY GONE.
THE ALGAE, ON THE OTHER HAND, IS COMPLETELY HEALTHY.
WHAT? BUT THE AIR IS ALREADY--
NO. ONLY THE DATA IS POISONED. AND THESE TWO FOOLS.
AND *YOU.*
DYING OF NOSTALGIA FOR SOMETHING NO ONE WANTED IN THE FIRST PLACE.
AT LEAST HOPE AND I TRIED. I...HAVE...NO REGRETS.

PLEASE... TAKE... MABEL?
GIVE HER A GOOD LIFE AS LONG...AS POSSIBLE.
YOU DID *THIS* TO TRY FOR A BETTER LIFE FOR YOUR *CAT?*
I...
THE ONLY SUGARCATS...IN THE UNIVERSE...ARE ABOARD THE *DODONA.*
WHO WOULD WANT TO LIVE...KNOWING THEY WERE ALL DOOMED?
I...
I CAN'T DENY YOU THAT.
SO ALL OF THIS WAS A LIE. NO SABOTAGE. THE AIR IS SAFE.
HOW DO WE STOP THE ORBITAL INSERTION?
THERE'S STILL TIME, KOA!
I'LL PING THE COUNCIL ELDER. SHE'LL KNOW HOW TO START--
UM, NO. DON'T.
OR DO, IF YOU NEED TO. I AM NO BOSS TO YOU.
BUT I THINK *I* AM FINALLY READY TO LEAVE HOME.

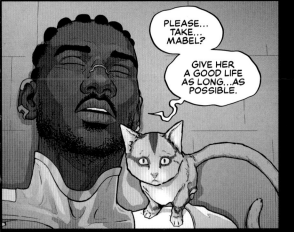

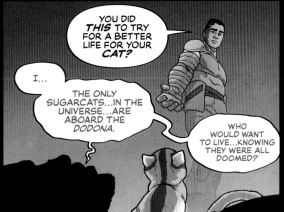

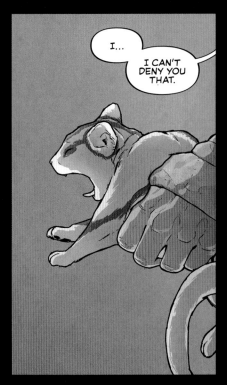

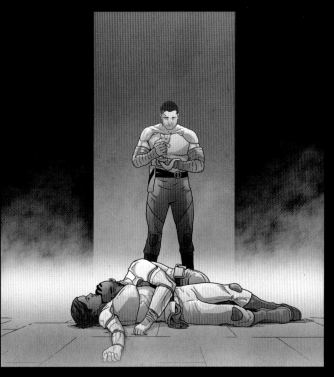

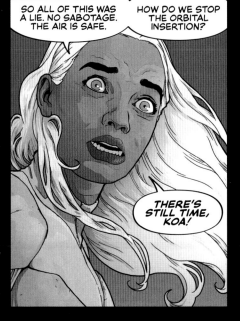

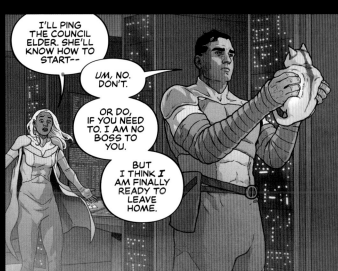

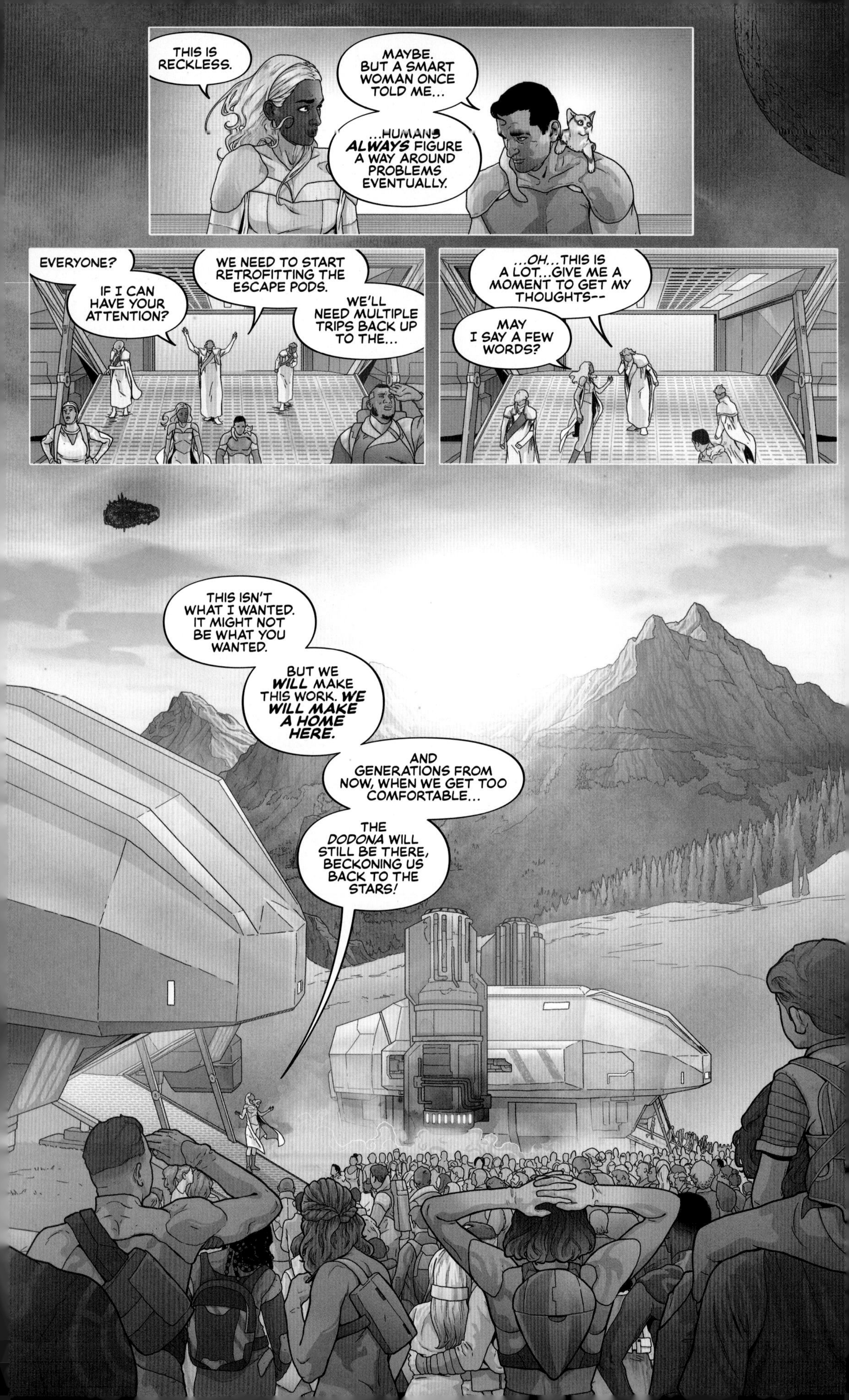

THIS IS RECKLESS.
MAYBE. BUT A SMART WOMAN ONCE TOLD ME...
...HUMANS ALWAYS FIGURE A WAY AROUND PROBLEMS EVENTUALLY.
EVERYONE?
IF I CAN HAVE YOUR ATTENTION?
WE NEED TO START RETROFITTING THE ESCAPE PODS.
WE'LL NEED MULTIPLE TRIPS BACK UP TO THE...
...OH...THIS IS A LOT...GIVE ME A MOMENT TO GET MY THOUGHTS--
MAY I SAY A FEW WORDS?
THIS ISN'T WHAT I WANTED. IT MIGHT NOT BE WHAT YOU WANTED.
BUT WE WILL MAKE THIS WORK. WE WILL MAKE A HOME HERE.
AND GENERATIONS FROM NOW, WHEN WE GET TOO COMFORTABLE...
THE DODONA WILL STILL BE THERE, BECKONING US BACK TO THE STARS!

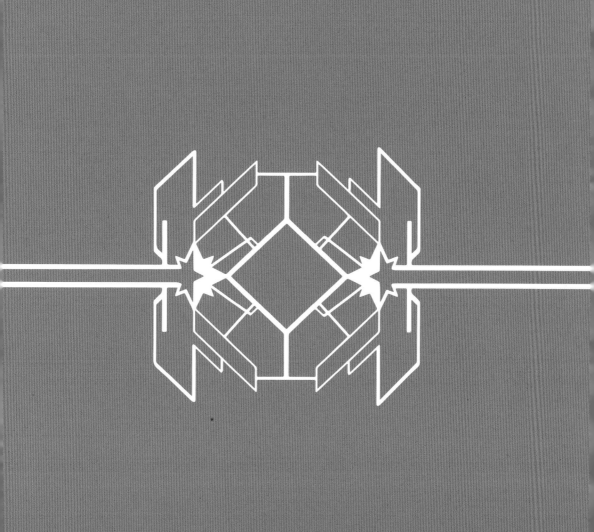

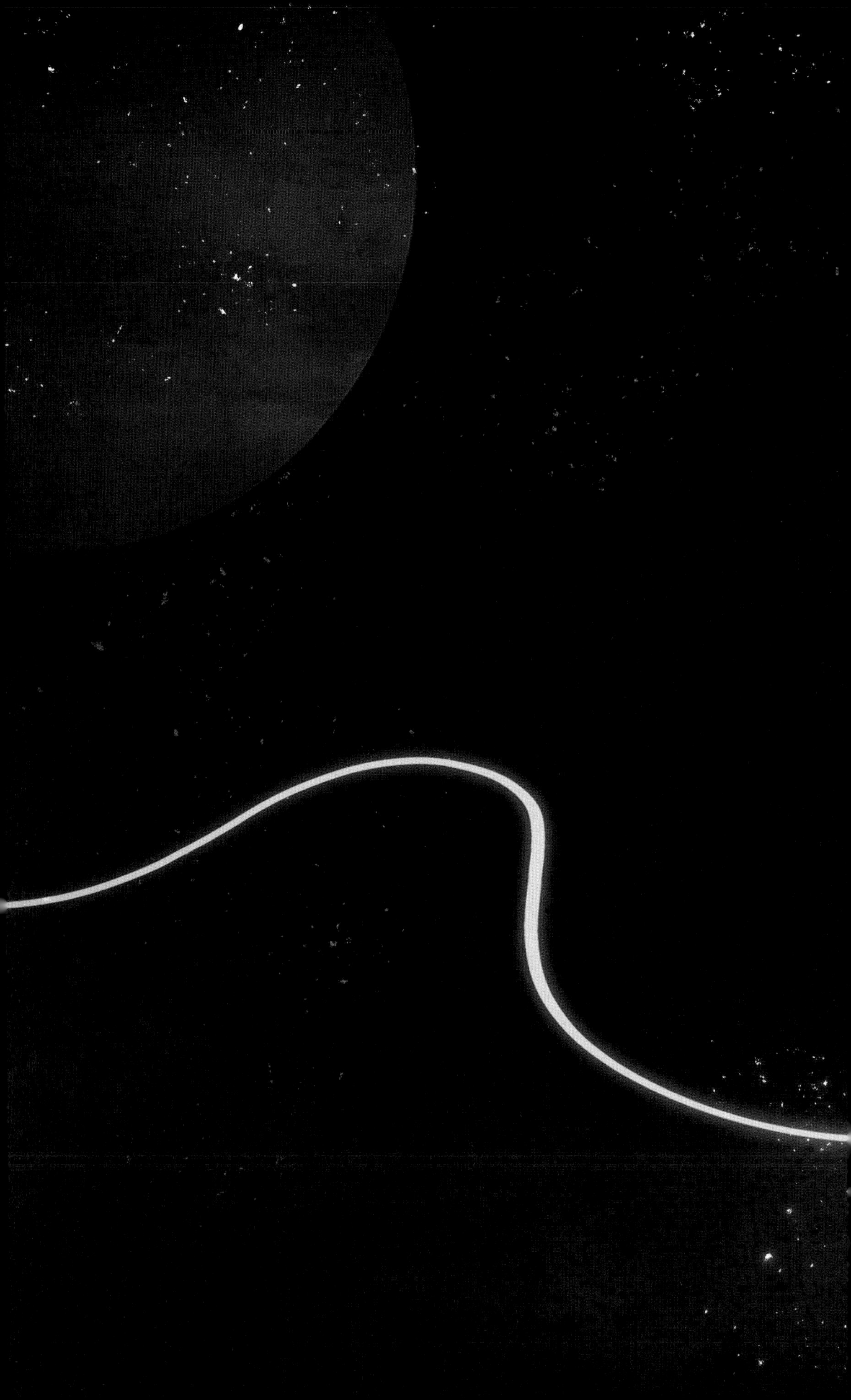

COVER
GALLERY

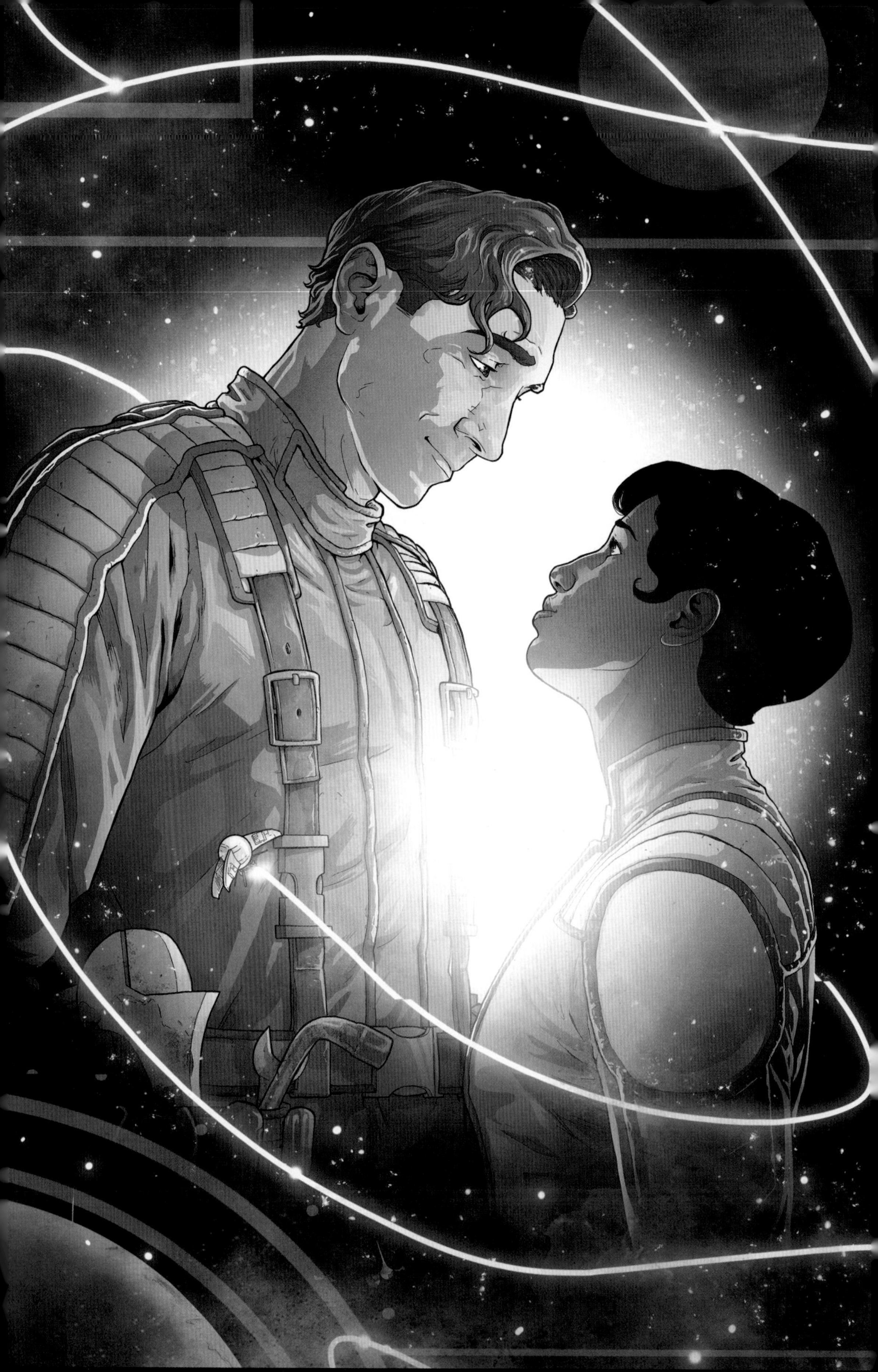

ISSUE #1 MAIN COVER BY **DANNY LUCKERT**

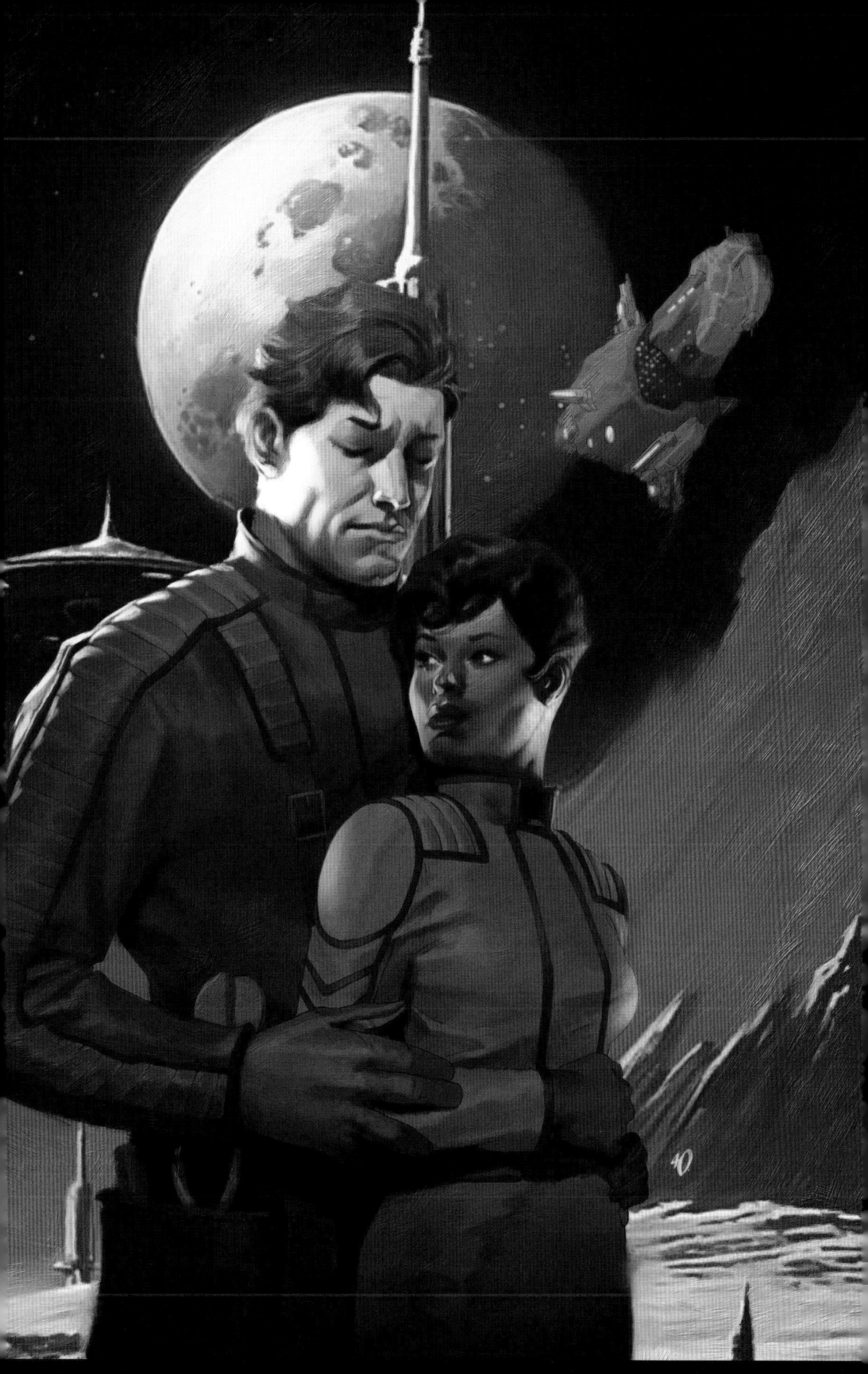

ISSUE #1 HOMAGE COVER BY **ARIEL OLIVETTI**

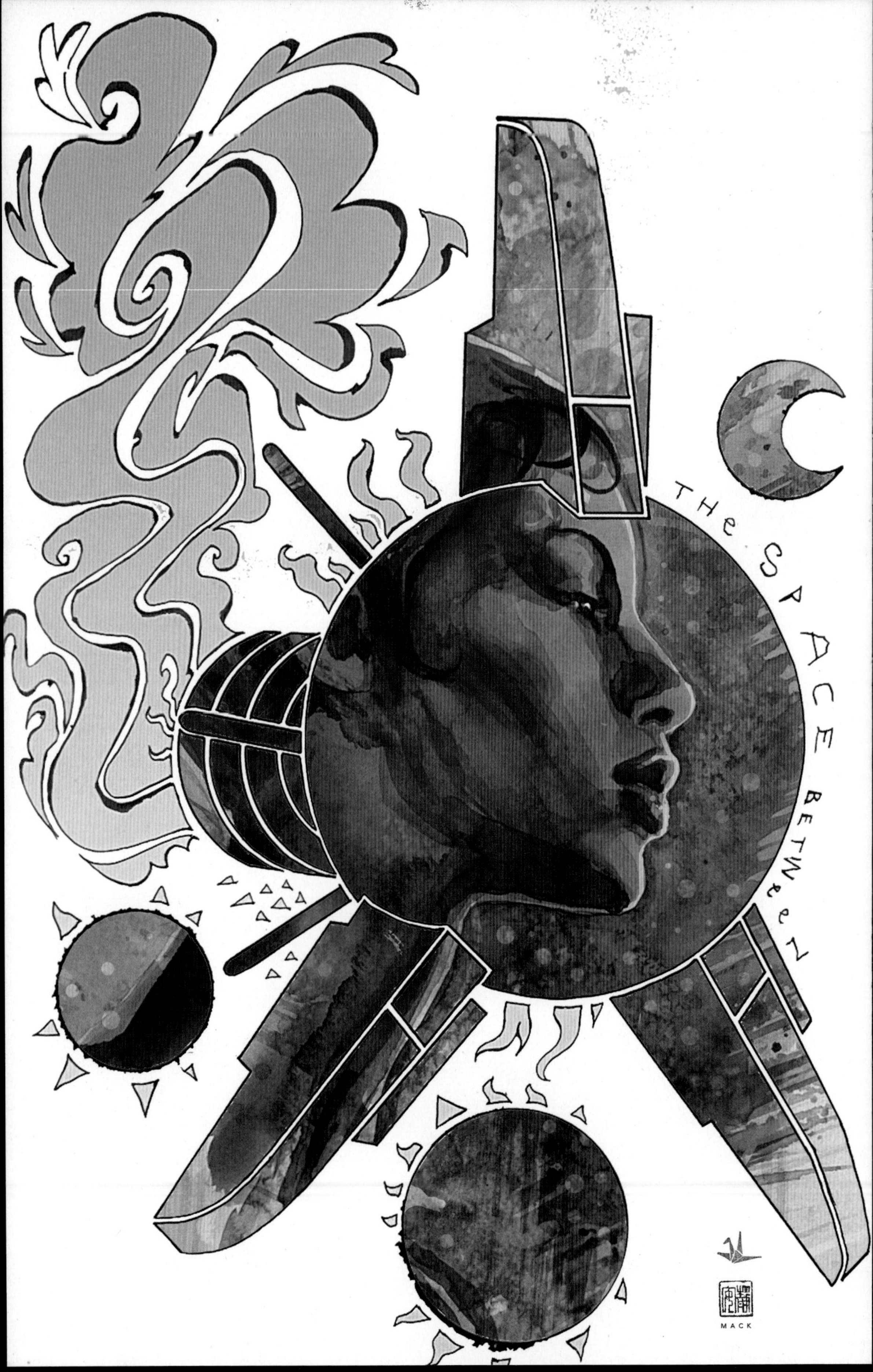
THE SPACE BETWEEN
MACK

ISSUE #1 VARIANT COVER BY **DAVID MACK**

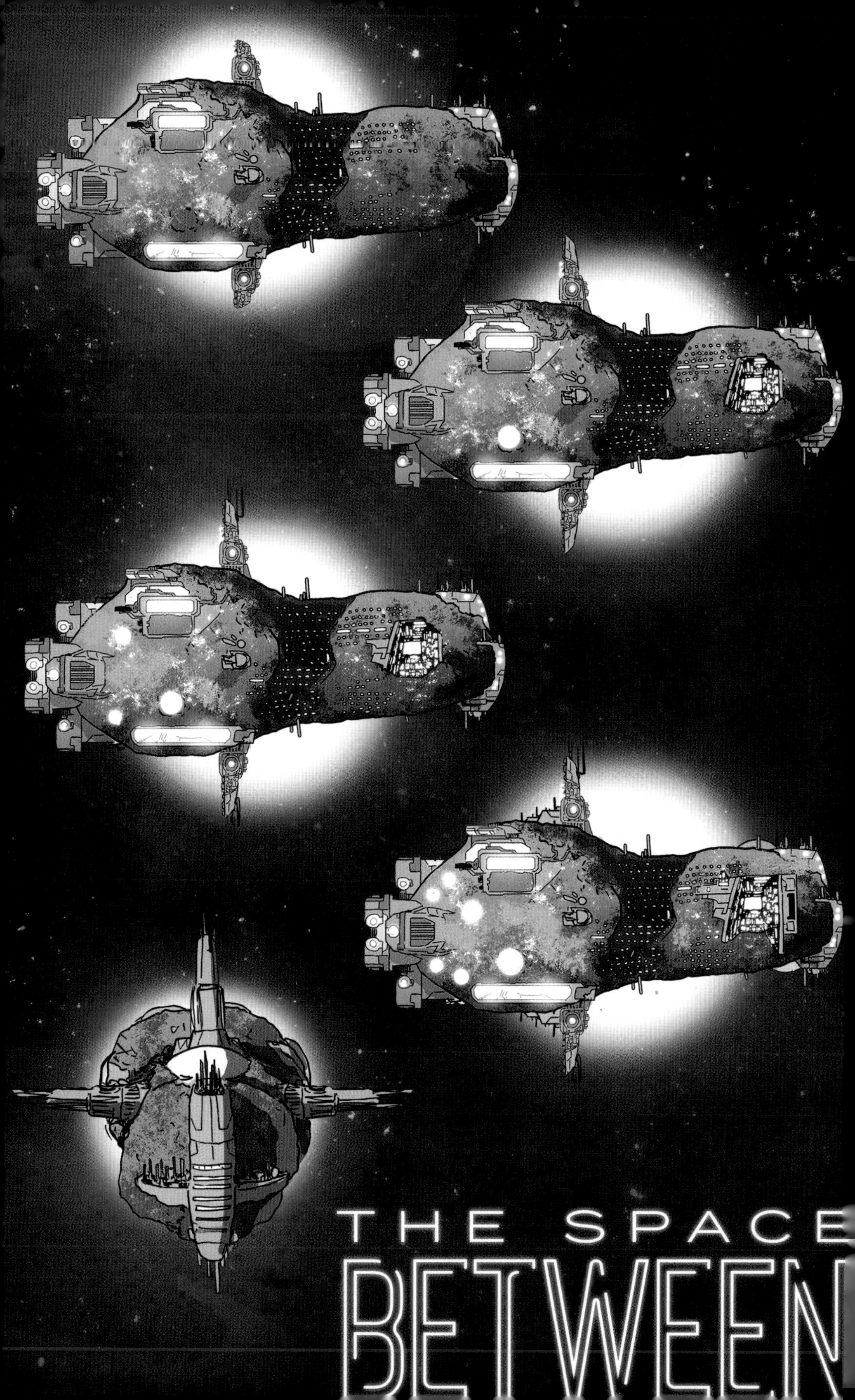
THE SPACE
BETWEEN

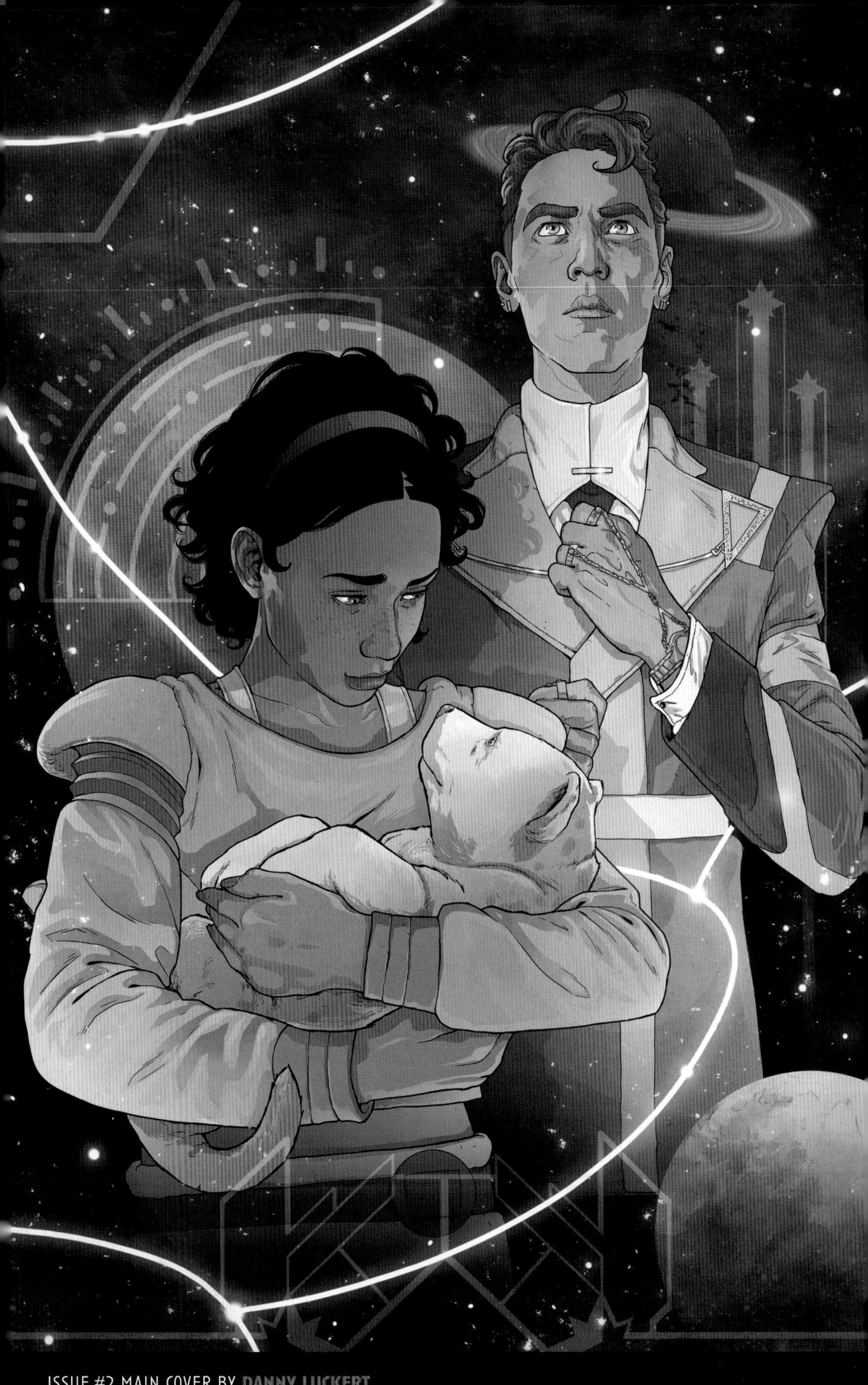

ISSUE #2 MAIN COVER BY **DANNY LUCKERT**

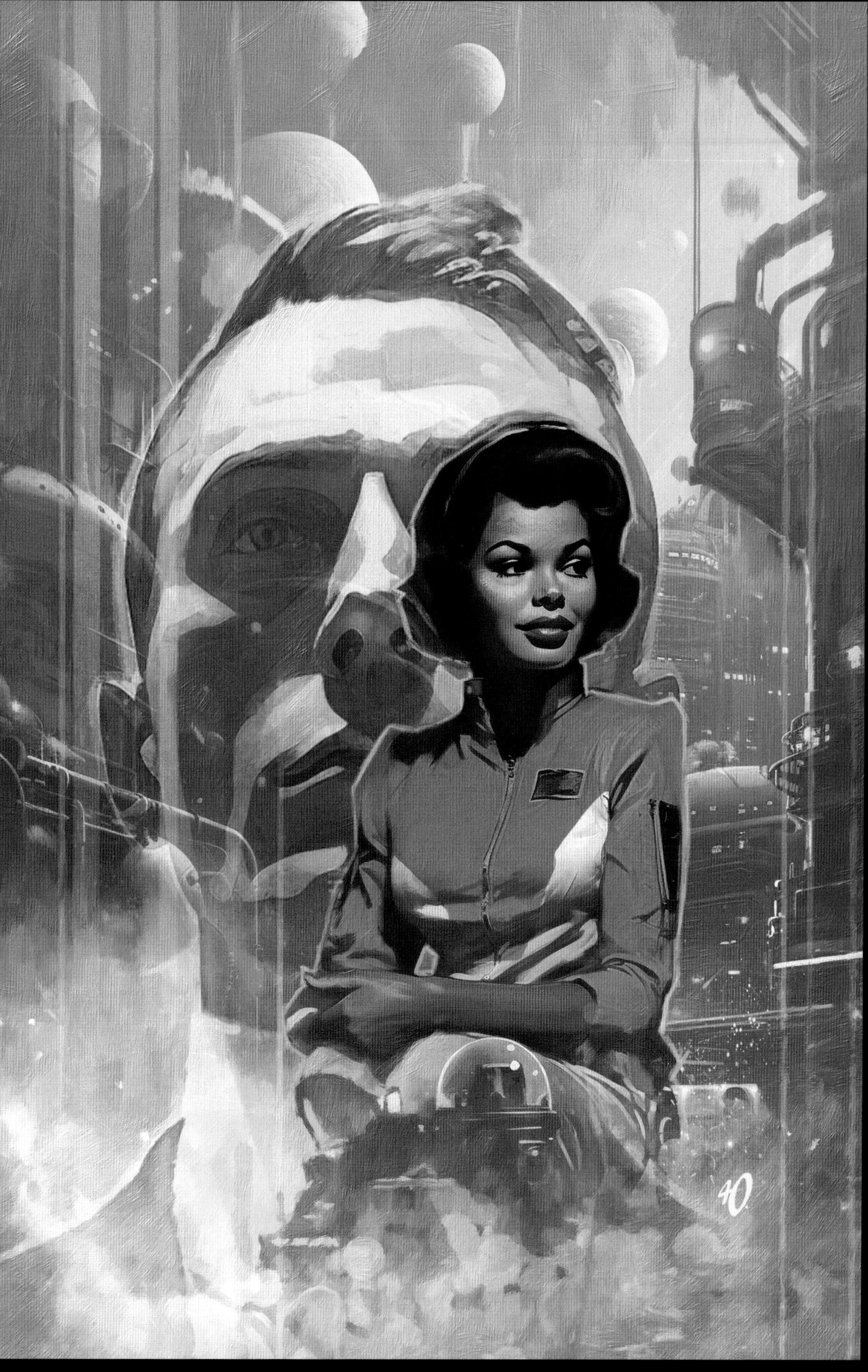

ISSUE #2 HOMAGE COVER BY **ARIEL OLIVETTI**

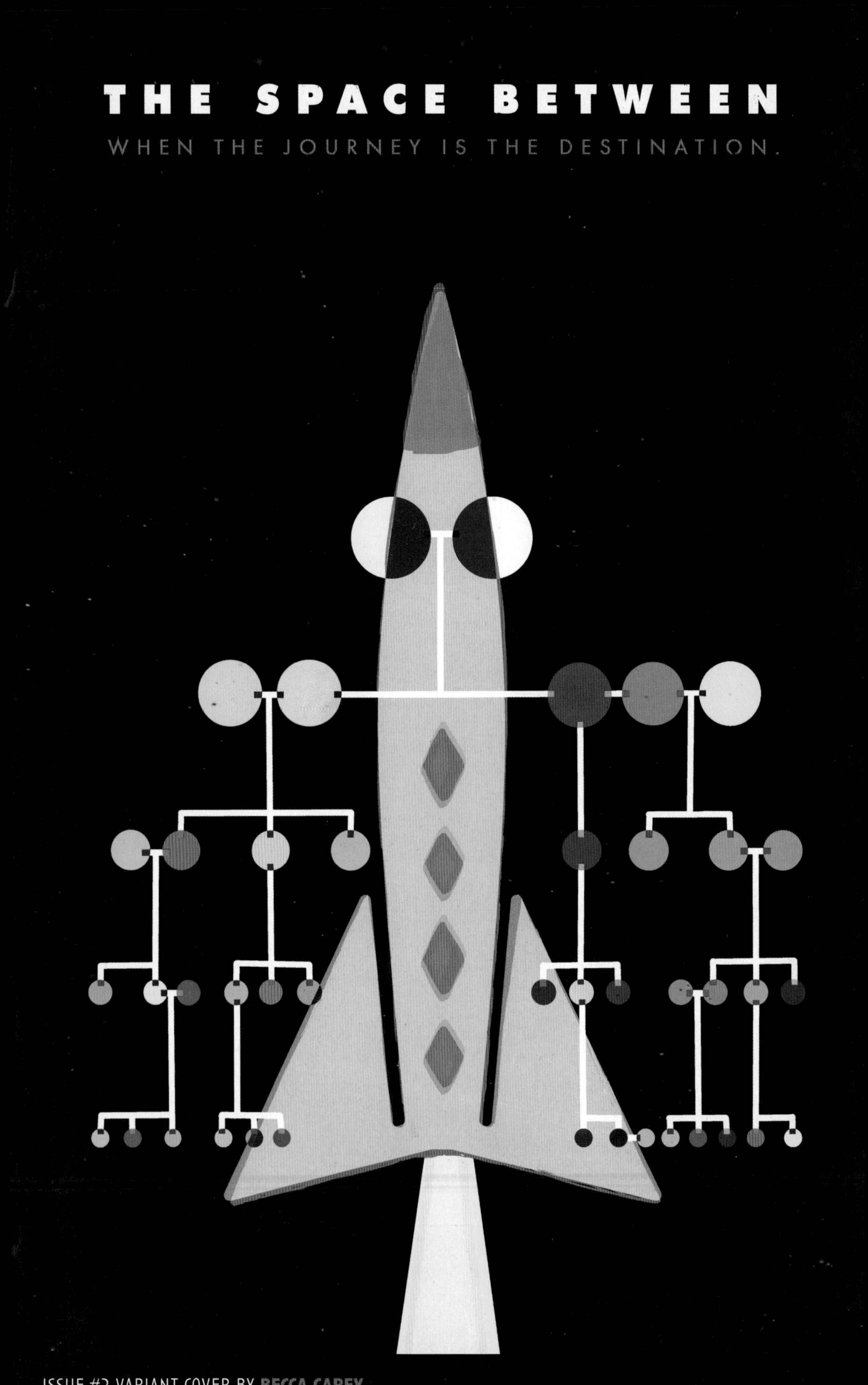
THE SPACE BETWEEN
WHEN THE JOURNEY IS THE DESTINATION.

ISSUE #2 VARIANT COVER BY **BECCA CAREY**

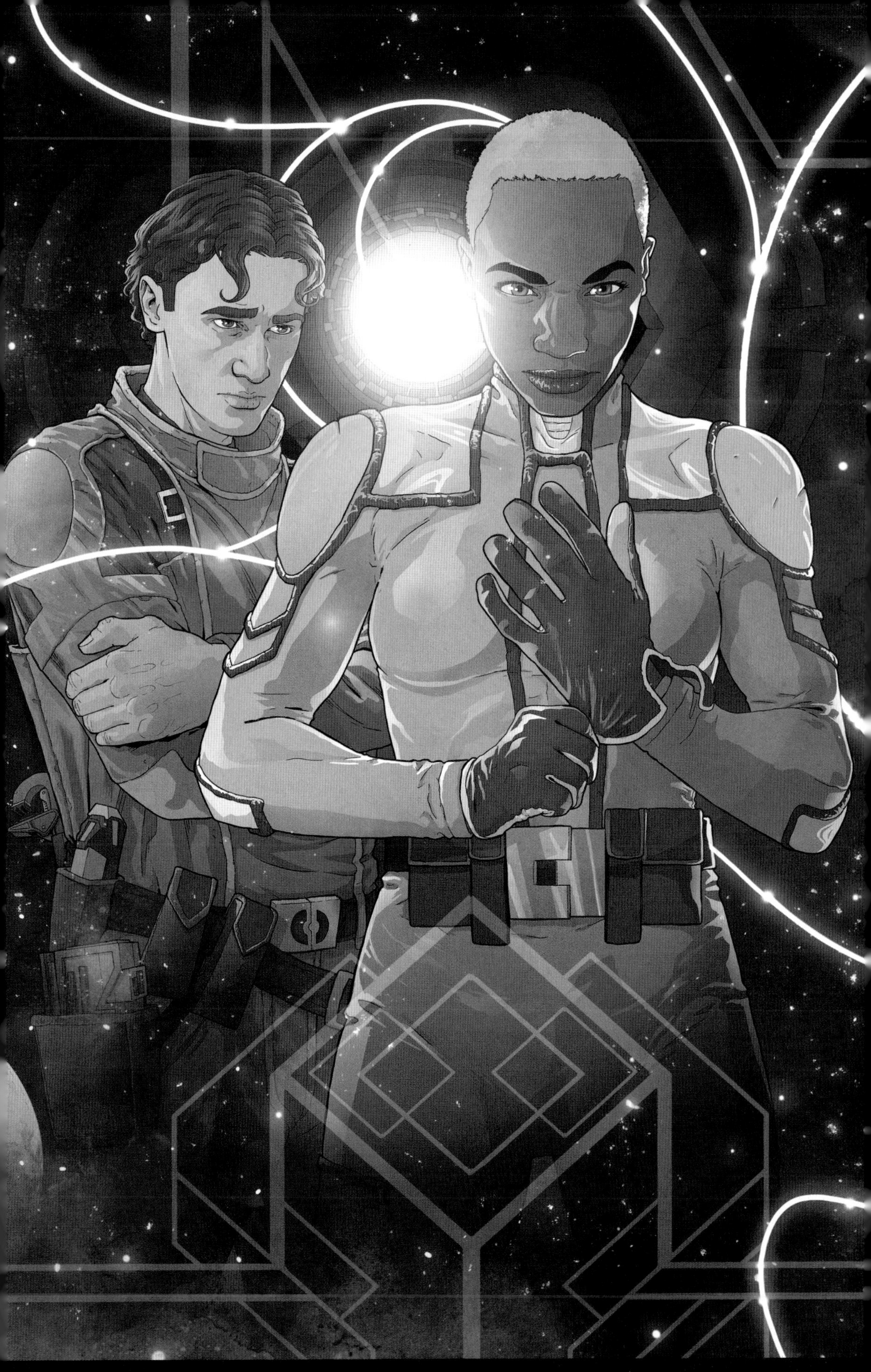

ISSUE #3 MAIN COVER BY **DANNY LUCKERT**

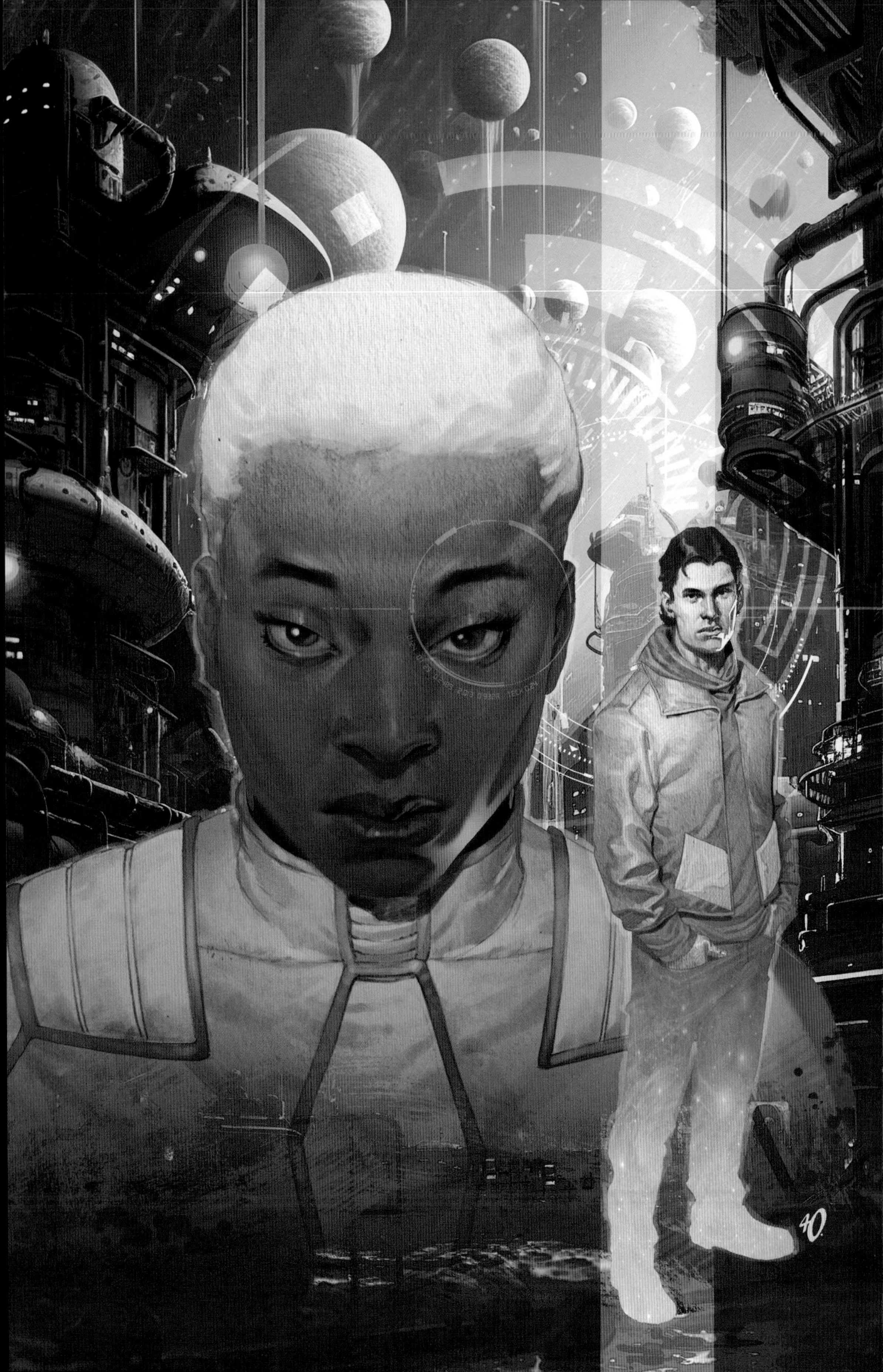

ISSUE #3 HOMAGE COVER BY **ARIEL OLIVETTI**

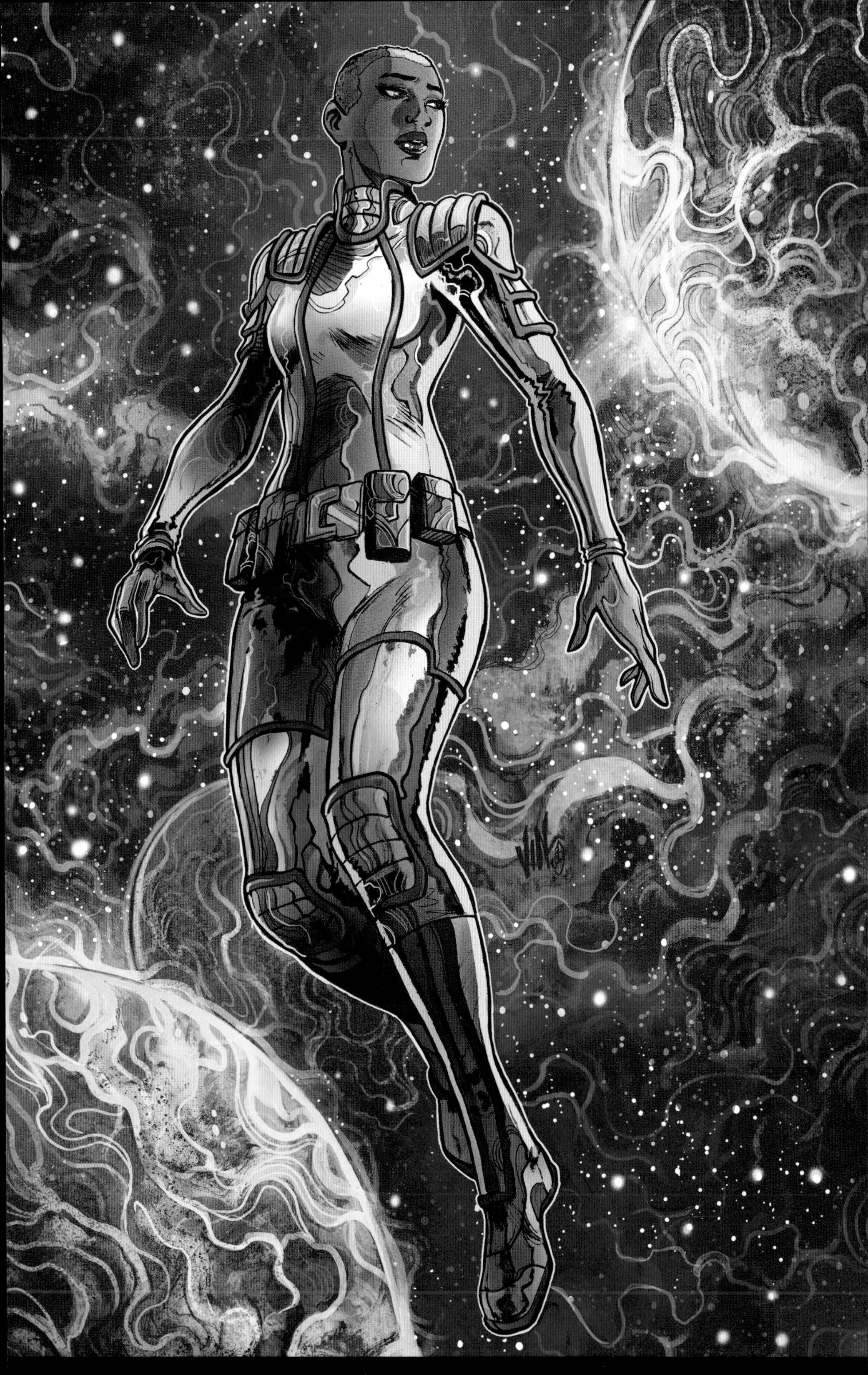

ISSUE #3 VARIANT COVER BY **VINCENZO RICCARDI**

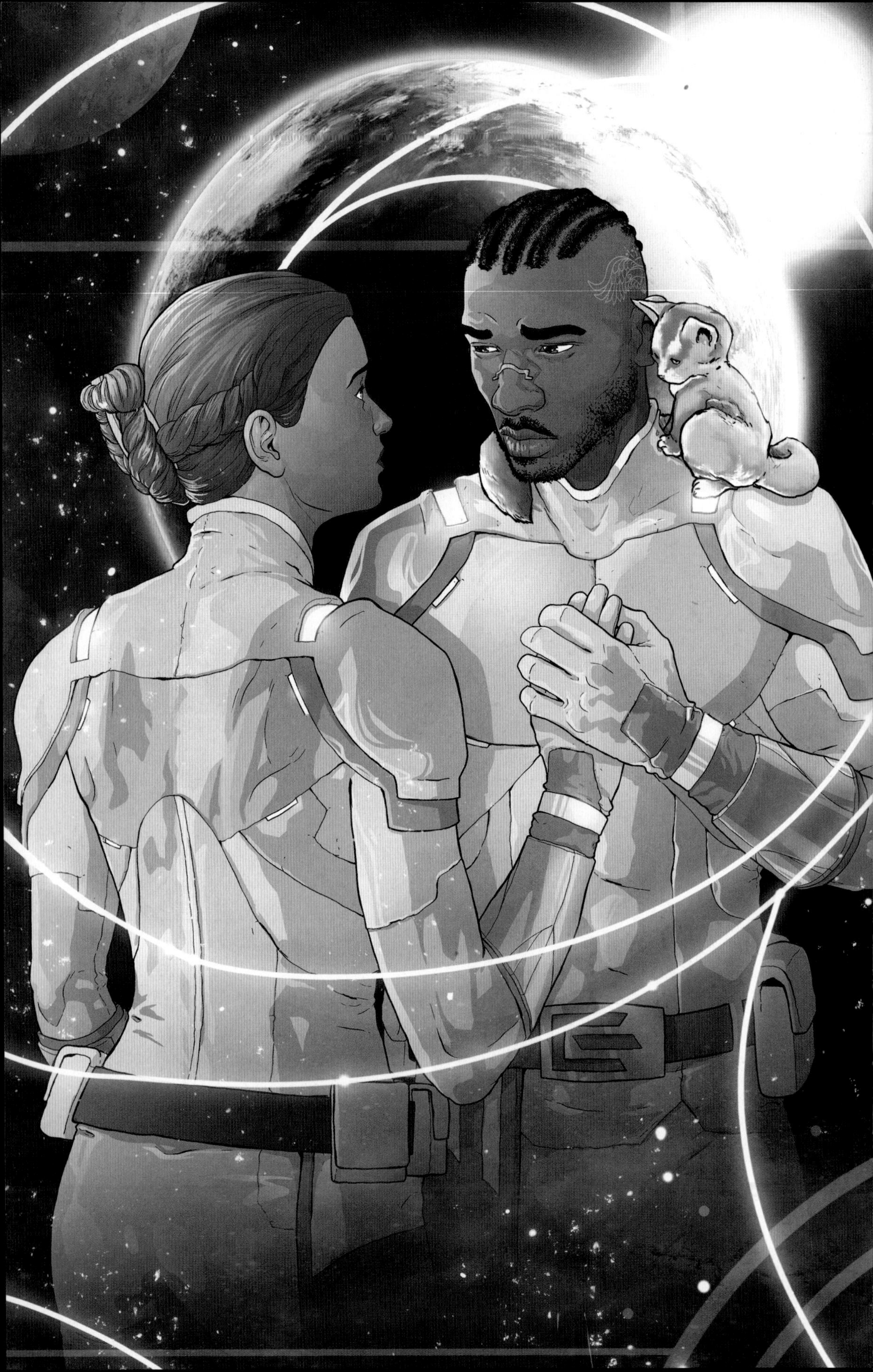

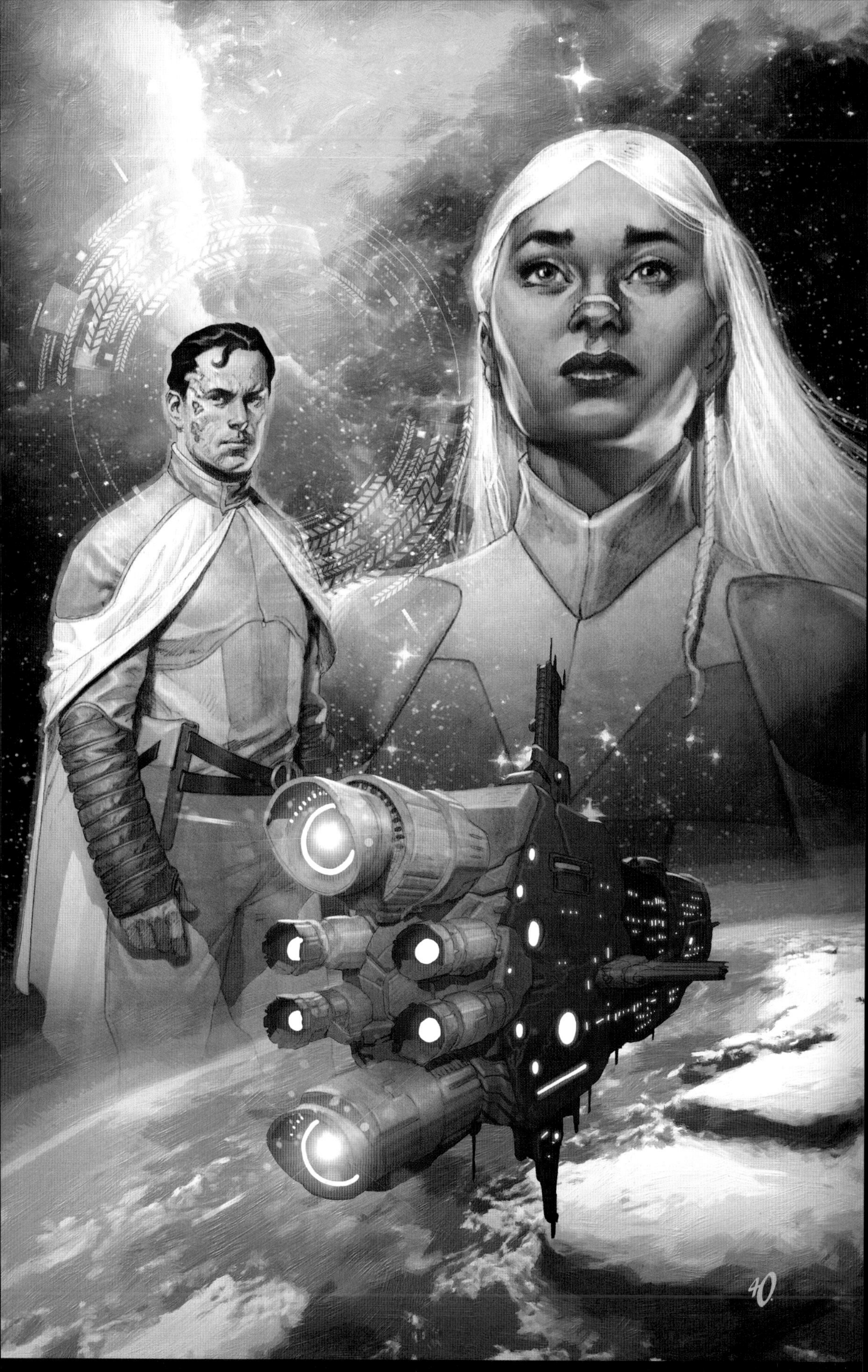

ISSUE #4 HOMAGE COVER BY **ARIEL OLIVETTI**

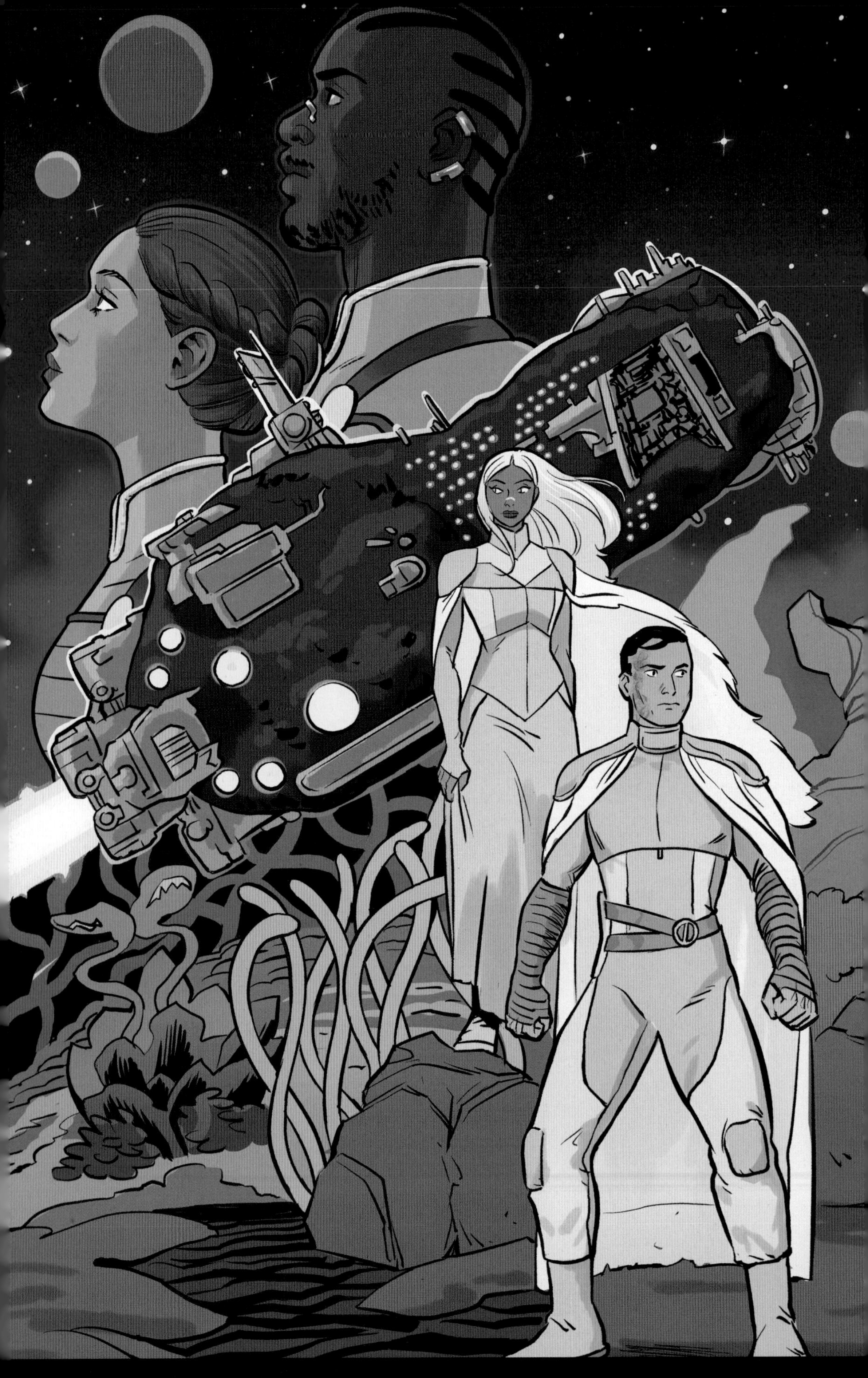

ISSUE #4 VARIANT COVER BY **NATACHA BUSTOS**

CHARACTER
DESIGN GALLERY

BY
DANNY LUCKERT

LES

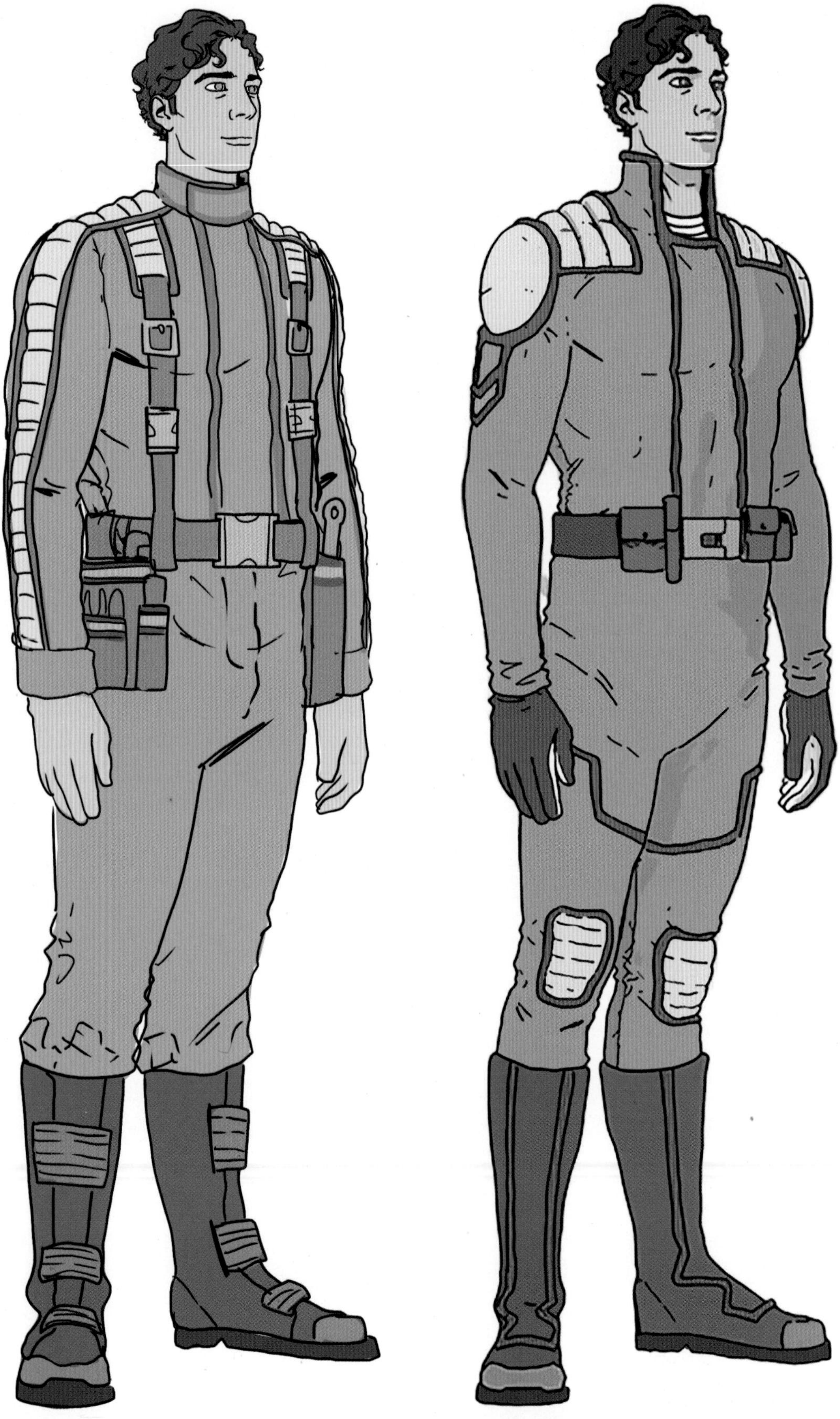

REVLA

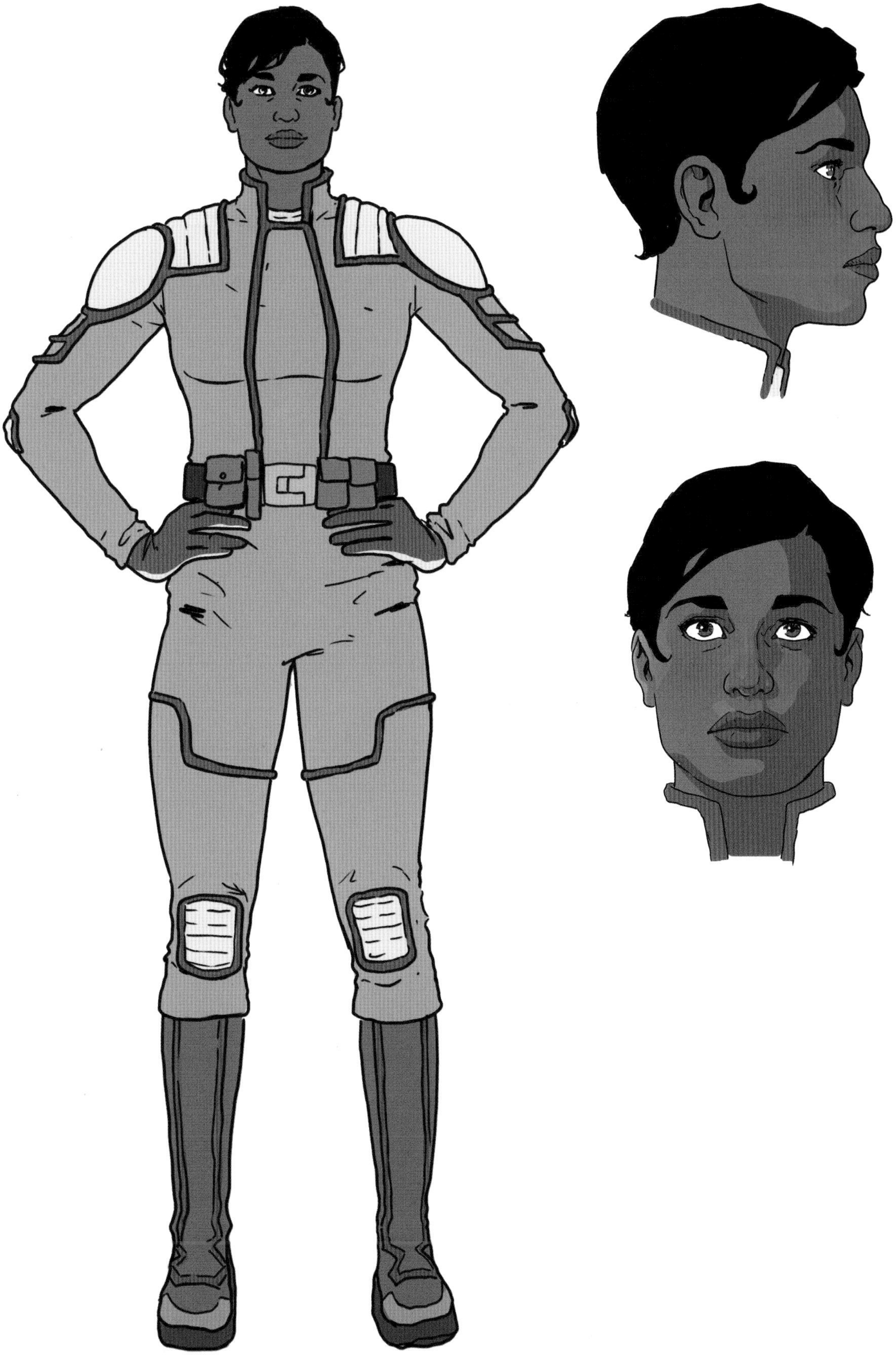

BEE

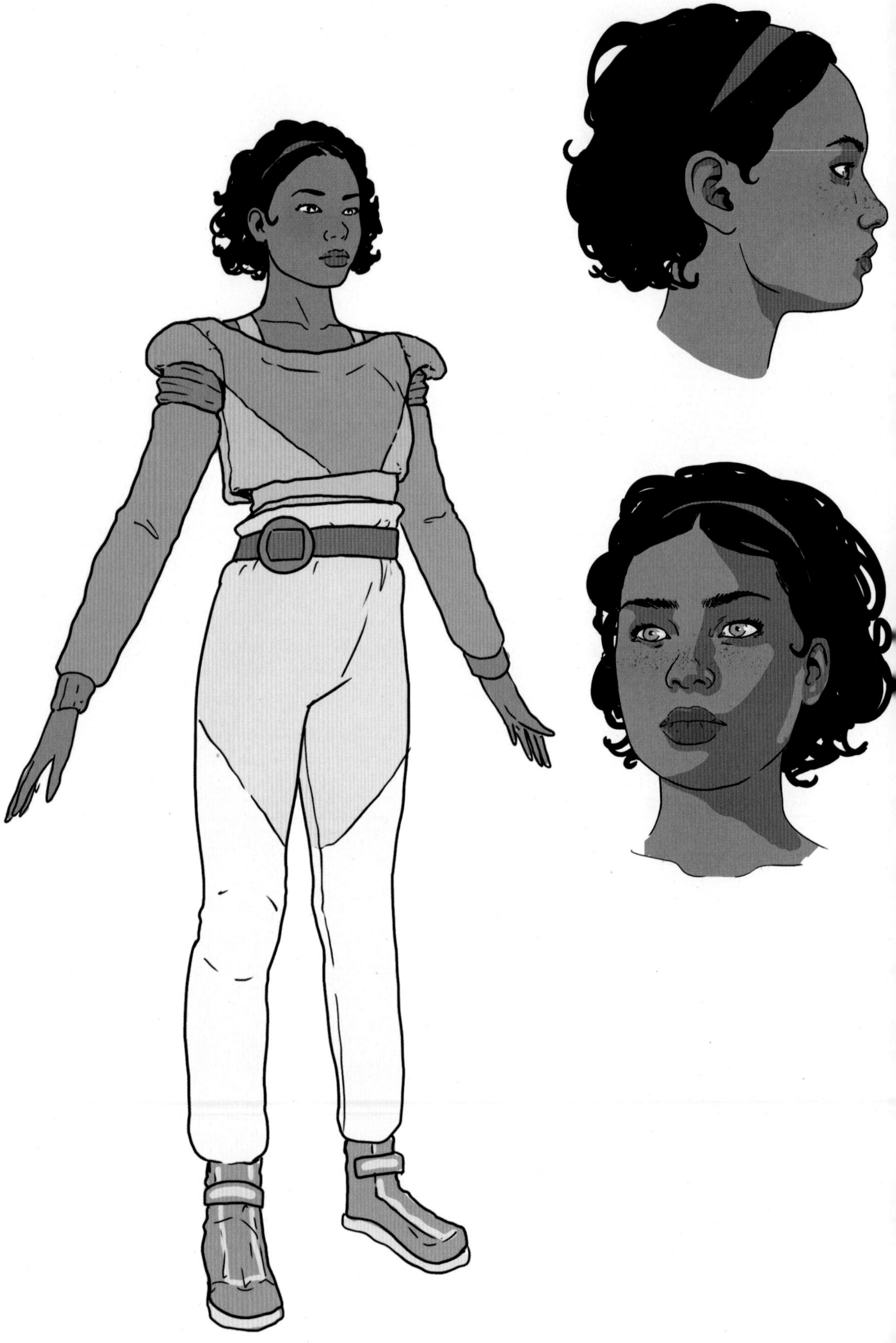

PARI

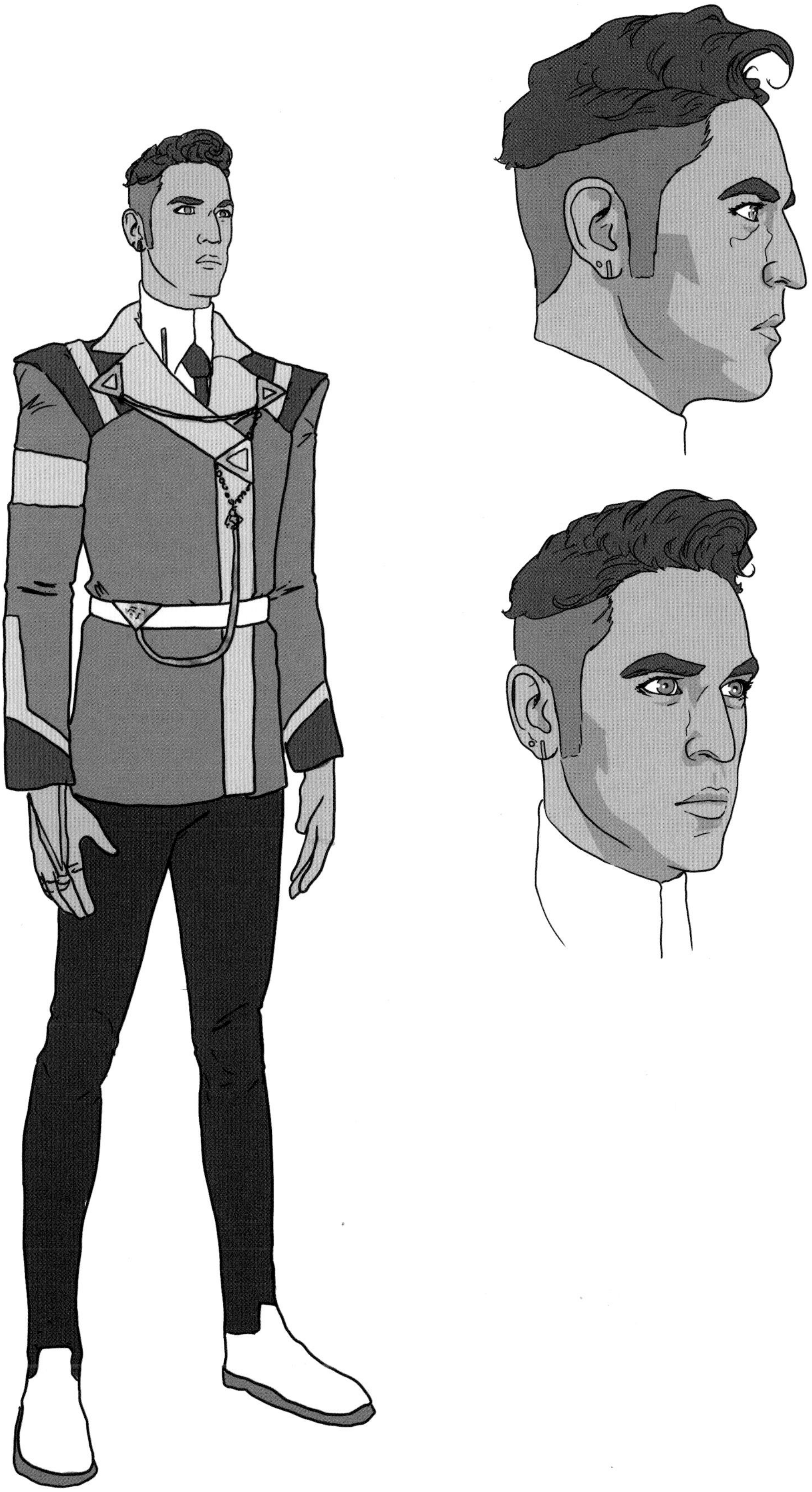

EDEN

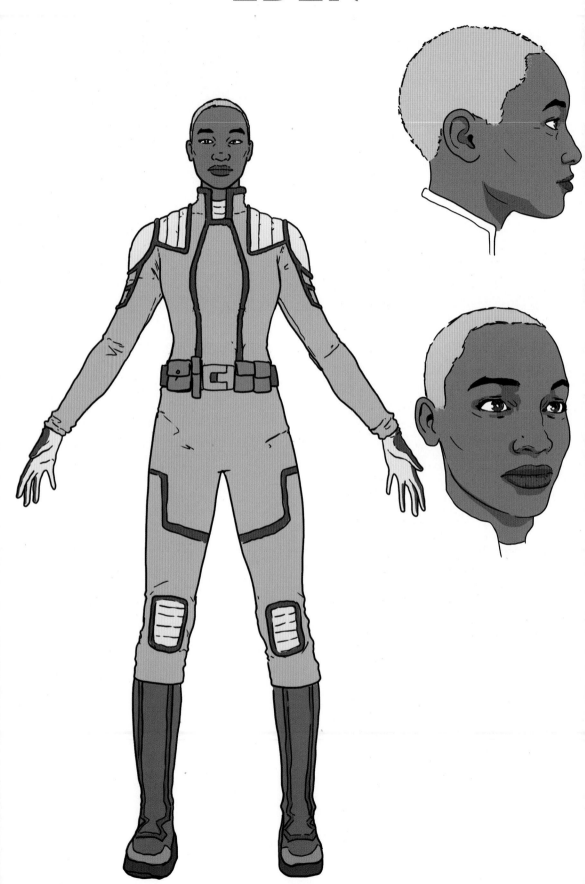

RUE

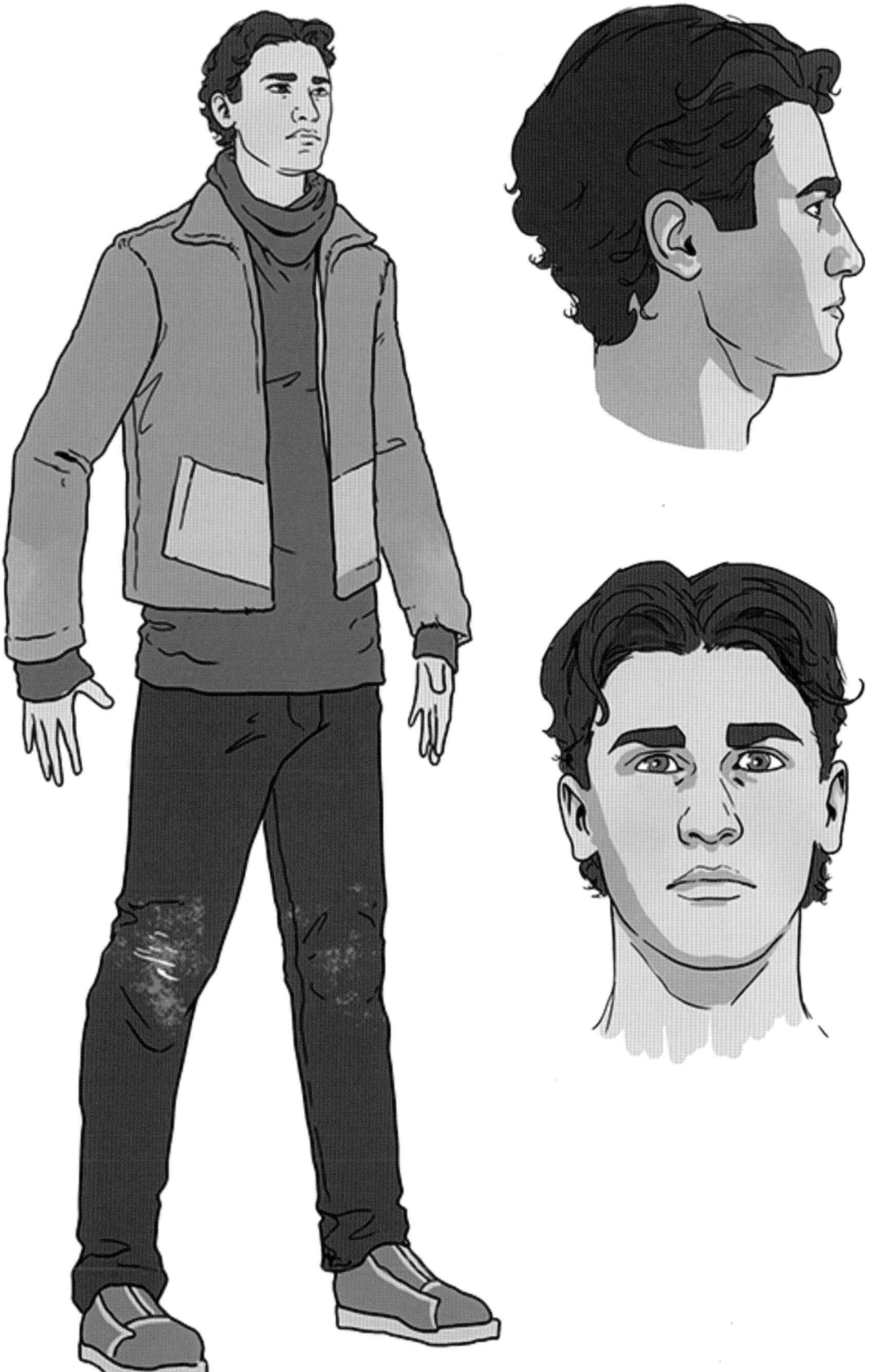

SKY

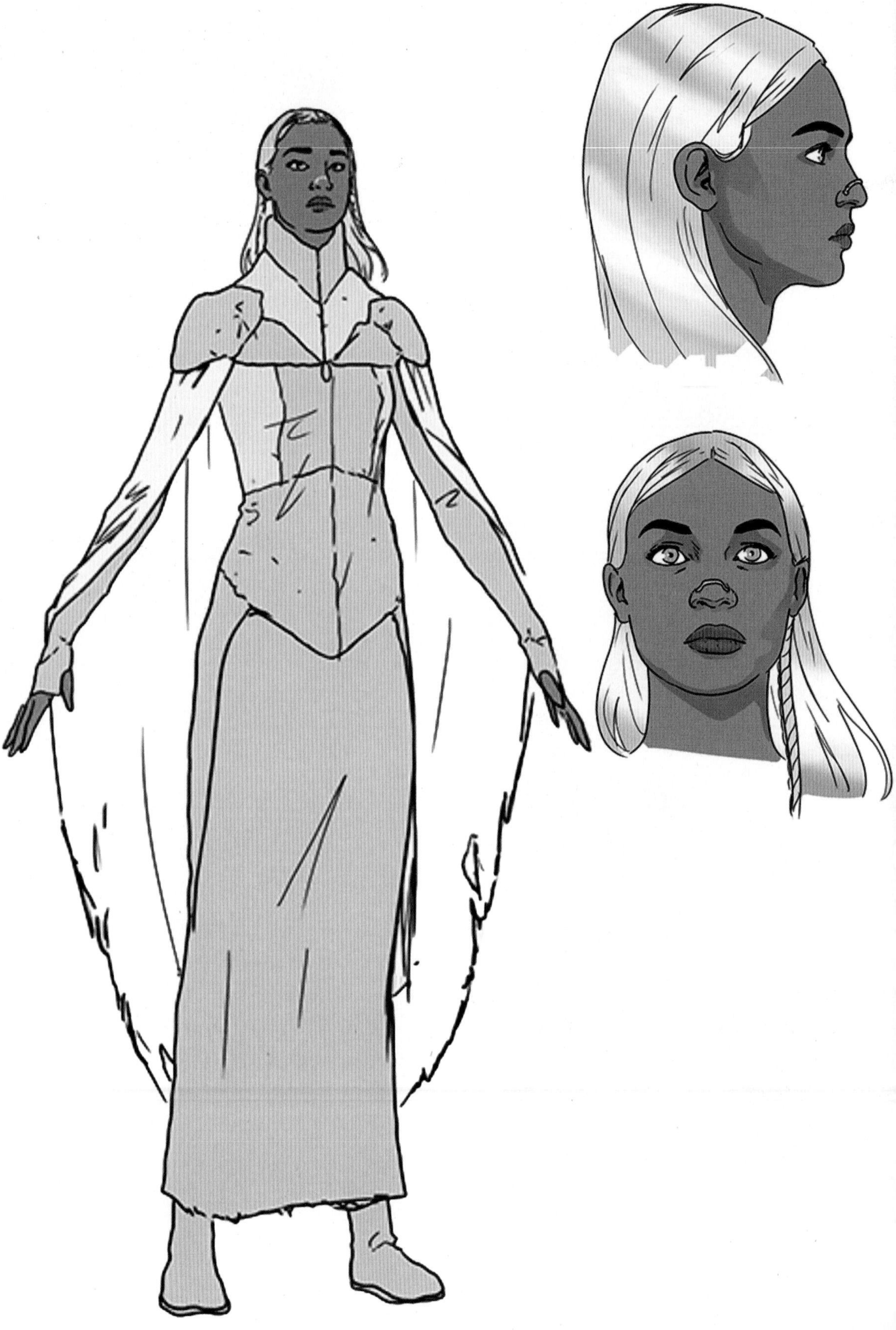

HOPE

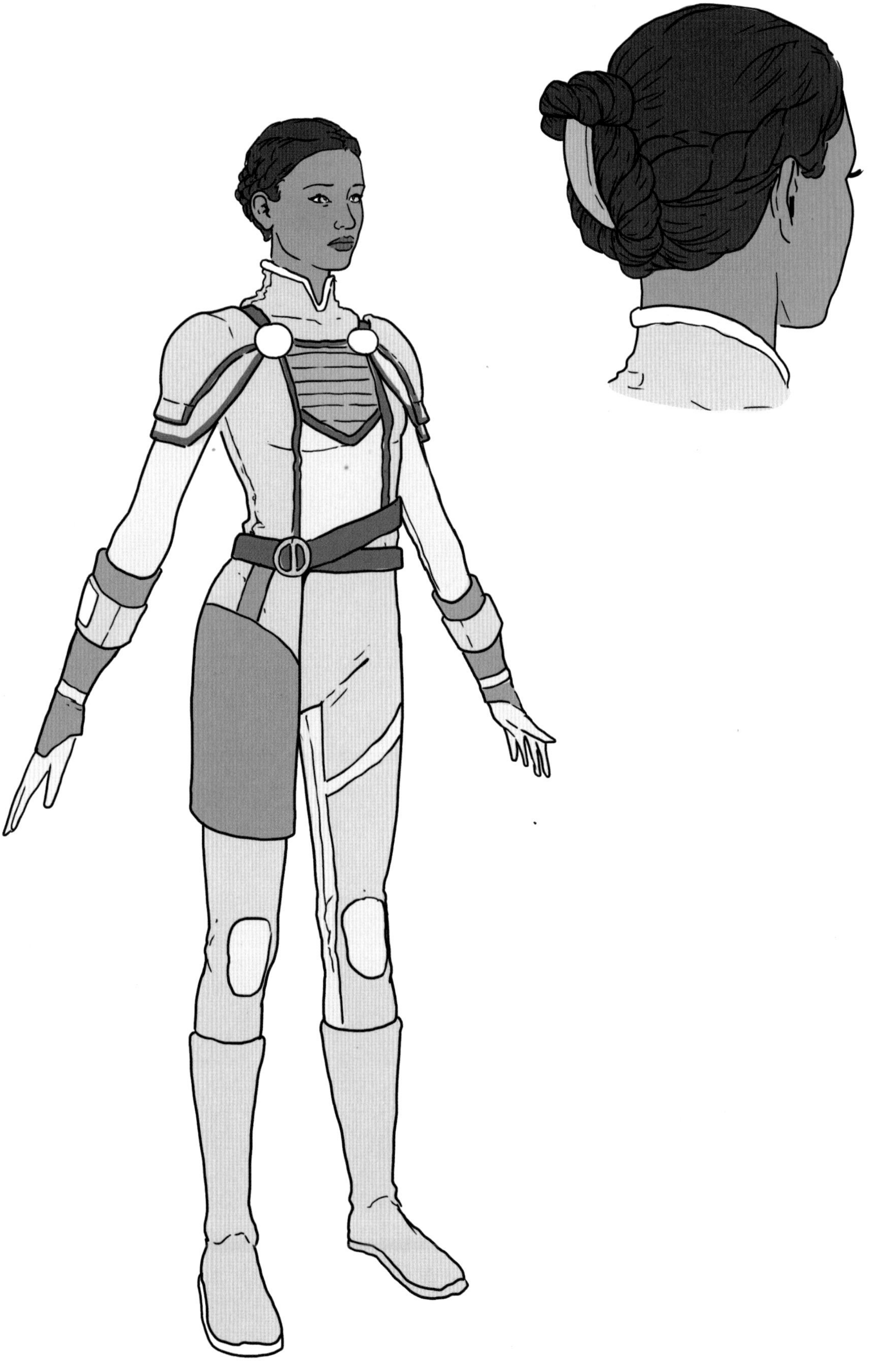

AULD

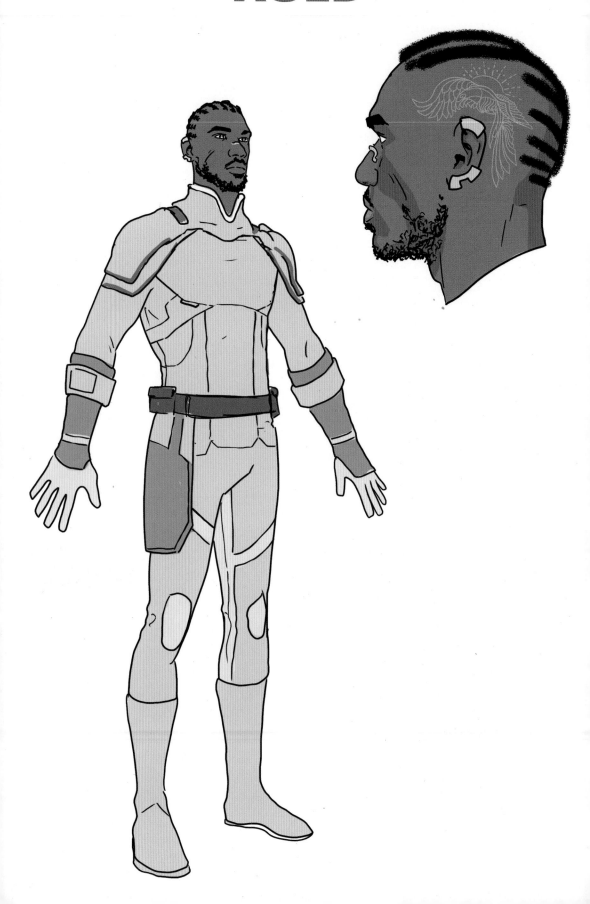

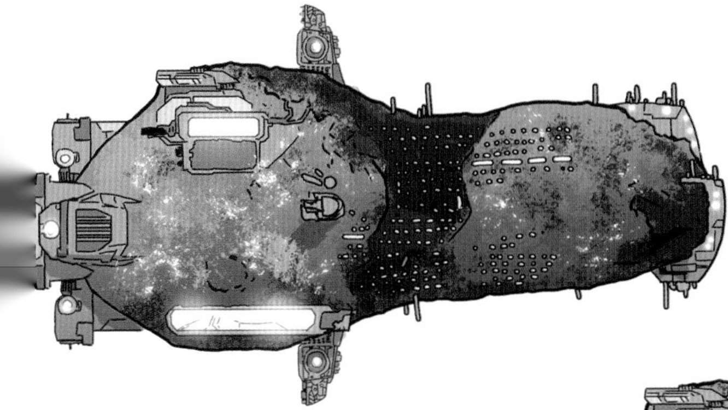

Dodona v1

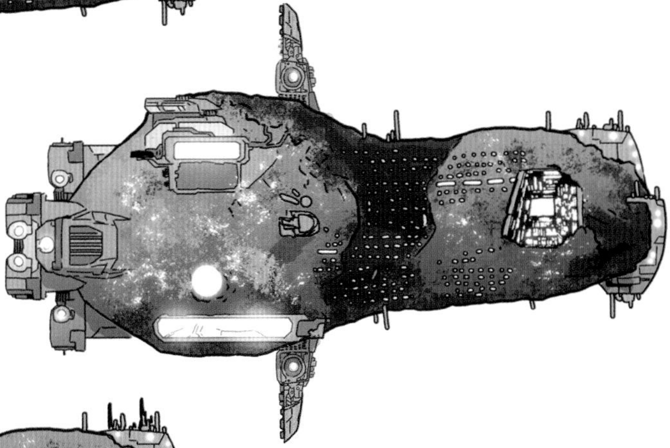

Dodona v2

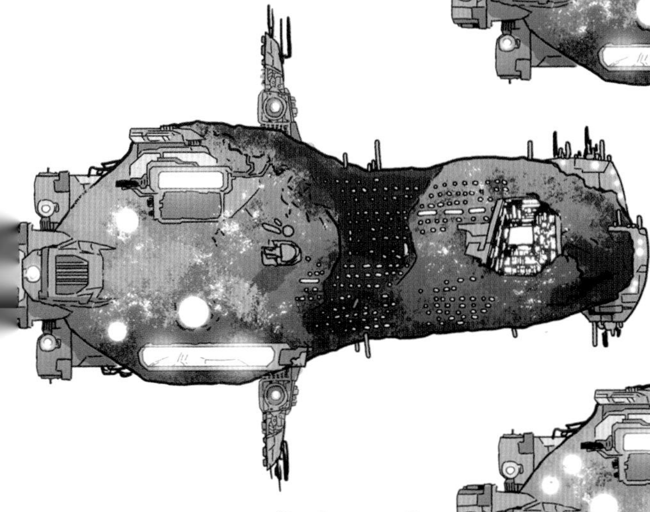

Dodona v3

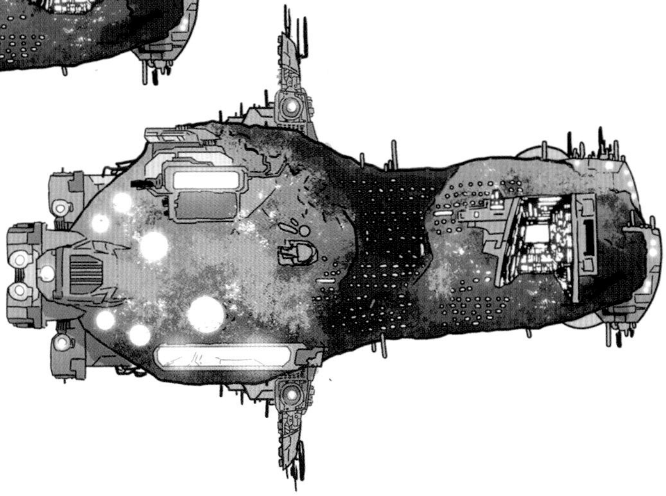

Dodona v4

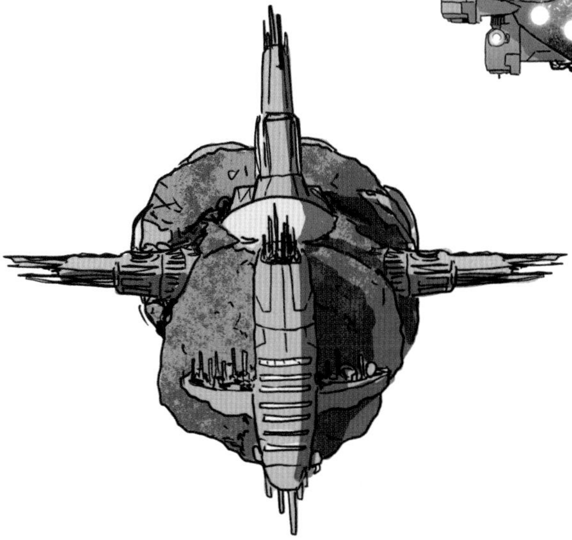

DISCOVER
THRILLING COLLECTIONS

BRZRKR
Keanu Reeves, Matt Kindt, Ron Garney
Volume 1
ISBN: 978-1-68415-685-6 | $16.99 US
Volume 2
ISBN: 978-1-68415-815-7 | $16.99 US
Volume 3
ISBN: 978-1-68415-712-9 | $16.99 US

Grim
Stephanie Phillips, Flaviano
Volume 1
ISBN: 978-1-68415-882-9 | $14.99 US
Volume 2
ISBN: 978-1-68415-905-5 | $14.99 US
Volume 3
ISBN: 978-1-60886-146-0 | $14.99 US

Damn Them All
Simon Spurrier, Charlie Adlard
Volume 1
ISBN: 978-1-68415-911-6 | $19.99 US

Coda
Simon Spurrier, Matías Bergara
Deluxe Edition
ISBN: 978-1-68415-945-1 | $49.99 US

Ghostlore
Cullen Bunn, Leomacs
Volume 1
ISBN: 978-1-60886-104-0 | $16.99 US

Once Upon A Time At The End of The World
Jason Aaron, Alexandre Tefenkgi, Leila del Duca, Nick Dragotta
Volume 1
ISBN: 978-1-68415-907-9 | $17.99 US
Volume 2
ISBN: 978-1-60886-152-1 | $17.99 US